Building High-Performance Web APIs with FastAPI

Build Scalable and High-Performance Web APIs Using Python, FastAPI, Pydantic, and SQLAlchemy with Practical Deployment Strategies

Girish Vas

www.orangeava.com

First Published: September 2025

Published By: Orange Education Pvt Ltd, AVA®

Address: 9, Daryaganj, Delhi, 110002, India

275 New North Road Islington Suite 1314 London,

N1 7AA, United Kingdom

ISBN (PBK): 978-93-49888-09-8

ISBN (E-BOOK): 978-93-49888-72-2

Scan the QR code to explore our entire catalogue

www.orangeava.com

Dedicated To

My Beloved Parents, ***Shri Gangadharan***
And ***Smt. Valsala****,*

Whose Unwavering Values and Blessings Have Been the Foundation of My Journey.

My Wife, ***Aparna****, for Her Enduring Support, Love, and Strength That Made This Endeavor Possible.*

My Sons, ***Agney*** *and* ***Amay****,*

Whose Curiosity and Boundless Energy Inspire Me Every Day to Keep Learning and Building.

And

The Vibrant ***Developer and Open-source Community****,*

Whose Collaboration, Innovation, and Shared Knowledge Have Shaped Not Just This Book, but the Very Spirit of FastAPI Itself.

About the Author

Girish Vas is a multi-domain Python expert, AI engineer, and backend architect with over 12 years of professional experience in software development. His career spans several industries–including healthcare, finance, wellness tech, e-commerce, edtech, and social media–where he has built scalable APIs, intelligent automation systems, and production-grade machine learning solutions.

Starting with a passion for writing clean, maintainable Python code, Girish evolved into a full- fledged problem solver with hands-on experience in FastAPI, Django, SQLAlchemy, PostgreSQL, Redis, Docker, Kubernetes, and modern DevOps practices. His journey has included architecting real-world solutions such as DNA-based wellness applications, mental health bots, e-commerce platforms, RAG pipelines for knowledge retrieval, social media APIs, and trading dashboards–each with a strong focus on performance, security, and developer ergonomics.

Girish's versatility stems from his ability to combine deep technical expertise with strong product sensibilities. He is proficient in integrating Large Language Models (LLMs), building personalized recommendation systems, designing scalable multi-tenant architectures, and deploying microservices to production. He has also led the development of AI-driven tools, and worked closely with data scientists as well as production teams to turn vision into value.

With this book, ***Building High-Performance Web APIs with FastAPI,*** Girish brings together his accumulated knowledge to guide Python developers from fundamentals to advanced concepts–equipping them to build robust APIs that are production-ready. His practical teaching style is rooted in real-world experience, making this book both a tutorial and a field manual for anyone building backend systems today.

Driven by curiosity, continuous learning, and a love for teaching, Girish is a strong advocate for open-source development, mentorship, and community-driven innovation. He hopes this book becomes your trusted guide as you explore and master the power of FastAPI in the evolving landscape of modern web development.

About the Technical Reviewer

Thinknyx® Technologies is a team of professionals with years of experience in Information Technology. Their expertise ranges from software development to the management of IT infrastructure, cloud, automation, container management, web and app development, security, and professional services. Recognized as a reputable brand, Think Nyx® Technologies provides IT consulting services, offering comprehensive information technology and soft skills' training. Additionally, they offer talent acquisition and recruitment solutions to diverse organizations worldwide.

Mr. Kulbhushan Mayer, the Co-Founder of Thinknyx® Technologies, is a certified expert in DevOps, SRE, Cloud, and Containerisation, with over 17 years of IT experience. He has expertise in technologies such as Public/Private Cloud, Containers, Automation tools, Continuous Integration/Deployment/Delivery tools, Monitoring and Logging tools, and more. Mr. Mayer is passionate about sharing his technical expertise with a global audience through various forums, conferences, webinars, blogs, and LinkedIn. Furthermore, he has reviewed multiple books on Automation, DevOps, DevTools, and more for different vendors.

Acknowledgments

There are several people whose support, encouragement, and guidance were instrumental in helping me to bring this book to life. First and foremost, I express my heartfelt gratitude to my parents, **Shri Gangadharan** and **Smt. Valsala**, whose values and constant encouragement have always been my foundation. I extend my deepest thanks to my wife, **Aparna**, for her unwavering patience and support, and to my sons, **Agney** and **Amay**, who continue to inspire me every single day with their curiosity and energy.

I would also like to express my sincere appreciation to my professors and teachers, whose early lessons laid the groundwork for my lifelong journey into technology and learning. Their influence continues to guide me in every line of code I write and every idea I try to communicate.

My thanks extend to my friends, colleagues, and professional peers who supported me throughout this process, offering feedback, motivation, and time, whenever it was most needed.

A special thanks to **Mr. Vibhu Bansal** for your technical review and feedback–it added great value to this work. I am equally grateful to **Ms. Medhavi Tanwar (Senior Editor) and the entire team at Orange Education Pvt Ltd** for their valued contribution to the publishing of this book, ensuring clarity, consistency, and accessibility of the book's material.

Finally, I am thankful to the developer community and contributors behind FastAPI as well as the tools it builds on. This book is a humble contribution to the ever-growing ecosystem of modern, clean, and high-performance web APIs.

Preface

Welcome to **Building High-Performance Web APIs with FastAPI.**

If you have embarked on this journey, you are likely to be eager to move beyond theory, and build modern, high-performance APIs–quickly, cleanly, and at scale. This book is structured to get you there–systematically.

We begin with "*Introduction to FastAPI and RESTful APIs*", laying the groundwork of what makes FastAPI, a unique choice for building web interfaces in Python. With a solid understanding of REST principles, you will be ready for "*Setting Up the Development Environment*" and "*Installing FastAPI*" steps designed to get your tools in place quickly.

From there, we dive deeper into "*Core Features of FastAPI*", where you will learn to create asynchronous routes, utilize decorators, and harness Python type hints effectively. "*Dependency Injection*" follows, teaching you how to design modular and testable code. Then comes "*Request and Response Models with Pydantic*"–a key chapter for mastering data validation and serialization.

Thus, once you are familiar with data flow and structure, we move to "*Authentication and Authorization*", implementing secure token-based and OAuth2 systems. The next is "*File Uploading*", exploring techniques for accepting, validating, and processing uploaded files securely. This is followed by "*Connecting to Databases*", where you will integrate SQLAlchemy and Tortoise ORM along with PostgreSQL, MySQL, or SQLite for full CRUD operations.

Quality matters most in production, so "*Testing and Debugging*" offers structured strategies, using **pytest**, integration testing, and debugging tools, including **pdb** and interactive IDE support. The final system-level chapter, "*Deployment and Scalability*", guides you through containerization with Docker, orchestration via Kubernetes, load balancing, caching, and monitoring.

With your application fully built, "*Managing Application Configuration*" teaches techniques to handle environment variables, encrypted secrets, and configuration libraries such as Pydantic Settings and Dynaconf. Then, in "*Building Practical Projects*", you can apply all the learning through three complete examples of APIs: To-Do, E-Commerce, and Social Media.

Lastly, "*Future of FastAPI*" chapter explores the roadmap ahead such as advanced async support, AI/ML APIs, serverless use-cases, and the vibrant open-source community, making it happen. This is followed by "*Appendices*" that round out the book with cheat sheets, recommended reading, and curated resources to help you explore further.

Each chapter is designed to build on the last—moving you from beginner topics to confident application, and deployment in real-world scenarios. My experience in building APIs for industries spanning finance, healthcare, and AI has taught me that clarity, structure, and real-world code examples matter. This is what the book delivers.

Hence, whether you are transitioning from Flask or Django, building a startup backend, or mentoring yourself in modern API design—this book is your ultimate guide. So, let us build your foundation, expand your skills, and help you confidently architect powerful APIs with FastAPI.

Get a Free eBook

We hope you are enjoying your recently purchased book! Your feedback is incredibly valuable to us, and to all other readers looking for great books.

If you found this book helpful or enjoyable, we would truly appreciate it, if you could take a moment to leave a short review with a 5 star rating on Amazon. It helps us grow, and lets other readers discover our books.

As a thank you, we would love to send you a free digital copy of this book, and a **30%** discount code on your next cart value on our official websites:

www.orangeava.com

www.orangeava.in (For Indian Subcontinent)

☑ **Here's how:**

Leave a review for the book on Amazon.

Take a screenshot of your review, and send an email to **info@orangeava.com** (it can be just the confirmation screen).

Once, we receive your screenshot, we will send you the digital file, within 24 hours.

Thank you so much for your support it means a lot to us!

Downloading the code bundles and colored images

Please follow the links or scan the QR codes to download the ***Code Bundles and Images*** of the book:

https://github.com/OrangeAVA/Building-High-Performance-Web-APIs-with-FASTAPI

The code bundles and images of the book are also hosted on ***https://rebrand.ly/gjgmshk***

In case there's an update to the code, it will be updated on the existing GitHub repository.

Errata

We take immense pride in our work at **Orange Education Pvt Ltd,** and follow best practices to ensure the accuracy of our content to provide an indulging reading experience to our subscribers. Our readers are our mirrors, and we use their inputs to reflect and improve upon human errors, if any, that may have occurred during the publishing processes involved. To let us maintain the quality and help us reach out to any readers who might be having difficulties due to any unforeseen errors, please write to us at :

errata@orangeava.com

Your support, suggestions, and feedback are highly appreciated.

DID YOU KNOW

Did you know that Orange Education Pvt Ltd offers eBook versions of every book published, with PDF and ePub files available? You can upgrade to the eBook version at **www.orangeava.com** and as a print book customer, you are entitled to a discount on the eBook copy. Get in touch with us at: **info@orangeava.com** for more details.

At **www.orangeava.com**, you can also read a collection of free technical articles, sign up for a range of free newsletters, and receive exclusive discounts and offers on Print Books and eBooks.

PIRACY

If you come across any illegal copies of our works in any form on the internet, we would be grateful if you would provide us with the location address or website name. Please contact us at **info@orangeava.com** with a link to the material.

ARE YOU INTERESTED IN AUTHORING WITH US?

If there is a topic that you have expertise in, and you are interested in either writing or contributing to a book, please write to us at **business@orangeava.com**. We are on a journey to help developers and tech professionals to gain insights on the present technological advancements and innovations happening across the globe and build a community that believes Knowledge is best acquired by sharing and learning with others. Please reach out to us to learn what our audience demands and how you can be part of this educational reform. We also welcome ideas from tech experts and help them build learning and development content for their domains.

REVIEWS

Please leave a review. Once you have read and used this book, why not leave a review on the site that you purchased it from? Potential readers can then see and use your unbiased opinion to make purchase decisions. We at Orange Education would love to know what you think about our products, and our authors can learn from your feedback. Thank you!

For more information about Orange Education, please visit **www.orangeava.com**.

Table of Contents

CHAPTER 1
Introduction to FastAPI and RESTful APIs

Introduction

The opening chapter will give a real introduction to FastAPI, a modern, fast performance, and high-level web API framework used for building Python APIs. FastAPI is absolutely incomparable in terms of performance, ease of use, and rich support for asynchronicity. The benefits of FastAPI compared to popular alternatives such as Flask and Django will be described, including how it differs from the other frameworks with interactive data APIs, use cases, and serializations supported by Pydantic.

This chapter is a primer on RESTful API, the base of today's services. It provides an overview of statelessness, client-server separation, and integration as the guiding principles of the REST architecture and clarifies their importance for making APIs scalable and maintainable. A few common patterns and best practices around the design of a RESTful API are touched upon as well, in order to put the reader on a sound footing toward building robust, efficient APIs.

By the end of this chapter, each reader will have crystal-clear reasons why FastAPI is the first choice today for developing an API, and will make clear the basic concepts that back RESTful services. The principles will lay the groundwork for further topics covered in the next section.

Structure

In this chapter, we will discuss the following topics:

- **Advantages of FastAPI Over Other Frameworks**
    - Key Features and Benefits of FastAPI

- Comparison with Other Frameworks (for example, Flask, Django)
- Real-World Use Cases and Industry Adoption

- **Principles and Benefits of RESTFul APIs**
  - Understanding RESTFul APIs
  - Principles RESTFul API Architecture
  - Benefits of RESTFul API Architecture
- **Common API Patterns and Practices**
  - Common RESTful Patterns and Practices
  - Best Practices in Designing RESTful Services
  - Examples of Well-Designed RESTful APIs

Advantages of FastAPI Over Other Frameworks

FastAPI has many advantages that make it the first choice for developing web APIs. The design concept emphasizes speed, simplicity, and powerful features to meet the needs of both novice and experienced developers. In the following section, we will detail the key features of FastAPI, and its advantages over other frameworks, its comparison with Flask and Django, and its real-world business applications.

Key Features and Benefits of FastAPI

FastAPI offers a range of features and benefits that make it a powerful and efficient framework for developing APIs, including:

- **Speed and Performance:**
  - **High Performance:** FastAPI is known for its speed and, in most aspects, ranks among the fastest Python web frameworks. This speed is borrowed from the underlying technologies in use that are in common use–Starlette for the web parts and Pydantic for the data parts. It can handle a large number of requests per second with very low latency, which makes it very suitable for applications requiring real-time processing and high throughput.
  - **Asynchronous Capabilities:** FastAPI fully supports asynchronous programming, giving developers the capability to write non-blocking codes with async/await syntax. Thus, when developing applications designed to handle a large number of simultaneous connections efficiently–for instance, chat applications, live data feeds, and other real-time services–

this would be very useful. This aids in optimizing system resource usage for better responsiveness of the application and overall performance.

 - **Efficient Use of Resources:** FastAPI is executed asynchronously; therefore, none of the tasks, such as I/O operations, block the execution of other tasks. This leads to better utilization of server resources and makes applications scale efficiently, not increasing the hardware requirements much with an increase in concurrent users.

- **Ease of Use:**
  - **Simple Syntax and Structure:** FastAPI is designed with respect to simplicity. FastAPI uses Python's type hinting system. These improve the readability of the code and reduce the possibility of a bug from within. This clean syntax makes it accessible to all developers, from the freshest of beginners to seasoned experts, and allows rapid development with easier maintenance.
  - **On-the-box Interactive API Documentation:** Another outstanding feature of FastAPI is the automatic generation of interactive API documentation with tools such as Swagger UI and ReDoc. This helps a lot in testing endpoints, provides live documentation, and makes the API really user-friendly for any developer who wants to integrate with the API. All this auto-documentation saves huge development time and helps in maintaining clear and up-to-date API references.
  - **Minimal Boilerplate Code:** FastAPI reduces boilerplate code to the minimum so that more time is spent on writing business logic rather than setup and configuration. This makes development faster with less complexity in the code.

- **Data Validation and Serialization:**
  - **Pydantic Integration:** FastAPI uses Pydantic for strong data validation and serialization. This means that the Pydantic models guarantee that the data coming in and out from the API will conform to the specified schema, thus minimizing runtime errors and maximizing integrity in data. This is automated validation, pretty significant in keeping reliable and secure applications.
  - **Automatic Type Checking:** FastAPI uses type hints, and thus, it provides automatic type checking. It confirms that all the data types are flowing perfectly in the application. This basically helps in detecting errors at a very early stage of development and ensures a smooth developer experience.

- **Scalability and Flexibility:**
  - **Modular Design:** It has a modular design, which promotes the reusability of components and clean architecture. This makes FastAPI very easy to maintain and scale applications. This modularity supports the development

of large and complex systems by allowing the separation of concerns and the possibility of independent development of parts of an application.

  - **WebSocket and GraphQL support:** FastAPI supports both WebSockets and GraphQL natively, thus giving flexibility when building a wide range of applications that include systems of real-time communications or complex query interfaces. This versatility makes FastAPI suitable for a large spectrum of projects.

- **Developer Experience:**
  - **Extensive Documentation:** FastAPI is fully documented with tutorials, guides, and references. At this level of documentation, it is easier for a developer to get up to speed with the framework quickly and find solutions for common problems.
  - **Community and Ecosystem:** FastAPI has a growing community and a rich ecosystem of extensions and tools with support for dependency injection, background tasks, and OAuth2 authentication. Through this active community and ecosystem, there are available resources and extensions that increase the functionality of FastAPI.
  - **Error Handling and Debugging:** FastAPI provides detailed error messages and tracebacks, thus making debugging easier. Moreover, it supports monitoring tools such as Sentry out-of-the-box for effective error tracking.

Comparison with Other Web Frameworks (For Example, Flask, Django)

- **Flask:**
  - **Simplicity versus Performance:** Flask is famous for its simplicity, and it becomes user-friendly. It is usually used in small and medium projects. However, it does not support asynchronous programming by itself, which makes it possibly not as good at high concurrency compared to FastAPI.
  - **Extensions:** Flask has a large number of extensions. At times, this becomes the root of complex configuration and compatibility problems. In contrast, some features of FastAPI remove the necessity for external packages.
  - **Documentation and Testing:** FastAPI has better documentation and more built-in testing support compared to Flask. The latter partially supports the former.
- **Django:**
  - **Full-Stack versus Microframework:** Django is a full-stack framework that holds a broad range of functionality for web development, much of which comes already integrated with an ORM, authentication system, and admin

interface. That makes it much more fitting for constructing full-fledged web applications instead of an API. The downside is that Django is much heavier and more complicated in comparison with the lightweight FastAPI.

- **Synchronous Nature:** By default, Django is synchronous. But there are ways to implement asynchronous views. However, FastAPI is asynchronously natively supported, hence giving it a huge performance benefit in I/O-bound tasks.
- **Learning Curve:** On the other hand, the large number of features and conventions within Django make for a steeper learning curve, while the simplicity and Pythonic design of FastAPI have a shallower learning curve, especially for getting started with API development.

Table 1.1 presents a comparison between FastAPI and other frameworks:

Feature	**FastAPI**	**Django REST Framework**	**Flask**	**Express.js**
Speed	High performance	Moderate	Moderate	High performance
Asynchronous Support	Built-in	Limited	Limited (requires extensions)	Built-in
Ease of Use	Easy with automatic documentation	Moderate (steeper learning curve)	Easy, minimalistic	Easy, minimalistic
Data Validation	Automatic with Pydantic	Manual or with third-party	Manual or with third-party	Manual or with third-party
Community and Support	Growing	Established	Established	Established
Best for	High-performance APIs	Full-stack web applications	Simple, flexible APIs	Web and API development

***Table 1.1:** Comparison of FastAPI with other popular web frameworks*

Real-World Use Cases and Industry Adoption

- **Microsoft:** Microsoft uses FastAPI in a number of internal projects and services due to the fast speed and ease of building high-performance APIs.
- **Netflix:** Netflix has adopted FastAPI for some of its microservices due to async capabilities and high performance.
- **Uber:** FastAPI is used by Uber in some of the backend services for high-throughput and real-time data processing.

Case Studies

- **Example 1:** A fintech company moved to FastAPI for their payment processing API and reduced the response time by 30%, improving its handling of concurrent requests.

- **Example 2:** A healthcare startup used FastAPI to build a telemedicine platform and used its data validation features to ensure the accuracy and integrity of medical data.

These examples show exactly how FastAPI's advantages realize real-world performance gains at the same time as improvements in developer productivity, making it ever more compelling for modern API development.

Principles and Benefits of RESTful APIs

RESTful APIs, or Representational State Transfer, create the basis for modern development due to their simplicity, scalability, and high performance. This chapter describes the basic principles of RESTful API and the major benefits provided by it. Such concepts need to be known and understood in order to create a powerful and reliable API that could easily integrate with any client or service.

Understanding RESTful APIs

- **Definition:** REST stands for Representational State Transfer, which is an architectural style used for designing networked applications. RESTful APIs create, read, update, and delete resources by sending HTTP requests.
- **Core Components:** Core components include resources, URIs, HTTP methods for interaction, that is, GET, POST, PUT, and DELETE, and finally the representations, usually JSON or XML.

Principles of RESTful APIs Architecture

- **Statelessness:**
  - **Definition and Explanation:** In a RESTful API, no client information is stored in the server session data. This means that a client request to the server contains all the information that is required to understand and process it. Under stateless architecture, a server does not need to maintain any kind of state for the client. It only forwards the client request to the intended service or resource.
  - **Benefits:** Stateless is essentially a server design principle that maintains interact requests as separate operations; therefore, they are resilient to scalability changes, and can easily scale out horizontally–the more, the merrier.
- **Client-Server Architecture:**
  - **Separation of Concerns:** The best way to separate this concern is through client-server architecture, which is basically a separation of concerns between the user interface and data storage. The separation

allows the user and server evolutions to take place independently, making development and deployment easier.

- **Benefits:** Features associated with this principle are mainly important because when developers can have most of their work concentrated on creating an efficient, scalable backend, most frontend developers can have most of their work on creating a user interface that is inducing and responsive.

- **Uniform Interface:**
  - **Standardized Interactions:** RESTful APIs usually adopt a uniform interface, primarily using standard HTTP methods such as GET, POST, PUT, DELETE, and, in some cases, PATCH. Accordingly, a uniform interface makes it straightforward to design an API, and ensures that the interface is predictable as well as easy to work with.
  - **Benefits:** A uniform interface reduces the learning curve for both consumers and developers of the APIs, thus making it easier for the user to understand the given service, and to integrate the API with various systems and services.
- **Resource-Based:**
  - **Identification of Resources:** In REST, each resource is identified with the help of a URI. A resource, whether a user or a product, should be unique in terms of its URL. The interactions with respect to these resources are performed using standard HTTP methods.
  - **Benefits:** Utilizing URIs for identification of resources makes the API more intuitive and easier to navigate. It also improves reading and using API documentation as a resource.
- **Representation of Resources:**
  - **Data Formats:** Data formats for resources can be represented in several formats: JSON, XML, or HTML. The flexibility of the client to request a representation based on a given format is carried out using corresponding headers in the communication based on HTTP, hence offering flexibility in how data ought to be consumed.
  - **Benefits:** Flexibility, such as it on the part of the client to request data representation in a form that is more useful from its point of view, such as it enhances the effective use and adaptability of an API.
- **Layered System:**
  - **Intermediary Servers:** The presence of intermediary servers as in a system, such as caching proxies and balancing load, makes the system quite scalable and easily implementable for increasing performance.

Each layer supports a specific responsibility and may be developed and maintained separately.

- **Benefits:** Making the entire system scalable, reliable, and secure, this principle distributes responsibilities into multiple layers.

- **Cacheability:**
  - **HTTP Caching Mechanisms:** RESTful APIs provide support for caching to possibly increase their performance and reduce server loads. That is, HTTP headers can define a server response to be cacheable or non-cacheable for the client to store and reuse a response.
  - **Benefits:** Caching reduces the need for repeated requests to the server, decreasing latency and improving the user experience.

Benefits of RESTful APIs Architecture

- **Scalability:**
  - **Horizontal Scaling:** Due to a stateless and layered architecture, it is easier to scale applications horizontally. It is done by adding more servers that may handle the increased load.
  - **Performance Optimization:** RESTful APIs make use of caching and other similar techniques for performance optimization; hence, a large number of requests can be handled efficiently.
- **Flexibility and Modularity:**
  - **Independent Evolution:** Separation of Concerns enables the different constituents of an application to evolve independently. Thus, front-end and back-end teams can work on their respective components without interfering with each other.
  - **Easier Maintenance:** The modular nature of RESTful APIs makes it comparatively easy to maintain and update them, as changes in one component do not necessarily affect others.
- **Interoperability:**
  - **Cross-Platform Integration:** Because a RESTful API utilizes ordinary HTTP protocols, it can be devoured by any customer fit for sending HTTP demands. This incorporates any internet browser, versatile applications, and different servers.
  - **Language Independent:** Since RESTful APIs use standard configurations such as JSON and XML, they might be used with any programming dialect, accordingly advancing interoperability crosswise over various stages and advances.

- **Security:**
  - **Standard Security Practices:** RESTful APIs can support some of the standard security practices, such as providing secure communication through HTTPS and supporting authorization using OAuth to safeguard sensitive information, and ensure secure interactions.
  - **Granular Access Control:** Fine-grained access control is ensured through the use of tokens and other authentication mechanisms to ensure access to resources by users who are only authorized to do so.
- **Ease of Use:**
  - **Clear and Intuitive:** RESTful APIs foster clear and intuitive design, making it easier than ever for a developer to use the API to its full potential.
  - **Extensive Tooling:** There are many tools and libraries available for development against RESTful APIs that cover areas from testing, debugging, and documentation, thus enriching the experience of a developer.
- **Robust Ecosystem:**
  - **Community and Resources:** Because of the high adoption of RESTful APIs, a strong ecosystem of community support, documentation, and resources has been developed. This exposes the developer to easy access to knowledge and tools necessary for fast and effective implementation, testing, and deployment of APIs.

It is the detailed overview of principles and benefits of RESTful API that gives an overall understanding of why RESTful design has become an integral part in the development of today's web. Following these principles, a developer will be able to create scalable, flexible, secure APIs that are easy to maintain and use.

Common API Patterns and Practices

The design of effective APIs follows certain standardized patterns and good practices that ensure consistency, scalability, and ease of use. The next section describes some of the common API patterns and best practices that developers can use to drive the building of robust, end-user-friendly APIs. These guidelines ensure improvement in maintainability, performance, and overall quality of an API for a developer.

Common RESTful Patterns and Practices

When designing RESTful APIs, following established patterns and best practices ensures consistency, scalability, and ease of use. Key practices include using standard HTTP methods, status codes, and ensuring statelessness and resource-based interactions.

RESTful Resource Naming Conventions

Resource naming conventions are crucial in RESTful APIs. Clear, consistent, and intuitive naming enhances readability and usability. Names should be nouns representing the resource, using plural forms for collections, and avoiding special characters and spaces.

- **Consistent Naming:**
  - Resources shall have names that are clear, consistent, and descriptive. This helps users understand the purpose and structure of an API.
  - Example: `/users, /orders, /products`.
- **Nouns for Endpoints**
  - Represent resources with nouns instead of verbs since RESTful APIs are resource-oriented.
  - Example: `/customers` instead of `/getCustomers`.
- **Hierarchical Relationships:**
  - Use nested paths of resources to relate one to another, thus representing hierarchy.
  - Example: `/users/{userId}/orders` to show that orders are related to users.
- **Plural Naming:**
  - All names of resources use plural nouns to show collections.
  - Example: `/users` rather than `/user`.

HTTP Methods and Status Codes

- **Standard HTTP Methods:**

  State an action in resource performance by using standard HTTP methods.
  - **GET:** Retrieve a resource.
  - **POST:** Create a new resource.
  - **PUT:** Update an existing resource.
  - **DELETE:** Remove a resource.
  - **PATCH:** Partially update a resource.
- **Appropriate Status Codes:**

  Use appropriate HTTP status codes to inform about the result of an operation.
  - **200 OK:** Successful GET, PUT, or DELETE.

- **201 Created:** Successful POST.
- **204 No Content:** Successful DELETE with no content to return.
- **400 Bad Request:** Invalid request parameters.
- **401 Unauthorized:** Authentication required.
- **403 Forbidden:** Insufficient permissions.
- **404 Not Found:** Resource not found.
- **500 Internal Server Error:** Server encountered an error.

Versioning

- **API Versioning:**

  Implement versioning to handle changes and maintain backward compatibility.

  - **URI Versioning:** Include the version number in the URI.
  - Example: `/v1/users`.
  - **Header Versioning:** Specify the version in the request header. Example: `Accept: application/vnd.api+json; version=1`.

- **Deprecation Strategy:**
  - Provide clear documentation and a timeline for deprecating older versions.
  - Communicate deprecation notices to users well in advance.

Pagination, Filtering, and Sorting

- **Pagination:**
  - Use pagination; this will be efficient for large data sets.
  - Example: Use query parameters such as `?page=2&limit=20`.
- **Filtering:**
  - Allow users to filter results based on specific criteria.
  - Example: `?status=active&role=admin`.
- **Sorting:**
  - Enable sorting of results by various fields.
  - Example: `?sort=created_at&order=desc`.

Best Practices in Designing RESTful Services

Adhering to best practices in designing RESTful services is essential for creating robust, scalable, and maintainable APIs. These practices include using appropriate

HTTP methods, designing intuitive URI structures, ensuring stateless interactions, and providing comprehensive documentation. Proper versioning and security measures are also critical for long-term API sustainability.

Error Handling

- **Consistent Error Responses:**
    - Provide consistent error responses and information to the user to aid troubleshooting.
    - Example: `{ "error": { "code": 400, "message": "Invalid request parameters" } }`.
- **Error Codes and Messages:**
    - Usage of standard error codes with clear error messages.
    - Add a link to documentation for details.

Authentication and Authorization

- **Secure Endpoints:**
    - Authenticate and authorize; protect sensitive data.
    - Use OAuth2, JWT, or API keys for authentication.
- **Role-Based Access Control (RBAC):**
    - Role definition and permission interaction with resources and actions are well explained.

Documentation and Testing

- **Comprehensive Documentation:**
    - Detailed and interactive API documentation in Swagger or ReDoc.
    - Endpoint examples - request/response formats, explanation
- **Automated Testing:**
    - Run unit tests and integration tests to check if the API works as expected.
    - Test using tools such as Postman, pytest, or unittest.

Caching

- **Implement Caching:**
    - The strategies for caching can be put in to enhance the performance and lighten the load on the server.

  - Example: Use HTTP headers such as `Cache-Control` and `ETag` for caching responses.
- **Invalidate Cache:**
  - Make sure caches are invalidated correctly as data changes.

Examples of Well-Designed RESTful APIs

Here are two notable examples of well-designed RESTful APIs:

- **GitHub API:** This is an API that has self-descriptive resource-based URLs and great documentation. It makes great use of HTTP methods and status codes.
- **Twitter API:** Easy to use, adhering to RESTful principles with well-structured endpoints and supporting pagination.

These common API patterns and practices drive the design and implementation of a good RESTful API, which ought to be solid, scalable, and convenient to use. If these guidelines are followed, it will not be hard to develop an API that can easily meet the demand of the users and integrate with other systems or services.

Conclusion

In this chapter, we explored the key advantages of FastAPI, such as its speed, simplicity, and asynchronous capabilities, making it an excellent choice for modern web API development. We also delved into the principles and benefits of RESTful APIs, emphasizing the importance of statelessness, scalability, and structured communication. Additionally, we examined common API patterns and practices that ensure robust, maintainable, and efficient API designs. This foundational knowledge sets the stage for leveraging FastAPI to build powerful web applications.

The upcoming chapter will provide a detailed guide to setting up your development environment for FastAPI projects. We will walk through the installation of Python, and the configuration of popular IDEs such as VSCode and PyCharm, ensuring an optimized setup for FastAPI development. We will also cover managing dependencies with `pip` and virtual environments, setting environment variables, integrating Docker for containerized development, and using Git and GitHub for version control. This comprehensive setup will prepare you for efficient and effective development with FastAPI.

Multiple Choice Questions

1. **What is one of the primary advantages of FastAPI?**
    a. High performance
    b. Synchronous support
    c. Complex setup
    d. Limited community support
2. **Which library does FastAPI use for data validation?**
    a. Marshmallow
    b. Pydantic
    c. SQLAlchemy
    d. Django ORM
3. **What is the key feature of RESTful APIs?**
    a. Stateful interactions
    b. Resource-based architecture
    c. Tight coupling of client and server
    d. Complicated URIs
4. **Which HTTP method is used to retrieve data in RESTful APIs?**
    a. POST
    b. PUT
    c. DELETE
    d. GET
5. **In RESTful APIs, what does statelessness mean?**
    a. Each request from client to server must contain all the information the server needs to fulfil that request.
    b. Server maintains client state.
    c. Client maintains server state.
    d. None of the above.

6. **Which of the following is NOT a common HTTP status code used in RESTful APIs?**
    a. 200 OK
    b. 404 Not Found
    c. 600 Invalid Request
    d. 201 Created
7. **What is the typical use of the POST method in RESTful APIs?**
    a. To retrieve a resource
    b. To update a resource
    c. To create a new resource
    d. To delete a resource
8. **Why is FastAPI considered to be fast?**
    a. It uses a compiled language
    b. It relies on synchronous operations
    c. It uses asynchronous capabilities
    d. It caches all responses
9. **Which of the following is an example of a well-formed RESTful resource URI?**
    a. /getBooks
    b. /books
    c. /books?get
    d. /fetchBooks
10. **What is the role of a Pydantic model in FastAPI?**
    a. To manage database interactions
    b. To validate and parse data
    c. To render HTML templates
    d. To handle HTTP requests

11. **What kind of documentation does FastAPI automatically generate?**
    a. Javadoc
    b. Swagger and ReDoc
    c. JSDoc
    d. None
12. **Which principle ensures that each resource in a RESTful API is identified by a unique URI?**
    a. Statelessness
    b. Client-server separation
    c. Uniform interface
    d. Resource-based architecture
13. **What HTTP method is typically used to update an existing resource in a RESTful API?**
    a. GET
    b. POST
    c. PUT
    d. DELETE
14. **Which HTTP status code indicates a successful POST request?**
    a. 200 OK
    b. 201 Created
    c. 400 Bad Request
    d. 401 Unauthorized
15. **Which of the following is a benefit of using RESTful APIs?**
    a. Tight coupling between client and server
    b. Scalability and flexibility
    c. Stateful interactions
    d. Platform dependency

Answers

Question	Answer
1	a
2	b
3	b
4	d
5	a
6	c
7	c
8	c
9	b
10	b
11	b
12	d
13	c
14	b
15	b

CHAPTER 2
Setting Up the Development Environment

Introduction

Setting up the development environment is one of the most important things any developer should do when starting a FastAPI project. The chapter will walk you through step-by-step to ensure that your environment is perfectly configured for FastAPI development.

We start with the installation of Python, since it is the main language used in FastAPI, covering installation processes on Windows, macOS, and Linux. It is basic to guarantee that Python is correctly installed and configured, since all the other development activities will be based on it.

The next topic will be the selection and setting up of a proper Integrated Development Environment (IDE) or text editor. An IDE or text editor would impact the amount of productive time and ease in development. We will look into some of the popular variants such as VSCode, PyCharm, Sublime Text, and Atom, and demonstrate in detail how to set them up with tips. These tools offer features such as code completion, active debugging, and integration with version control that are very critical for efficient FastAPI development.

Apart from setting up IDEs, the chapter inspects crucial parts of dependency management using pip and virtual environments. Correct dependency management provides consistency in projects and avoids potential conflicts. We will walk you through how to create and use **`requirements.txt`** and set up and manage virtual environments with both **`venv`** **`virtualenv`** and.

We also put some concentration on the need for setting up environment variables and added instructions for different operating systems. Environment variables are important in configuration settings, securing them, and making their management efficient across a number of development, testing, and production environments.

Apart from this, we will introduce integration with Docker, which contributes to the enhancement of your development workflow. Docker provides you with the possibility of having consistent development environments and making the process of deployment smoother. We will walk through how to set up a Dockerfile for a FastAPI project and finally run your application in a Docker container.

Finally, we will look into version control with Git and GitHub. Version control is a tool for managing changes to your code. It makes it easier to collaborate with other developers and gives you an overview of your project's history. We will go through the basic Git commands, setting up a GitHub repository, best practices for commit messages, and branching.

Structure

In this chapter, we will discuss the following topics:

- Installing Python
- **Choosing and Configuring IDEs and Text Editors**
    - Popular IDEs and Text Editors
    - Configuring Visual Studio Code (VSCode)
    - Configuring PyCharm
    - Configuring Sublime Text
    - Configuring Atom
- **Managing Dependencies with Pip**
    - Explanation of the `requirements.txt` File
    - How to Generate and Use `requirements.txt` for Dependency Management
- **Using Python Virtual Environments Effectively**
    - Differences between `venv` and `virtualenv`
    - Best Practices for Managing Virtual Environments
- **Setting Up Environment Variables**
    - Importance of Environment Variables in Development
    - How to Set Environment Variables in Different Operating Systems
- **Integrating Docker for Development**
    - Basics of Docker and Its Benefits
    - Setting Up a Dockerfile for a FastAPI Project

  - Running FastAPI in a Docker Container
- **Using Git and GitHub**
  - Basic Git Commands for Version Control
  - Setting Up a GitHub Repository
  - Best Practices for Commit Messages and Branching
- **IDE Specific Tips and Tricks**
  - Customizing Themes and Layouts for Better Productivity
  - Using Plugins and Extensions for Specific Needs
  - Shortcuts and Tools for Debugging and Testing Within the IDE

Installing Python

Python is the core language that will be used for FastAPI development. This chapter explains how to download, install, and configure Python on various operating systems. You will also learn about configuring a virtual environment, very important in keeping order among project dependencies.

Detailed Steps

The detailed installation steps will be explained here, along with all the operating system variants as well.

Downloading Python

1. Go to the official Python website `https://www.python.org/`
2. Head to the download section and acquire the latest stable version compatible with your OS, whether it be Windows, macOS, or Linux.
3. Installers are available in Python under different operating systems, so whatever development environment is used, a user can get up and run.

Installing Python on Windows

1. Download the executable installer.
2. Run the installer and make sure to select the option to "`Add Python to PATH`". This setting allows you to run Python from any command prompt without specifying the full path.
3. Follow the on-screen instructions to complete the installation. You can optionally customize the installation, but for the most part, the default settings should be fine.

4. Open Command Prompt after installation and test it by running:

   ```
   python --version.
   ```

5. You should see the version of Python you installed. Otherwise, ensure that Python is added to your PATH environment variable correctly.

Installing Python on macOS

1. MacOS comes with Python pre-installed, but most of the time, it is way outdated. The latest version needs to be installed. macOS.
2. Download a macOS Installer from the Python website.
3. Download either an installer package, run it, and follow the setup instructions.
4. You can also use Homebrew to install Python.

   ```
   brew install python
   ```

5. After installation, open Terminal and test it:

   ```
   python3 --version
   ```

6. Note that on macOS, you may need to use **`python3`** instead of **`python`** to avoid conflicts with the pre-installed version.

Installing Python on Linux

1. Most of the Linux distributions actually come with Python already installed. However, you may be required to update or upgrade Python to the latest version.
2. Update the package list and install Python by calling the package manager for your distribution. For instance, on Debian-based systems such as Ubuntu:

   ```
   sudo apt-get update
   sudo apt-get install python3
   ```

3. Verify if it installed correctly:

   ```
   python3 --version
   ```

Setting Up a Virtual Environment

1. It is necessary to have virtual environments for handling dependencies and avoiding conflicts between different projects.
2. Create a new directory for your FastAPI project and navigate into it:

   ```
   mkdir fastapi-project
   cd fastapi-project
   ```

3. Create a virtual environment:

   ```
   python -m venv fastapi-env
   ```

4. Activate the virtual environment:
   - On Windows:
     ```
     fastapi-env\Scripts\activate
     ```
   - On macOS/Linux:
     ```
     source fastapi-env/bin/activate
     ```
5. Notice that, after activation, your terminal prompt changes to let you know that you are now working in a virtual environment.
6. To deactivate the virtual environment, you simply need to type:
   ```
   deactivate
   ```

Verifying the Virtual Environment

1. To ensure your virtual environment is set up correctly, install a sample package, such as `requests`
   ```
   pip install requests
   ```
2. Verify the installation:
   ```
   pip list
   ```
3. You should see `requests` listed among the installed packages. This confirms that your virtual environment is functioning correctly.

By the end of this section, you will have installed and configured Python on your system and set up a virtual environment for the FastAPI project. It will enable you to manage all the dependencies cleanly and keep your development environment completely separated from other projects.

Choosing and Configuring IDEs and Text Editors

The right IDE or text editor can make all the difference in the development experience with FastAPI. In this section, we will review some of the popular tools, with detailed setup instructions and additional configuration tips to help you improve your development workflow. We will cover Visual Studio Code, PyCharm, Sublime Text, and Atom so you can pick and configure one of them that serves you the best.

Popular IDEs and Text Editors

Here are the four most used and famous text editors. We will discuss the installation and configuration of FastAPI based on these text editors' point of view.

- Visual Studio Code (VSCode)

- PyCharm
- Sublime Text
- Atom

Configuring Visual Studio Code (VSCode)

VSCode is a very powerful and flexible text editor; it is widely applied in the developer community. It provides full support for Python and FastAPI development with a combination of extensions and built-in features. This section will walk you through setting up VSCode for the best possible development experience with FastAPI.

1. **Installation**
    a. From the following link, download and install VSCode `https://code.visualstudio.com/`
    b. Open VSCode once the installation is done.
2. **Essential Extensions**
    a. Install the Python extension by Microsoft. It provides IntelliSense, linting, debugging, and more.
        i. Open the Extensions view by clicking the square icon in the left sidebar or pressing *Ctrl+Shift+*X.
        ii. Search for "Python" and click Install.
    b. Install Pylance for language support with improved performance.
        i. In the Extensions view, search for "**Pylance**" and click Install.
3. **Setting Up a FastAPI Project**
    a. Open your project folder in VSCode.
        i. Click on **File > Open Folder** and select your project directory.
    b. Set up the Python interpreter to use your virtual environment.
        i. Open the Command Palette with *Ctrl+Shift+P* and type "**`Python: Select Interpreter`**".
        ii. Choose the interpreter from your virtual environment (**`fastapi-env`**).
4. **Creating a Launch Configuration for Debugging**
    a. Create a launch configuration file to enable FastAPI applications to be debugged.

i. In the sidebar, click on the Run view or press *Ctrl+Shift+D*.

ii. Click on "**create a launch.json file**" and select **Python**.

iii. Add the following configuration:

```
{
    "name": "Python: FastAPI",
    "type": "python",
    "request": "launch",
    "program": "${workspaceFolder}/main.py",
    "args": ["run", "app:app", "--reload"],
    "console": "integratedTerminal"
}
```

b. Replace `main.py` and `app:app` with the appropriate entry point for your FastAPI application.

Additional Tips for VSCode

- Customize Settings for an Improved Development Experience:
  - Open the Settings view with *Ctrl+*, and search for relevant settings (for example, auto-save, linting options).
- Use integrated terminals:
  - Open an integrated terminal with *Ctrl+* and run commands directly within VSCode.
- Create and Use Code Snippets for Common FastAPI Boilerplate Code:
  - Go to **File > Preferences > User Snippets** and create a new snippet file for Python.

Configuring PyCharm

PyCharm is a rather popular IDE for Python development, considerable for its features and great support for web development frameworks. The following section provides an in-depth guide on how to set up PyCharm to perform FastAPI development, so you can make the most out of it.

1. **Installation**

   a. Download and install PyCharm from the official website `https://www.jetbrains.com/pycharm/`

   b. Open PyCharm after installation is complete.

2. **Setting Up a Project**
    a. Open PyCharm and create a new project.
        i. Click on "**Create New Project**" and select "**Pure Python**".
        ii. Choose your project location and click "**Create**".
    b. Set the project interpreter to your virtual environment.
        i. Go to **File > Settings > Project: [Your Project] > Python Interpreter**.
        ii. Click on the gear icon and select "**Add Interpreter**".
        iii. Choose "**Existing environment**", and select the interpreter from your virtual environment (`fastapi-env`).
3. **Configuring Run/Debug Configurations**
    a. Configure run/debug configurations for FastAPI.
        i. Go to **Run > Edit** Configurations.
        ii. Click on the "+" icon and select "**Python**".
        iii. Set the script path to your FastAPI entry point (for example, **`main.py`**).
        iv. Add script parameters to run FastAPI with `uvicorn`:

```
run app:app - reload
```

    b. Replace **`main.py`** and **`app:app`** with the appropriate entry point for your FastAPI application.

Additional Tips for PyCharm

- Customize keymap and settings for a better development experience.
    - Go to **File > Settings** and explore various options (for example, editor settings, keymap customization).
- Use integrated version control.
    - PyCharm offers built-in support for Git and other version control systems.
    - Go to **VCS > Enable Version Control Integration**, and follow the prompts.

Configuring Sublime Text

Sublime Text is an ultra-light, highly extensible text editor; it is one of the most-used text editors among developers because of its speed and agility. Now, this section will walk you through configuring Sublime Text for FastAPI development.

1. **Installation**
   a. Download and install Sublime Text from the official website. `https://www.sublimetext.com/`
   b. Open Sublime Text after installation is complete.
2. **Installing packages**
   a. Install Package Control for easy package management.
      i. Open the Command Palette with *Ctrl+Shift+P*, and type "**Install Package Control**".
   b. Use Package Control to install the Anaconda package for Python support.
      i. Open the **Command Palette** again, type "**Package Control: Install Package**", and search for "**Anaconda**".
   c. Install additional packages for better productivity, such as SublimeLinter and GitGutter.
3. **Project Setup**
   a. Open your project folder.
      i. Go to **File > Open Folder** and select your project directory.
   b. Set up build systems for running and debugging FastAPI applications.
      i. Go to **Tools > Build System > New Build System**, and add the following configuration:

```
{
    "cmd": ["uvicorn", "main:app", "--reload"],
    "selector": "source.python"
}
```

      ii. Save the file with a descriptive name, such as **`FastAPI.sublime-build`**.

Additional Tips for Sublime Text

- Customize settings for a better development experience.
  - Go to **Preferences > Settings** and adjust various options (for example, font size, tab width).
- Create and use code snippets for common FastAPI boilerplate code.
  - Go to **Tools > Developer > New Snippet** and create snippets for frequently used code patterns.

Configuring Atom

Atom is a hackable text editor made by GitHub that is known for its flexibility and its huge package ecosystem. The following section helps to guide you in the configuration of Atom for FastAPI development to ensure that everything goes smoothly and productively.

1. **Installation**
    a. Download and install Atom from the official website. **`https://atom.io/`**
    b. Open Atom after installation is complete.
2. **Installing Packages**
    a. Install essential packages for Python development.
        i. Open the Settings view with *Ctrl+Comma* and go to the Install tab.
        ii. Search for and install the **`ide-python`** package for enhanced Python support.
        iii. Install the **`atom-ide-ui`** package for a better development experience.
3. **Project Setup**
    a. Open your project folder.
        i. Go to **File > Add Project Folder**, and select your project directory.
    b. Configure the Python interpreter to use your virtual environment.
        i. Create a **`.env`** file in your project root, and add the following line:

```
VIRTUAL_ENV=path/to/your/fastapi-env
```

Additional Tips for Atom

- Customize themes and layouts for a better development experience.
    - Go to **File > Settings > Themes** and explore various options.
- Use integrated terminals.
    - Install the **`platformio-ide-terminal`** package to run commands directly within Atom.
- Create and use code snippets for common FastAPI boilerplate code.
    - Go to **File > Snippets** and create snippets for frequently used code patterns.

This section will put you in a good position to select and set up an Integrated Development Environment or text editor best adapted to your workflow, thus offering you a smooth and productive environment for FastAPI projects. Detailed step-by-step installation and setup instructions are given for popular tools such as Visual Studio Code, PyCharm, Sublime Text, and Atom.

Managing Dependencies with Pip

Proper dependency management is essential for any Python project, including FastAPI applications. One of the ways to do this is through pip, Python's package installer, to install and then manage packages. In the next section, we will learn how to handle such dependencies using pip, and explain why and how to use the requirements.txt file. This will help to keep your project organized, but also makes it easy to reproduce the development environment either on another machine or when working with collaborators.

Explanation of the `requirements.txt` File

The **`requirements.txt`** is a text file containing all the packages your project needs to run, along with the particular version needed. The contents of this file will enable you to:

- **Dependency sharing:** Simply share dependencies for your project
- **Environment reproducibility:** Install the same packages across dev, CI, and other environments.
- **Maintain consistency:** Keep track of the versions of the packages your project is using, which is especially useful in updating or deploying your app.

How to Generate and Use `requirements.txt` for Dependency Management

Managing dependencies efficiently ensures consistency across different environments, and makes it easier to share your project with others. The **`requirements.txt`** file helps track installed packages and allows for quick installation of dependencies.

It helps in maintaining a stable and reproducible environment by specifying the exact versions of dependencies required for your project. This prevents compatibility issues and ensures that your application runs smoothly across different systems

1. **Installing Packages with Pip**

    a. To install a package using `pip`, simply run:

    ```
    pip install package_name
    ```

   b. For example, to install FastAPI and Uvicorn (a fast ASGI server for FastAPI), run:

      ```
      pip install fastapi uvicorn
      ```

   c. **`pip`** will download and install the specified packages and their dependencies.

2. **Generating `requirements.txt`**

   a. Once you have installed all the necessary packages for your project, you can generate a **`requirements.txt`** file that lists them.

   b. Navigate to your project directory and run:

      ```
      pip freeze > requirements.txt
      ```

   c. This command will create a **`requirements.txt`** file containing a list of installed packages and their versions, like this:

      ```
      fastapi==0.65.2
      uvicorn==0.14.0
      ```

3. **Using `requirements.txt`**

   a. To install all the packages listed in a **`requirements.txt`** file, use the following command:

      ```
      pip install -r requirements.txt
      ```

   b. This command reads the file and installs all the listed packages, ensuring that the exact versions specified are used.

4. **Updating `requirements.txt`**

   - If you add new packages to your project or update existing ones, you should regenerate the **`requirements.txt`** file to reflect these changes.
   - Simply run **`pip freeze > requirements.txt`** again to update the file with the current state of your installed packages.

Best Practices

- **Pinning versions**: Always specify exact versions of packages in **`requirements.txt`** to avoid unexpected changes that might break your application.
- **Virtual environments**: Use virtual environments to manage dependencies for each project separately. This avoids conflicts between packages required by different projects.
- **Regular updates**: Regularly update your dependencies to benefit from bug fixes and new features. Test your application thoroughly after updates to ensure compatibility.

By following these steps and best practices, you can effectively manage dependencies in your FastAPI project, ensuring consistency, reproducibility, and ease of collaboration.

Using Python Virtual Environments Effectively

Amongst the key tools in isolating the dependencies of a project and keeping the development setup clean and manageable are Python virtual environments. A virtual environment assists in avoiding incompatibilities related to different projects' requirements for specific packages. Additionally, it keeps you consistent between development, test, and production environments. This section aims to provide an overview of how **venv** differs from **virtualenv** and some best practices, when using them to effectively manage virtual environments.

Differences Between venv and virtualenv

1. **venv**
    - **Built-in: venv** comes by default with Python's standard library from Python 3.3 onwards, so it is easy to get to without any additional package installations.
    - **Basic functionality**: It is the version with the very least functionality that only provides basic functionality to create and manage virtual environments. It thus lacks some features of the popular **virtualenv** package.
2. **virtualenv**
    - **Standalone package**: **virtualenv** is a package independent of Python, so it must be installed using **pip**.
    - **Compatibility**: It works with both Python 2 and Python 3, so it is okay for projects that require backward compatibility.
    - **Advanced features**: Enhanced isolation, more comprehensive support for a variety of Python interpreters, and, most importantly, faster times while creating environments.

Example Usage

- Creating a virtual environment with **venv**

```
python -m venv myenv
```

- Creating a virtual environment with **virtualenv**

```
pip install virtualenv
virtualenv myenv
```

Best Practices for Managing Virtual Environments

- Creating Virtual Environments
  - Always create a new virtual environment for each project to ensure dependency isolation.
  - Use meaningful names for virtual environments to easily identify their purpose.
- Activating and Deactivating Virtual Environments
  - Activate the virtual environment before working on your project to ensure you are using the correct dependencies.
    - On Windows:

      ```
      myenv\Scripts\activate
      ```
    - On macOS/Linux

      ```
      source myenv/bin/activate
      ```
  - Deactivate the environment when you are done:

    ```
    deactivate
    ```
- Managing Dependencies
  - Install dependencies only after activating the virtual environment to ensure they are correctly scoped.
  - Use a **`requirements.txt`** file to keep track of your dependencies and share them with others.
- Updating Virtual Environments
  - Regularly update your virtual environment's dependencies to benefit from the latest features and security fixes.
  - Test your application thoroughly after updating to ensure compatibility.
- Version Control Integration
  - Exclude the virtual environment directory from version control by adding it to your **`.gitignore`** file:

    ```
    myenv/
    ```
  - Include the **`requirements.txt`** file in version control to allow others to replicate your environment.

- Automating Environment Setup
    - Use tools such as **`Makefile`** or shell scripts to automate the creation and activation of virtual environments, making it easier for new developers to set up their workspace.

Example `Makefile`

```
setup:
    python -m venv myenv
    source myenv/bin/activate && pip install -r requirements.txt

activate:
    source myenv/bin/activate
```

By following these best practices, you can effectively manage Python virtual environments, ensuring a clean, consistent, and conflict-free development setup for your FastAPI projects.

Setting Up Environment Variables

Environment variables play a crucial role in software development, especially when dealing with configuration settings that differ between development, testing, and production environments. They allow you to keep sensitive information secure and make your application more flexible and portable.

Importance of Environment Variables in Development

Environment variables enable you to:

- Store sensitive information securely (for example, API keys, database credentials).
- Configure application settings without hardcoding values.
- Simplify deployment across different environments.

How to Set Environment Variables in Different Operating Systems

Environment variables are used to store configuration settings, secrets, and system paths without hardcoding them into the application. Setting them correctly ensures smooth operation across different environments, and enhances security.

- Windows
  1. Open the **Start menu** and search for "**Environment Variables**".
  2. Click on "**Edit the system environment variables**".
  3. In the **System Properties** window, click "**Environment Variables**".
  4. Click "**New**" to add a new variable, or select an existing one to edit.
  5. Enter the variable name and value, then click "**OK**".
- macOS/Linux
  1. Open a terminal window.
  2. To set a variable temporarily, use:
     ```
     export VARIABLE_NAME=value
     ```
  3. To set it permanently, add the export command to your shell's configuration file (for example, `~/.bashrc, ~/.zshrc`):
     ```
     echo 'export VARIABLE_NAME=value' >> ~/.bashrc
     ```
  4. Apply the changes:
     ```
     source ~/.bashrc
     ```

Integrating Docker for Development

Docker simplifies the setup and deployment of applications by packaging them in lightweight, portable containers. This section covers the basics of Docker and how to set up a Docker environment for FastAPI development.

Basics of Docker and Its Benefits

Docker allows you to:

- Isolate applications in containers.
- Ensure consistency across development, testing, and production environments.
- Simplify dependency management and deployment.

Setting Up a Dockerfile for a FastAPI Project

A **Dockerfile** helps in containerizing a FastAPI application, making it portable and easy to deploy across different environments. By defining dependencies and configurations within the Dockerfile, you can ensure consistency and scalability for your application.

1. Create a Dockerfile in your project directory:

```
FROM python:3.9-slim
WORKDIR /app
COPY . .
RUN pip install -r requirements.txt
CMD ["uvicorn", "main:app", "--host", "0.0.0.0", "--port",
"8000"]
```

2. Build the Docker image:

```
docker build -t fastapi-app .
```

Running FastAPI in a Docker Container

Running a FastAPI application inside a Docker container ensures a consistent environment across different systems. This approach simplifies deployment, improves scalability, and helps manage dependencies efficiently.

1. Run the Docker container:

```
docker run -d -p 8000:8000 fastapi-app
```

2. Access your FastAPI application at http://localhost:8000.

Using Git and GitHub

Git is a version control system that helps you track changes in your code, collaborate with others, and manage different versions of your project. GitHub is a cloud-based platform that hosts your Git repositories, and provides collaboration tools.

Basic Git Commands for Version Control

Git is a powerful version control system that helps track changes, collaborate with others, and manage code efficiently. Understanding basic Git commands allows developers to maintain a structured workflow and avoid code conflicts.

- Initialize a repository:

```
git init
```

- Clone a repository:

```
git clone <repository_url>
```

- Commit changes:

```
git add .
git commit -m "Commit message"
```

- Push changes to GitHub:

```
git push origin main
```

Setting Up a GitHub Repository

A GitHub repository allows you to store, manage, and collaborate on your code with version control. Setting it up properly ensures seamless tracking of changes and easy collaboration with others.

1. Create a repository on GitHub:
   a. Go to GitHub and click on "**New repository**".
   b. Enter the **repository name**, **description**, and **settings**.
   c. Click "**Create repository**".
2. Connect your local repository to GitHub:

```
git remote add origin <repository_url>
git push -u origin main
```

Best Practices for Commit Messages and Branching

Clear and descriptive commit messages help maintain a readable project history, making it easier to track changes. Effective branching strategies, such as feature branching and Git Flow, improve collaboration and streamline development workflows.

- **Write clear, concise commit messages**: Summarize changes in the present tense (for example, "Add feature X").
- **Use branches for features and fixes**: Create a new branch for each feature or bug fix to keep the main branch stable.

IDE Specific Tips and Tricks

Customizing your IDE can significantly improve your productivity. This section covers tips and tricks for popular IDEs such as VSCode and PyCharm.

Customizing Themes and Layouts for Better Productivity

Customizing themes and layouts in development environments can enhance focus, reduce eye strain, and improve overall productivity. Choosing the right color schemes, fonts, and workspace organization helps create a comfortable and efficient workflow.

- **VSCode**: Install themes from the marketplace (for example, "One Dark Pro") and customize the layout through the settings.
- **PyCharm**: Use the "**Appearance and Behavior**" settings to change themes and configure the toolbar and window layout.

Using Plugins and Extensions for Specific Needs

Plugins and extensions enhance functionality by adding specialized features tailored to your workflow. Selecting the right tools can streamline development, automate tasks, and improve overall efficiency.

- **VSCode**: Install extensions such as Python, Pylance, and Docker for enhanced functionality.
- **PyCharm**: Use plugins such as `.env files support` for environment variable management and **Docker** for container integration.

Shortcuts and Tools for Debugging and Testing Within the IDE

Using shortcuts and built-in debugging tools in an IDE can significantly speed up the development process. Features such as breakpoints, step-by-step execution, and automated testing integrations help identify and resolve issues efficiently.

- **VSCode:**
  - Use the integrated terminal (`*Ctrl+*`) to run commands.
  - Set breakpoints and use the debugger to step through code.
- **PyCharm**:
  - Use the "**Run**" tool window for running and debugging applications.
  - Set breakpoints, inspect variables, and step through code with the built-in debugger.

By following these guidelines, you can create a highly efficient development environment tailored to your needs, enabling you to build and deploy FastAPI applications effectively.

Conclusion

In this chapter, we explored the essential steps to set up an efficient development environment for FastAPI projects. We began by installing Python, and then discussed the importance and practicalities of managing dependencies with **`pip`** and the **`requirements.txt`** file. We also covered how to use Python virtual environments to isolate project dependencies and ensure consistency. Additionally, we walked through the process of choosing and configuring IDEs and text editors to enhance productivity. By following these guidelines, you can establish a robust and efficient setup that will support your FastAPI development journey.

The next chapter will delve into the specifics of installing FastAPI. We will guide you through the installation process, ensuring that you have all the necessary tools and libraries set up correctly. We will also discuss the initial configuration and basic setup needed to get your first FastAPI application up and running. This foundational knowledge will be crucial as you start developing APIs with FastAPI, enabling you to leverage its full potential for building high-performance web applications.

Multiple Choice Questions

1. **What is the primary purpose of using virtual environments in Python?**
    a. To improve performance
    b. To isolate project dependencies
    c. To increase security
    d. To enable multi-threading
2. **Which command is used to create a virtual environment using venv?**
    a. **`python -m venv create`**
    b. **`python -m venv newenv`**
    c. **`python -m venv myenv`**
    d. **`python -m venv setup`**
3. **How can you set an environment variable temporarily on macOS/Linux?**
    a. **`env VARIABLE_NAME=value`**
    b. **`export VARIABLE_NAME=value`**
    c. **`set VARIABLE_NAME=value`**
    d. **`define VARIABLE_NAME=value`**

4. **How do you install all dependencies listed in a `requirements.txt` file?**
    a. `pip install -r requirements.txt`
    b. `pip install requirements.txt`
    c. `pip import requirements.txt`
    d. `pip setup -r requirements.txt`
5. **What is the benefit of using Docker for development?**
    a. Faster execution of code
    b. Application isolation and consistency
    c. Enhanced security features
    d. Better debugging capabilities
6. **Which command is used to activate a virtual environment on Windows?**
    a. `activate myenv`
    b. `myenv\activate`
    c. `myenv\Scripts\activate`
    d. `start myenv`
7. **What file should you add your virtual environment directory to in order to exclude it from version control?**
    a. `.gitignore`
    b. `requirements.txt`
    c. `env_exclude.txt`
    d. `config.ignore`
8. **What is the purpose of the `requirements.txt` file?**
    a. To list Python version requirements
    b. To list all the packages and their versions required for the project
    c. To specify environment variables
    d. To configure IDE settings

9. **Which IDE is mentioned for customizing themes and layouts for better productivity?**
   a. Eclipse
   b. NetBeans
   c. VSCode
   d. IntelliJ IDEA
10. **What is a key advantage of using Python virtual environments?**
   a. Simplified code syntax
   b. Isolating dependencies for different projects
   c. Improved graphics support
   d. Enhanced error handling

Answers

Question	Answer
1	b
2	c
3	b
4	a
5	b
6	c
7	a
8	b
9	c
10	b

CHAPTER 3
Installing FastAPI

Introduction

This chapter covers the basics of setting up FastAPI—a foundation that secures your development environment, and truly equips you to develop web APIs efficiently. In fact, FastAPI has gained rapid momentum, and for reasons such as its high performance, intuitiveness in design, and automatically generated interactive API documentation. Considering that you are about to unlock the potential of this modern framework, it is important that you first do a full and appropriate installation and configuration to lay the foundation for successful project development.

FastAPI is based on Python 3.7 and above, taking advantage of the feature of Python type hinting and asynchronous programming to provide unprecedented speed and efficiency in development. Before delving into the core features of FastAPI, this chapter will walk you through the installation process to make sure all necessary components are set up. This step-by-step guide will have you up and running even if you're migrating from another framework or starting completely from scratch, guiding you through how to avoid some common pitfalls while creating a clean, reliable setup.

One of the key elements introduced in this chapter is the use of virtual environments. Virtual environments are a must for any dependency management: they keep your development environment nice and tidy, separated from other projects. By creating a dedicated environment for FastAPI, you won't run into problems caused by different package versions, so your setup will be coherent and stable. We are going to walk you through setting up a virtual environment, specifically for FastAPI, describing the advantages and best practices that will help you maintain your development environment with ease.

In this chapter, we go through how you can create the basic project structure after performing the installation and setting up of your virtual environment. Proper structuring of a project is critical in ensuring code quality and scalability as your application grows. We are going to look at how you can create directories, configuration files, and basic setup that forms the skeleton of any FastAPI project. Then, we will also implement a simple "Hello, World!

This will be an "application" to verify that everything is working correctly; it will give you the confidence that your setup is sound and ready for further development. This chapter will be comprehensive and easy to follow, with detailed instructions and explanations suitable for all levels of developers. The idea is that you will, at the end of this chapter, have a complete FastAPI environment, with a well-structured setup for a project and all the necessary tools for developing your APIs.

Well, this is a basic knowledge that will be important in going further into more advanced topics, and it will set the path for a good start of your development journey with FastAPI.

Structure

In this chapter, we will discuss the following topics:

- **Installation Guide**
  - Detailed Instructions on Installing FastAPI Using **`pip`**
  - Overview of Additional Required Packages, such as **`uvicorn`** for Running the FastAPI Application
  - Troubleshooting Common Installation Issues
- **Setting Up a Virtual Environment**
  - Importance of Using a Virtual Environment for FastAPI Projects
  - Step-by-Step Guide to Creating and Activating a Virtual Environment
  - Installing FastAPI Within the Virtual Environment to Isolate Project Dependencies
- **Initial Project Setup**
  - Creating the Initial Folder Structure for a FastAPI Project
  - Setting Up Configuration Files and Environment Variables
  - Writing a Basic "Hello, World!" FastAPI Application to Verify the Setup

The chapter will therefore be key in ensuring the readers are equipped with the skills and confidence needed for fast API installation, together with the management of their development environments. It will help the readers learn how to install Python, create and activate virtual environments, and finally install FastAPI using `pip`. The chapter will also guide readers on how to structure their FastAPI projects in a way that will be easily maintainable and scalable. By the end of this chapter, the reader will have a solid foundation for starting any development in FastAPI because it will show how to properly structure your project.

Installation Guide

Before being able to create web APIs with FastAPI, you would have installed it along with its dependencies. FastAPI is a modern Python web framework for building APIs with high speed and performance in mind. Among the main advantages are ease of installation via **`pip`**, Python's package installer.

Detailed Instructions on Installing FastAPI Using `pip`

Prerequisites: First, you will require Python on your system. Once you have Python up and running, you can straightforwardly install FastAPI. You would go ahead with the **`pip`** command, which is normally present in any standard Python installation, in order to install FastAPI and perhaps, some other third-party packages that might be necessary.

The following section will guide you through the step-by-step installation of FastAPI, including the use of `pip` to handle all the dependencies, setting up a development environment, and basic troubleshooting of common installation problems. Be it for your very first project or if you are an established developer, this section will have you up and running with FastAPI in no time.

Installation with **`pip`** is very easy using pip, Python's package installer. First of all, make sure the Python environment is set up and updated. **`pip`** is a multifunctional tool that makes it very easy to download and install packages from the Python Package Index. For this reason, let us go through the installation of FastAPI and its core components and make sure your setup is ready for development.

Introduction to pip

`pip` is an indispensable utility for any Python developer; it is the de facto package manager for Python libraries and frameworks. **`Pip`** lets you install, upgrade, or delete packages to set up your development environment correctly for your projects. More than a convenience, **`pip`** is essential in keeping your development environment clean and neat. Working with FastAPI, `pip` is especially helpful in that it will let you easily install FastAPI and its dependencies, so that you will know from the very beginning that your project is set up with everything it could need.

With pip, developers grant access to a large repository of Python packages hosted in the Python Package Index. That means you are only a few commands away from integrating various libraries into your FastAPI application–be it database support, handling asynchronous tasks, or even security features. Pip also affords ease regarding managing package versions, which is important to maintain compatibility and stability within FastAPI applications.

Apart from installation, updating packages with `pip` is relatively easy to newer versions–which is how one keeps their projects updated with the latest bug fixes and security patches. On the flip side, **`pip`** can also be used to downgrade a package to any previous version in case of a newer update that introduces bugs. It leaves room for either scenario, so you can adapt it to the ever-changing needs of your project, not necessarily tampering with your workflow.

In short, pip is not just a utility to install software, but part of the Python ecosystem to keep you working effectively and efficiently with the dependencies of your project, making it ready for development using FastAPI.

Installing FastAPI

FastAPI has been designed as a lightweight; therefore, the setup should be sleek and quick. Our first action will be to verify that our system has at least Python 3.7 to run FastAPI. Start by opening a terminal or command prompt, and checking your Python version with the following command:

```
python --version
```

If your version of Python is 3.7 or later, then you are good to go ahead with the installation of FastAPI. Thanks to pip - the package manager for Python, it would be easy to install FastAPI. You can install it by executing:

```
pip install fastapi
```

`pip` will then connect to the **Python Package Index called PyPI**, and it will download the latest version of FastAPI, downloading dependencies required by FastAPI. Since FastAPI was designed to be lightweight, it will not only be fast in installation but also very light on your system. This is one of the many reasons FastAPI became popular among developers who needed to rapidly get web APIs up and running without the feeling of heavyweight frameworks.

That means that after installation, FastAPI is immediately ready within your Python environment. It is one of the first steps for your FastAPI development projects, making sure you have all the packages and tools necessary to create modern, high-performance web APIs. In addition to installing the core FastAPI package, you might also want to consider an ASGI server such as Uvicorn, which makes serving your application much easier. You can install it using:

```
pip install "uvicorn[standard]"
```

This command will install Uvicorn, a lightning-fast ASGI server, along with some extra dependencies that improve its performance and functionalities. With both FastAPI and Uvicorn installed, your environment will have all the paraphernalia necessary to cope with modern API development requirements, from handling asynchronous tasks to serving requests efficiently.

All in all, setup with FastAPI is fast and painless: Verify the Python version your system is running, install FastAPI via pip, and optionally set up Uvicorn for running your FastAPI applications. Now you are off to a great start in building robust and scalable APIs with FastAPI.

Installing Uvicorn

FastAPI requires an ASGI server to serve your applications. Uvicorn is a lightning-fast ASGI server, powered by uvloop and httptools. It runs asynchronous Python web applications, including FastAPI applications. For installing Uvicorn with pip:

```
pip install uvicorn
```

This command installs Uvicorn along with its dependencies. Once installed, Uvicorn can be used to serve your FastAPI applications.

Installing Optional Packages

Therefore, when building a FastAPI application, sometimes your project might need additional features that are probably not provided out of the box by it. The requirements differ based on your application. Thus, there exist several complementary packages that would enhance your application to greater heights. Of course, some of the most commonly used complementary packages alongside FastAPI include:

- **Pydantic**: Pydantic is a crucial package for FastAPI because it deals with validation, together with managing settings. FastAPI uses Pydantic models to validate data that is coming into and being sent out of your application to ensure that it conforms to a set schema and constraints. This becomes helpful when working with complicated data structures to maintain integrity across your application.
- **SQLAlchemy**: In case your project needs to interact with any kind of database, it is a great and flexible **Object-Relational Mapping (ORM)** tool to define the models of the database and interact with it using Python code. Due to SQLAlchemy, all the complexity of SQL queries is abstracted, which enables you to work with your database in a more Pythonic way. This makes integrating databases into your FastAPI applications much easier.
- **Jinja2**: In projects that require the rendering of dynamic HTML, such as web applications based on server-side templates, Jinja2 is an excellent templating engine. Under Jinja2, you can write HTML templates with placeholder dynamic data; thus, it would be rendered on the server side before actually being sent to the client. This is of great help in order to make web pages that have to show the data from your FastAPI application.

These packages you can install using pip, which is Python's package installer. For instance, to install SQLAlchemy on your computer, you execute this command in the terminal:

```
pip install sqlalchemy
```

For any other package you need, you can install it similarly. These surely are packages that would add more power to your FastAPI project, where it gets robust tools for data validation, database interaction, and web templating that permit developing larger applications, full of features.

Verifying the Installation

To ensure that both FastAPI and Uvicorn are installed correctly, you can run a quick test by creating a minimal FastAPI application, and serving it with Uvicorn. Create a file named **`main.py`** with the following content:

```
from fastapi import FastAPI

app = FastAPI()

@app.get("/")
async def read_root():
    return {"message": "Hello, World!"}
```

Run the application using Uvicorn:

```
uvicorn main:app --reload
```

Visit http://127.0.0.1:8000 in your browser to see the output. If everything is set up correctly, you should see the message "Hello, World!" displayed.

Overview of Additional Required Packages, such as Uvicorn for Running the FastAPI Application

Setting up a FastAPI application involves not only the installation of FastAPI but also understanding and incorporating other packages that would make your application run smoothly and meet the specific requirements of your current project. These packages provide critical functionalities for running an application server, data validation, and database interactions, amongst others, including rendering HTML templates. The following are a few of those key dependencies, and how they really help in reaping the overall performance and capability in a FastAPI project.

Uvicorn

Uvicorn is a lightning-fast ASGI server that is commonly used to run FastAPI applications. It's an essential component, since FastAPI is an ASGI-compatible framework; this means FastAPI needs an ASGI server to handle web requests asynchronously. Uvicorn supports both HTTP/1.1 and WebSocket protocols, enabling your FastAPI application to easily deal with real-time communication, long-lived connections, and background tasks. Uvicorn is a fully asynchronous server, meaning your application will handle more concurrent requests. It is an ideal choice where performance is critical.

You would run your FastAPI application, using Uvicorn, with a command like this:

```
uvicorn main:app --reload
```

In this command:

- **`main:app`** specifies the module (**`main.py`**) and the FastAPI application instance (`app`) to be run.
- The **`--reload`** flag allows the server to restart automatically whenever changes in the code are detected, which is particularly useful during development.

Starlette

Starlette is a lightweight ASGI framework that FastAPI is built upon. Although it gets installed automatically when you install FastAPI, understanding its role could be essential to unleashing the full power of FastAPI. Starlette provides a lot of foundational features that FastAPI builds on top of, including:

- **Routing**: Starlette is responsible for routing incoming HTTP requests to the correct path in your FastAPI application. This makes sure that the right endpoint logic is executed based on the request URL.
- **Middleware**: The middleware in Starlette allows you to process requests and responses globally, which enables all sorts of cross-cutting concerns: logging, security, and modifications of requests or responses before they reach your FastAPI routes.
- **Background Tasks**: Starlette enables you to execute tasks in the background. This is particularly useful in activities that have to occur outside the normal flow, including the sending of an email, and any other general data processing tasks.

Due to the feature-rich nature of Starlette, FastAPI can be very performant and flexible. Thus, it can be applied for simple and complex applications out of the box.

Pydantic

Pydantic is the other core dependency of FastAPI, and it is highly used to perform major tasks for data validation and setting management. FastAPI uses Pydantic models for:

- **Validate Incoming Data**: Pydantic validates that the data received by your application, through query parameters, request bodies, or form submissions, matches the predefined schema. In case of wrong data structure or types, FastAPI would automatically return an informative error message regarding the same.

- **Manage Settings:** Pydantic allows one to define the settings for an application in a typed way, and loads them from environment variables, configuration files, or directly from Python objects. This makes configuration across environments, namely development, testing, and production, much easier.

A mix of FastAPI and Pydantic will make your application robust, secure, and strongly data integrity-focused.

Databases

Most real-world FastAPI applications require some sort of persistent data storage and, thus, integration with a database. As it stands currently, an out-of-the-box FastAPI application does not support out-of-the-box database management. The good news, though, is that it is pretty easy to implement the support of any database with the use of various drivers and/or ORMs. Common tools to use include:

- **SQLAlchemy**: SQLAlchemy is arguably one of the most popular ORMs in the Python ecosystem. It allows the developer to define database schemas with Python classes while offering an easy way to interact with your database without actually writing raw SQL queries. At this time, it supports quite a broad variety of databases: from PostgreSQL and MySQL to SQLite; it also has tools for complex queries, migrations, and relationship management.
- **Tortoise ORM**: Another ORM that was built with full asynchrony in mind, so it is well-suited to FastAPI's async superpowers. Lightweight and easy to use, it supports migrations out of the box, and relational database management.

You would typically install the packages you need to connect FastAPI with your database via `pip`. For instance:

```
pip install sqlalchemy
```

This enables you to seamlessly integrate your FastAPI application with the database of your choice, ensuring efficient data storage and retrieval.

Jinja2 and Templates

While FastAPI is designed to make API development easy, there are times when you might want to render HTML templates, most especially in web applications with dynamic content. **Jinja2** can be used together with FastAPI for server-side rendering of HTML.

- **Dynamic HTML Generation:** Jinja2 allows the developer to write HTML templates with placeholders to hold dynamic content. Such templates can then be used by FastAPI, which merges the static content with dynamic information–for example, user data, or lists of products–before sending the finished HTML to the client.

- **Separation of Concerns:** Because of templating, this decouples the business logic of an application from its presentation layer and, therefore, makes your code more maintainable and modular.

In order to begin working with Jinja2 for your FastAPI application, you would install it via **pip**:

```
pip install jinja2
```

Finally, you will be able to include it in your FastAPI routes, and you will be enabled to serve complicated web pages that may need some server-side processing.

Troubleshooting Common Installation Issues

Even with installation instructions at their most detailed, challenges during the installation of FastAPI and its dependencies are still rampant. Issues can range from Python version incompatibilities to dependency conflicts and permission errors. This section goes into some of the most common problems developers encounter during installation and also covers strategies to effectively troubleshoot and resolve these issues.

Python Version Issues

One of the most common mistakes that people make when installing FastAPI is using a Python version that is not compatible. FastAPI requires Python 3.7 or higher to work, and trying to install it with any version older than this brings up errors. The most common mistakes involving Python version incompatibilities are syntax errors or features missing because they are available only in newer versions of Python.

How to Check Your Python Version:

You can verify your Python version by running the following command in your terminal or command prompt, depending on your system:

```
python --version
python3 --version    #if using python3
```

If your Python version is lower than 3.7, you need to update it. On most systems, updating Python is straightforward:

- **Windows**: Download the latest Python installer from the official Python website (https://www.python.org/downloads/) and run it. Ensure you check the option to add Python to your PATH during installation.
- **macOS**: Use Homebrew to update Python by running **brew install python3**.
- **Linux**: Use your distribution's package manager, such as **apt-get** for Ubuntu (**sudo apt-get install python3**) or **dnf** for Fedora (**sudo dnf install python3**).

After updating, re-run the Python version command to confirm the upgrade.

pip Version Issues

Another common issue arises from using an outdated version of **pip**, Python's package installer. Older versions of **pip** might not support some of the dependencies required by FastAPI or Uvicorn, leading to installation errors.

How to Update pip:

To avoid these issues, it is a good practice to ensure that **pip** is up to date before installing any packages. You can update **pip** using the following command:

```
pip install --upgrade pip
pip3 install --upgrade pip    # if using pip3
```

After updating **pip**, retry installing FastAPI or other dependencies.

Dependency Conflicts

Dependency conflicts occur when packages required by FastAPI are incompatible with those already installed on your system. This is especially common, if you are working on multiple Python projects that have different dependency requirements.

Using Virtual Environments to Prevent Conflicts:

The best way to prevent dependency conflicts is to use a virtual environment. A virtual environment isolates your project's dependencies from the global Python environment, ensuring that each project has its own set of packages.

To create a virtual environment:

```
python -m venv env
```

Activate the virtual environment:

- **Windows: `.\env\Scripts\activate`**
- **macOS/Linux: `source env/bin/activate`**

With the virtual environment activated, you can install FastAPI and its dependencies without worrying about conflicts with other projects.

Uvicorn Installation Errors

Uvicorn, the ASGI server for running FastAPI applications, sometimes encounters installation issues due to missing system dependencies. These issues are particularly common on Linux systems, where certain libraries might be required.

Common Missing Dependencies:

- **libffi-dev**: This library is required for compiling some Python packages that Uvicorn depends on.

- `python3-dev`: Provides the headers and libraries needed to build Python modules.

If you encounter errors while installing Uvicorn, you can resolve them by installing the necessary system packages:

- **Ubuntu/Debian**: `sudo apt-get install libffi-dev python3-dev`
- **Fedora:** `sudo dnf install libffi-devel python3-devel`

After installing these dependencies, retry installing Uvicorn using `pip`.

Resolving Permission Issues

Permission-related errors can occur, when attempting to install packages globally on your system.

These errors typically manifest as "permission denied" messages during installation.

Using the `--user` Flag:

One way to resolve these issues is by installing packages for the current user only, using the `--user` flag:

```
pip install --user fastapi
```

This command installs the package in your user directory, bypassing the need for administrative permissions.

Using Virtual Environments to Avoid Permission Issues:

A more robust solution is to use a virtual environment, which avoids permission issues altogether by isolating your project's environment from the system-wide Python installation. As mentioned earlier, create and activate a virtual environment before installing FastAPI and other dependencies.

Verifying Installations

After installing FastAPI and Uvicorn, you might encounter issues when trying to run your application. These problems are often due to incomplete installations or the environment not being correctly activated.

Steps to Verify Installations:

1. **Check Installed Packages:** Run the following command to see if FastAPI and Uvicorn are installed in your environment:

   ```
   pip list
   ```

   Look for `fastapi` and `uvicorn` in the list of installed packages.

2. **Activate Virtual Environment:** Ensure that your virtual environment is active. Your terminal prompt should change to indicate the environment is activated. If not, activate it using the commands provided earlier.

3. **Run a Simple FastAPI Application:** Create a simple **main.py** file with the following content:

```
from fastapi import FastAPI
app = FastAPI()

@app.get("/")
def read_root():
    return {"Hello": "World"}
```

Start the application using Uvicorn: **uvicorn main:app --reload**

If everything is set up correctly, Uvicorn should start the FastAPI application, and you can access it in your browser at **http://127.0.0.1:8000.**

Debugging Installation Problems

Use pip's verbose mode to gather more information about installation errors:

```
pip install fastapi --verbose
```

This will help you find the very root of the problem, hence, making it rather easier to find a solution.

In this tutorial, you will learn how to install FastAPI, set up your development environment, and, if something goes wrong, how to find the problem. The foundation will keep your projects on solid and stable ground; hence, there will be little chance that the installation troubles will distract you from its development.

More persistent problems might be better diagnosed by using pip's verbose mode. We will demonstrate how to turn this on, and interpret the output so that you understand how to diagnose and solve installation issues.

The extended version now includes connecting sentences between sections so that it flows nicely, and reads accordingly in the chapter.

Setting Up a Virtual Environment

One of the very first things you should start with when working with a new project on FastAPI is creating a virtual environment. **Virtualenv** is an isolated Python environment that allows you to manage dependencies for your project independently of the global Python installation on your system. This becomes crucial, when more than one Python application is being developed or maintained in parallel-it avoids breakages among different package versions.

Importance of Using a Virtual Environment for FastAPI Projects

Working with virtual environments is really important to keep your project stable and reproducible. Isolation of dependencies prevents conflicts between versions, adding ease in sharing projects with others. Moreover, virtual environments let you easily deal with different projects that have different sets of requirements: Each project can keep a set without affecting others.

Virtual environments are important for software development in general, and when working with Python, they are important to manage dependencies by making a project operate within its own isolated environment. In such cases, this is quite crucial for projects that involve FastAPI, considering that the underlying dependencies may differ significantly from one project to another. Virtual environments make conflicts between the libraries non-viable. Thus, your project stays steady and predictable. It also makes deploying your application easier, as the environment can then easily be replicated on other machines for development, testing, or production.

Virtual environments help maintain the integrity of your setup, when working on various projects. It does so by isolating the dependencies for each project independently so that in case different projects require different versions of the same library, version conflicts do not occur. Also, the use of virtual environments is related to best practices in Python development, and will make your FastAPI project maintainable and scalable over time.

Step-by-Step Guide to Creating and Activating a Virtual Environment

Simple, but the creation and activation of a virtual environment is the first part in setting up any FastAPI project. The virtual environment allows you to isolate all dependencies required by your project. That is, whatever libraries and packages you install for one project will not affect another. This is especially important in Python development, given that different projects may require different versions of the same packages. In the following, you will find the step-by-step process for creating and managing a virtual environment across different operating systems.

1. **Installing Python and pip:**

   First, before you get started with the creation of a virtual environment, Python and pip need to be installed on your system. You would want to use Python 3.7 or greater, because FastAPI uses many of its features. Pip is Python's package installer, which you will be using for maintaining packages for your project.

To check that Python and pip are installed on your system, open a terminal or command prompt and run the following commands:

```
python --version
pip --version
```

If Python is installed, these commands will display the versions of Python and pip installed on your system. If Python or pip is not installed, you will need to download the latest version of Python from the official Python website (https://www.python.org/downloads/) and follow the installation instructions provided for your operating system.

2. **Creating a Virtual Environment:**

   Once both Python and pip are correctly installed, it is time to configure a virtual environment. This will be specific to your FastAPI project; it will have its own installation of Python with all packages that might be needed by your project.

   Open a terminal or command prompt. If your project directory does not exist, you can create it. From your project directory, you will then create a virtual environment. To do so, run this in the terminal or command prompt:

   ```
   python -m venv env
   ```

   Here is what this command does:

   - **`python -m venv`**: This instructs Python to run the **`venv`** module, which is used to create virtual environments.
   - **`env`**: This is the name of the directory where your virtual environment will be stored. You can name this directory anything you like, but it is common to use names such as **`env`**, **`venv`**, or **`.venv`**.

   The result of this command is that it will create a new directory, which will be named **`env`**, or whatever name you chose in your project folder. This folder contains a copy of the Python interpreter, the standard library, and also a site-packages directory where any libraries that you install will be stored.

3. **Activating the Virtual Environment:**

   Once you have created the virtual environment, you will want to activate it before you can start working in it. The activation step is crucial because it notifies your operating system to use the interpreter and packages of Python that are situated within the virtual environment and not globally on the system where Python is installed.

The activation command varies depending on your operating system:

- **Windows**

  Open your command prompt and run:

  ```
  .\env\Scripts\activate
  ```

- **macOS/Linux**

  Open your terminal and run:

  ```
  source env/bin/activate
  ```

Once activated, your command prompt or terminal will now reflect the name of the virtual environment in parentheses, for example: **`(env)`**. This acts as an indicator that a virtual environment is activated, and any commands in Python are utilizing the Python interpreter and libraries residing in the env directory.

4. **Deactivating the Virtual Environment:**

   Once, you are done working in your virtual environment, you may deactivate it and go back to working in your global Python environment. This is important because you may forget you have the virtual environment activated and start installing packages into it, when really you want to install packages into the global Python installation.

   To turn off the virtual environment, just execute the following command in the terminal or command prompt:

   ```
   deactivate
   ```

   This command restores your system's PATH to its previous state and hence turns off the virtual environment. Your prompt or terminal will revert to normal sans the prefix-almost **`(env)`**, and you are now back to using the global Python environment.

Installing FastAPI Within the Virtual Environment to Isolate Project Dependencies

Now that your virtual environment is activated successfully, let us install FastAPI and any other additional dependencies for your project. This virtual environment will keep all packages and libraries isolated to that space, avoiding package conflicts installed globally on your system, and making your life much easier.

1. **Installing FastAPI:**

   First of all, to begin working with FastAPI, you have to install it into your virtual environment. FastAPI is a modern, fast web framework for building APIs with Python 3.7+, based on standard Python type hints. Installing into a virtual environment just means setting this installation apart from other projects.

And that is the important point in maintaining a clean and conflict-free setup of the development environment.

You can install FastAPI using the following command:

```
pip install fastapi
```

This command will tell pip, Python's package installer, to download FastAPI and all of its dependencies from the PyPI, and install them into the env directory. The installation process will handle all the necessary packages that FastAPI requires to function correctly.

2. **Installing Uvicorn:**

   FastAPI applications require an **ASGI** server to run. It is very common to use Uvicorn, one of the **ASGI** servers that works well with FastAPI, because it is fast and supports asynchronous operations. First, you will need to install Uvicorn:

   ```
   pip install uvicorn
   ```

   This command will install Uvicorn to the same virtual environment, so that it can be used only for your FastAPI project. You will use Uvicorn to serve your FastAPI application, handle HTTP requests, and support real-time features such as WebSockets.

   By installing both FastAPI and Uvicorn, now is the time to configure the development environment, and start building as well as running FastAPI applications.

3. **Managing Dependencies with a `requirements.txt` File:**

   A best practice in Python projects is to manage and document your project's dependencies using a `requirements.txt` file. This file lists all the packages and their versions installed in your virtual environment, which is helpful for sharing your project with others or deploying it to production environments.

   To create a `requirements.txt` file, use the following command:

   ```
   pip freeze > requirements.txt
   ```

   This command generates a **`requirements.txt`** file containing a snapshot of all the installed packages and their exact versions. This ensures that anyone who sets up your project will have the same package versions, leading to consistent behavior across different environments.

   To recreate the environment on another machine or deploy your project, you can use the **`requirements.txt`** file by running:

   ```
   pip install -r requirements.txt
   ```

   This command installs all the packages listed in the **`requirements.txt`** file into your virtual environment, matching the setup from the original development environment.

4. **Best Practices for Managing Virtual Environments:**
   - **Naming Conventions**: Use consistent and descriptive names for your virtual environments. Common names include `env`, `venv`, or more descriptive names such as `fastapi_env`. Consistent naming helps you quickly identify the purpose of each virtual environment, especially when managing multiple projects.
   - **Environment Variables**: Store environment-specific settings such as database credentials, API keys, and configuration parameters in environment variables rather than hardcoding them into your code. This approach enhances security by keeping sensitive information out of your source code and makes your project more portable. You can use a `.env` file in conjunction with libraries such as `python-dotenv` to manage these variables effectively.
   - **Regular Updates**: Regularly update your virtual environment by upgrading installed packages to their latest versions. This practice helps ensure that your project remains compatible with the latest features and security patches provided by package maintainers. Use commands such as `pip list --outdated` to check for outdated packages and `pip install --upgrade <package>` to update them.

By adhering to these steps and best practices, you can effectively manage virtual environments for your FastAPI projects, leading to a more organized, secure, and scalable development process.

Initial Project Setup

Before digging deep into developing your FastAPI application, set up a project in an organized and scalable manner. Having the project well-structured will make your development process easier to manage, thus, allowing your code to be maintained, extended, and worked on by others more easily. Setup includes creating a clear folder structure, setting up version control, and configuring your environment.

While scaffolding the project, design for the needs of your application and how it will scale in the future. It can be a very simple API or a complex web application, but just having an idea of how to structure your project will save so much time in the future. Anticipating what your project will need–like different environments such as dev, test, prod, or certain services—can help you visualize how the design of the folders and subfolders could support those aspects from the beginning.

Creating the Initial Folder Structure for a FastAPI Project

Set up your environment, then create the basic folder structure that you will need for a FastAPI project. A logical folder structure will help you keep your project organized in the process of growth, where it will be easy to manage routes, models, configuration files, and other components. Early definition sets the stage for a clean, maintainable codebase.

While building your folder structure, you are supposed to have a feel for how different parts of your application interact. Perhaps, you would want to separate your business logic from your data models and API routes in various folders. Not only does this allow for easy maintenance while coding, but it is also much easier to scale, when adding new features to your application. This also helps in establishing clear, separate folders for configuration files, static assets, and templates that keep your application's core logic clean, giving your project a more modular and understandable structure.

Any worthy project starts with proper organization. It works exactly in the same way, when it comes to projects created with FastAPI. Because your project will grow, you have to keep your logical and understandable folder structure in order.

When creating a FastAPI project, it is a good practice to follow directory layout common practices or standards within the Python and web development communities. A very basic folder structure of a FastAPI project could look something like this:

```
my_fastapi_project/
│
├── app/
│   ├── __init__.py
│   ├── main.py
│   ├── api/
│   │   ├── __init__.py
│   │   ├── v1/
│   │   │   ├── __init__.py
│   │   │   ├── endpoints.py
│   ├── core/
│   │   ├── __init__.py
│   │   ├── config.py
│   ├── models/
│   │   ├── __init__.py
│   │   ├── user.py
│   ├── schemas/
│   │   ├── __init__.py
│   │   ├── user.py
│   ├── services/
│   │   ├── __init__.py
```

```
│   │   ├── auth.py
│   ├── tests/
│   │   ├── __init__.py
│   │   ├── test_main.py
│
├── .env
├── .gitignore
├── requirements.txt
├── Dockerfile
└── README.md
```

Explanation of Folder Structure

Creating a well-organized folder structure is crucial for maintaining and scaling a FastAPI project. Here is a detailed breakdown of a typical FastAPI project structure and the purpose of each component:

- **app/**: This is the main directory containing all your FastAPI application code. It serves as the root for your application's business logic, routes, models, and configuration. You can rename this directory based on your project's naming conventions, but `app/` is a common choice for clarity.
- **app/main.py**: This file is the entry point of your FastAPI application. It is where you create an instance of the FastAPI application and define your API routes. **main.py** typically includes:
    - The instantiation of the FastAPI app object.
    - Route definitions and their corresponding handlers.
    - Application-level configurations and middleware.
- **app/api/**: The `api/` directory organizes your API routes. This is particularly useful when your application grows and you need to manage multiple versions or sets of endpoints. Inside this directory, you might have:
    - **v1/**: A subdirectory for version 1 of your API. You can add more versions as needed (e.g., **v2/**) to handle backward-compatible changes.
    - **endpoints/**: A directory for grouping related routes into separate files. For instance, you might have files for user routes, product routes, and so on.
- **app/core/**: The **core/** directory typically contains configuration files and core components essential for the application's operation. This might include:
    - **config.py**: Configuration settings such as database connections, third-party service keys, and application settings.
    - **security.py**: Security-related components such as authentication and authorization mechanisms.
- **app/models/**: This directory holds your database models or data representations. If you are using an Object-Relational Mapping (ORM) tool

such as SQLAlchemy, this is where you define your database schemas. These models map to database tables and manage interactions with the database.

- **`app/schemas/`**: Schemas define the structure and validation rules for the data your API will handle. FastAPI uses Pydantic models for this purpose. In the **`schemas/`** directory, you define:
    - **`request schemas`**: Models that describe the expected structure of incoming requests.
    - **`response schemas`**: Models that describe the structure of outgoing responses.

  These schemas ensure data validation and serialization/deserialization, helping to maintain data integrity and consistency.

- **`app/services/`**: The **`services/`** directory is where you place the business logic of your application that is not directly tied to the routes. This can include:
    - **`authentication.py`**: Services for user authentication and authorization.
    - **`payment_processing.py`**: Services for handling payments or other external integrations.

  Separating business logic into services helps keep your route handlers clean and focused on handling HTTP requests and responses.

- **`app/tests/`**: This directory contains your unit and integration tests. Testing is crucial for ensuring that your application behaves as expected. This folder might include:
    - **`unit_tests/`**: Tests for individual components or functions.'
    - **`integration_tests/`**: Tests that cover interactions between different components or services.

  Tests help catch bugs early and ensure that changes to the codebase do not introduce regressions.

- **`.env`**: The **`.env`** file is used to store environment-specific settings such as database URIs, API keys, and other configuration parameters. This file is loaded into your application's environment variables, making it easier to manage sensitive information and configuration settings without hardcoding them into your code.

- **`.gitignore`**: The **`.gitignore`** file specifies which files and directories should be ignored by version control systems such as Git. This typically includes:
    - **`env/`**: The virtual environment directory.
    - **`__pycache__/`**: Python's bytecode cache files.
    - **`.env`**: The environment variables file, to avoid committing sensitive information.

- **`requirements.txt`:** The **`requirements.txt`** file lists all the Python dependencies needed to run your application. This file is generated using **`pip freeze`** and is essential for:
    - **Reproducing environments**: Ensuring that other developers or deployment environments can install the exact versions of packages used in your project.
    - **Deployment**: Facilitating the installation of dependencies in production environments.
- **`Dockerfile`:** If you use Docker for containerization and deployment, the **Dockerfile** defines the image for your FastAPI project. It specifies:
    - **Base image**: The Python version and OS to use.
    - **Dependencies**: Commands to install required packages and libraries.
    - **Application setup**: Instructions to copy application code, set environment variables, and specify entry points.
- **`README.md`:** The **`README.md`** file provides an overview of your project, including:
    - **Project description**: What the project does and its purpose.
    - **Setup instructions**: How to install and run the project.
    - **Usage examples**: How to use the API or application features.
    - **Contributing guidelines**: Information on how others can contribute to the project.

Setting Up Configuration Files and Environment Variables

In FastAPI projects, environment variables are very useful for managing different settings of the same application: testing or production. This abstraction of configuration settings to environment variables alone allows sensitive information such as API keys or database credentials not to be hard-coded into the source code of your application.

Using `.env` for Environment Variables

The **`.env`** file is a common approach to storing environment variables.

It is a simple text file where each line represents a key-value pair, like so:

```
DEBUG=True
DATABASE_URL=postgres://user:password@localhost/dbname
SECRET_KEY=your-secret-key
```

These variables can then be accessed in your FastAPI application using the **os** module or a configuration library such as **pydantic** or **python-dotenv**.

Creating config.py for Centralized Configuration:

In the **app/core/** directory, you can create a **config.py** file that centralizes the configuration for your application. Here is an example:

```
import os
from pydantic import BaseSettings

class Settings(BaseSettings):
    debug: bool = os.getenv("DEBUG", True)
    database_url: str = os.getenv("DATABASE_URL")
    secret_key: str = os.getenv("SECRET_KEY")

settings = Settings()
```

You can then import **settings** into your application files and access these variables as needed.

Writing a Basic "Hello, World!" FastAPI Application to Verify the Setup

Once you have your folder structure and configuration files set up, it is time to write a simple "Hello, World!" application to ensure that everything is functioning correctly.

In **app/main.py**, write the following code:

```
from fastapi import FastAPI

app = FastAPI()

@app.get("/")
def read_root():
    return {"message": "Hello, World!"}
```

This basic FastAPI application creates a single route (/) that returns a JSON response with the message **"Hello, World!"**. To run this application, you can use the Uvicorn server. First, ensure that your virtual environment is active and all dependencies are installed. Then run:

```
uvicorn app.main:app --reload
```

Navigate to `http://127.0.0.1:8000/` in your web browser, and you should see the message **"Hello, World!"** displayed. This verifies that your FastAPI project is set up correctly and is ready for further development.

Conclusion

This chapter has enabled you to create a robust and scalable FastAPI development environment–a good foundation for project management efficiency and ease of deployment. You will now be well-equipped with the knowledge of setting up a clear folder structure, environment variables, and creating a simple "Hello, World!" application that will see you through more interesting aspects of FastAPI development. The steps followed in this chapter ensure that your project is well organized, secure, and ready for growth.

Moving into the next chapter, *Core FastAPI Concepts*, we will be explaining in detail the most salient features of FastAPI that make it so effective at modern web development. Such topics as how one could create and handle asynchronous requests, path and query parameters, and building a full-fledged FastAPI application will be discussed in the following section. Of course, it is in the understanding of these core concepts that one will be able to implement scalable, high-performance APIs to handle real-world use cases efficiently. Development environment firmly in place, you are now perfectly positioned to explore the rich feature set of FastAPI, and start building your applications with confidence.

Multiple Choice Questions

1. **What is the primary reason for setting up a virtual environment in a Python project?**
    a. To improve performance.
    b. To manage dependencies and prevent conflicts between packages.
    c. To enable faster coding.
    d. To simplify the installation process.
2. **Which file is commonly used to store environment variables in a Python project?**
    a. `config.py`
    b. `settings.py`
    c. `.env`
    d. `environment.py`
3. **What is the main function of the requirements.txt file in a Python project?**
    a. To list all installed Python packages and their versions.
    b. To configure environment variables.

   c. To document the project requirements.
   d. To manage the folder structure.

4. **Which command is used to activate a virtual environment in Python on a Unix-like system?**
   a. `activate venv`
   b. `source venv/bin/activate`
   c. `venv activate`
   d. `activate env`
5. **What is the purpose of the `__init__.py` file in a Python directory?**
   a. To initialize the Python environment.
   b. To declare a directory as a Python package.
   c. To manage dependencies.
   d. To configure IDE settings.
6. **Which of the following is a popular IDE for Python development that can be used with FastAPI?**
   a. NetBeans
   b. Visual Studio Code
   c. Dreamweaver
   d. IntelliJ IDEA
7. **What does the DEBUG variable in the .env file typically control?**
   a. The database connection string.
   b. Whether debug mode is enabled or disabled in the application.
   c. The secret key for encryption.
   d. The server hostname.
8. **Why is Docker often used in FastAPI projects?**
   a. To simplify the setup of development environments across different systems.
   b. To enhance the speed of Python code execution.
   c. To manage dependencies.
   d. To write unit tests.

9. **Which command installs FastAPI using pip?**
    a. `pip install fastapi`
    b. `pip install uvicorn`
    c. `pip install fastapi-setup`
    d. `pip install python-fastapi`
10. **What is the primary benefit of using Git for version control in a FastAPI project?**
    a. It automates the deployment process.
    b. It allows multiple developers to collaborate on the same codebase.
    c. It speeds up the application.
    d. It manages environment variables.
11. **What is ASGI, and why is it important for FastAPI?**
    a. A type of database.
    b. A web server gateway interface that supports asynchronous communication, crucial for FastAPI's performance.
    c. A templating engine used for rendering HTML.
    d. A debugging tool for Python applications.
12. **Which command is used to create a new virtual environment in Python?**
    a. `python -m venv myenv`
    b. `create venv myenv`
    c. `python venv create`
    d. `python myenv --create`
13. **In FastAPI, what does the `@app.get("/")` decorator signify?**
    a. It defines a route that handles POST requests to the root URL.
    b. It defines a route that handles GET requests to the root URL.
    c. It is used to import a package.
    d. It configures the application settings.

14. **Which package is often used alongside FastAPI for interacting with relational databases?**
    a. `Flask-SQLAlchemy`
    b. `Django ORM`
    c. `SQLAlchemy`
    d. `SQLite`
15. **What is the purpose of the Pydantic library in FastAPI?**
    a. To render HTML templates.
    b. To handle routing and middleware.
    c. To manage background tasks.
    d. To validate and parse data models.

Answers

Question	Answer
1	b
2	c
3	a
4	b
5	b
6	b
7	b
8	a
9	a
10	b
11	b
12	a
13	b
14	c
15	d

CHAPTER 4
Core Features of FastAPI

Introduction

This is where we go through the major features that make FastAPI one of the latest innovations in regard to the construction of web APIs. FastAPI is primarily designed to be light and fast, having support for asynchronous operations out of the box. These aspects make the technology a good fit for developers who wish to create high-performance applications. The objective of this chapter is to give you a strong understanding of these basic features so that you might use FastAPI to its fullest advantage.

First, we walk through the process of creating a basic FastAPI application. This step is important to understand the very structure of a FastAPI project: how one defines routes, manages requests, and sends responses. You will learn by example how you can set up your first FastAPI application and understand the importance of decorators such as **`@app.get`** and **`@app.post`**, used to handle routes in FastAPI.

Next in this book, we make a deep dive into one of the most distinctive features of FastAPI-asynchronous programming natively out of the box. Asynchronous requests are a cornerstone of modern web development, as they let applications do many tasks without blocking, and thus slowing down other tasks. In this chapter, you will learn in detail how FastAPI uses **`async`** and **`await`** keywords of Python to offer better performance. Well-review some real examples that exactly show how to create asynchronous API calls so your apps are not only efficient but quick to respond.

Other important concepts treated in the chapter are path and query parameters, which become very fundamental when capturing and then processing a user's input that emanates from APIs. You will learn how to declare and validate these parameters in FastAPI so you can create dynamic endpoints that answer users' requests for different kinds of information. In learning the use of path and query parameters, you will be able to create more interactive and flexible APIs that can serve a wider range of client needs.

By the end of this chapter, you will have gained foundational knowledge on the core features that FastAPI has to offer. These foundational skills set the basis on which more advanced topics will be covered through successive chapters as you go about developing your expertise in API development with FastAPI. Whether a developer has just started their journey with FastAPI or needs to firm up their fundamentals, this chapter will equip them with the necessary tools and knowledge to create robust, scalable, and high-performance APIs.

Structure

In this chapter, we will discuss the following topics:

- **Creating a Basic FastAPI Application**
    - Detailed Steps for Setting Up Your First FastAPI Application
    - Explanation of the **`@app.get`** and **`@app.post`** Decorators
    - Implementing Basic Route Handling and Returning Responses
- **Handling Asynchronous Requests**
    - Understanding Python's `async` and `await` Keywords
    - How FastAPI Leverages Asynchronous Programming for Improved Performance
    - Practical Examples of Handling Asynchronous API Calls
- **Path and Query Parameters**
    - Introduction to Path and Query Parameters in FastAPI
    - Techniques for Capturing and Validating User Input
    - Examples Demonstrating How to Use Parameters in API Endpoints

Creating a Basic FastAPI Application

FastAPI is intended for building high-performance APIs with great ease and should leave you rapid with your Python type system, and some core features set it apart as a standout option among developers who can help improve the performance and scalability of their applications.

One of the greatest attractions of FastAPI is that it automatically creates interactive API documentation. You define the endpoints and the models; you are not required to write additional code or to document the API manually because FastAPI manages to produce automatic, interactive documentation with Swagger UI and ReDoc, nearly an absolute necessity in the testing and exploration of your API.

In addition to documentation, FastAPI built-in validation and serialization capabilities help you ensure your API data handling is consistent and safe. FastAPI is run on Pydantic, which automates validation of incoming request data according to your data models. It lets you just get on with designing the application logic, while FastAPI sorts out the messiness of data validation, serialization, and error handling for you.

To truly appreciate these core features, it is really worthwhile to see them in action. In the following are instructions that will walk you through the creation of your very first FastAPI application, which demonstrates how these features work together to give you a powerful and very developer-friendly development experience. At the end, you will have a good understanding of how FastAPI can make the creating of robust APIs with little effort possible.

Detailed Steps for Setting Up Your First FastAPI Application

Setting up your very first FastAPI application is quite a bit of fun, and lets you take full advantage of this new modern framework. Whether it is building a simple API or complex web applications, FastAPI offers a solid rock foundation with speed, ease of use, and an amazing set of features. To get you going, it is important that the environment setup for development and all the steps that need to be gone through for getting your FastAPI application running are well understood.

1. **Installing FastAPI and Uvicorn**

Before you can start building with FastAPI, ensure that Python is installed on your machine. FastAPI supports versions of Python above 3.7 due to its use of some modern features, such as type annotations and asynchronous type of programming. You might check if you have Python installed on your machine as well as the version using:

```
python --version
```

For installing Python, in case you need to download it or update it, here is how to get it. You can download Python from the official Python website here: https://www.python.org/downloads/. Installation of Python and activating it are quite straightforward, but its version will depend on the operating system used. Installing it also adds it to the PATH of the system, and then you can run Python from the command line.

First, you will install FastAPI using **`pip -m install FastAPI`**. FastAPI has a light footprint; hence, installation should be very straightforward. Then you also install Uvicorn, which is the lightning-fast ASGI server powering FastAPI applications.

```
pip install fastapi[all]
```

The **`[all]`** tag ensures that all necessary dependencies, including **`uvicorn`**, are installed. `uvicorn` is an ASGI server used to run FastAPI applications.

2. **Setting Up a Virtual Environment**

Once you have installed Python, you will next want to create a virtual environment. An environment is useful in keeping the dependencies of your project separate from other projects on your machine. This means that any libraries or packages installed for your FastAPI application will not conflict with other Python projects.

It is a good practice to have a virtual environment for your FastAPI project in order to handle dependencies efficiently. You can have your virtual environment created with

```
python -m venv fastapi-env
```

This command creates a new directory named env (you can choose any name) that contains the virtual environment. Inside this directory, you will find a copy of the Python interpreter and the standard library, along with scripts that make it easy to activate and deactivate the environment.

Once the virtual environment is created, the next step is to activate the virtual environment with the following command.

- **On Windows:** `.\fastapi-env\Scripts\activate`
- **On macOS/Linux:** `source fastapi-env/bin/activate`

When activated, the command prompt changes to indicate that you are working inside the virtual environment. This is where you install FastAPI, and any other dependencies for your project.

3. **Setting Up the Project Structure**

To keep your code tidy, scalable, and manageable, organizing your FastAPI project with a well-defined structure is very important. Such a project structure not only helps you keep your files organized but will also be very helpful in guiding other developers–or even you sometime in the future–through navigating the project. Let us now walk through the process of getting the bare basics of the structure set up for your FastAPI project.

Initialize a new directory for your FastAPI project. This will be the root directory of your project, containing all files and nested directories needed in order to complete your application. Start by initializing a new project directory, and then entering with:

```
mkdir fastapi_project
cd fastapi_project
```

The **`fastapi_project`** directory should be the main directory for all of your own project files, your main application logic, your configuration files, and also all of your additional resources such as templates, static files, or documentation.

Then, inside your project directory, you are going to create a Python file that will serve as an entry for your FastAPI application. In this case, the name is usually main.

py. There, you will define your FastAPI instance and set up some initial routes or API endpoints exposed by the application.

Create the **main.py** file within the **fastapi_project** directory:

```
touch main.py
```

The `main.py` file, which starts it all, will almost certainly begin very simply with just the core FastAPI application instance and a basic route. But as your project grows, this file will morph into something much more complex, with logic and routing that just will not disappear.

The **requirements.txt** file is a fundamental part of any Python project. In it, you list all of the external Python packages and libraries that your project requires, specifically their versions when required. It makes installing those dependencies quickly from the command line possible for every developer who works on the project.

To generate this file, you will need to have the following:

```
touch requirements.txt
```

You will add new packages to your project in each step and update **requirements.txt**. For example, after installing FastAPI and Uvicorn, you can add them to the file running:

```
pip freeze > requirements.txt
```

It will capture your virtual environment's currently installed packages into your virtual environment, and write to **requirements.txt**. It is of most use when you share your project with people and deploy it in different environments.

The **.env** file is an optional but highly advisable part of your project structure. This utility is for storing environment-specific variables: database connection strings, API keys, and the like, not hard-coded into your source. Keeping these settings in the **.env** file lets you handle them separately from your application logic, thereby making it easier to switch between environments–for example, development, staging, or production.

Create the **.env** file:

```
touch .env
```

You can then define your environment variables in the **.env** file like this:

```
DEBUG=True
DATABASE_URL=postgres://user:password@localhost/dbname
SECRET_KEY=your-secret-key
```

These variables can be accessed within your FastAPI application using libraries such as **python-dotenv** or **Pydantic**.

After completing the steps above, your project directory should have the following structure:

```
fastapi_project/
├── main.py
├── requirements.txt
└── .env
```

- **`main.py`**: This is the entry-point of your FastAPI application, where you define your app instance and routes.
- `requirements.txt`: This is a listing of all your dependencies used in your application. You would need this to reproduce your development environment elsewhere.
- **`.env`**: This file contains critical environmental variables that your application might need but should not be put directly in the codebase because of security reasons.

As your FastAPI project grows, you may want to expand this basic structure by adding more directories and files. For example:

- **`app/`**: Directory where all your application core will reside, such as routers, models and schemas.
- **`app/api/`**: Where you could organize your API routes, potentially grouping them by version.
- **`app/core/`**: For configuration and the core essentials, such as settings and security.
- **`app/models/`**: Where you would define your database models if you were using an ORM like SQLAlchemy..
- **`app/schemas/`**: This will hold your Pydantic models, which define the structure of data your API will handle.

This clear, structured layout of a project at the start allows for a truly scalable and maintainable FastAPI application, as extended project support naturally underpins your development workflow - it becomes easier to add features, deploy dependencies, and work with other developers.

1. **Writing Your First FastAPI Application**

Having set up the project structure, now it is the turn to get writing for your very first FastAPI application. A very important aspect, as this will expose you to some basic syntax and core concepts that FastAPI works under. By the end of this section, you will have a simple yet viable API that could handle HTTP requests and return responses.

```
from fastapi import FastAPI

app = FastAPI()
```

```
@app.get("/")
async def read_root():
    return {"message": "Hello, World!"}
```

In this code:

- **`FastAPI()`**: The **`FastAPI()`** class is the starting point for any FastAPI application. When you call **`FastAPI()`**, you are creating an instance of the FastAPI application, which serves as the central object that manages your application's routes, middleware, and configurations. This instance is crucial because it provides the methods and decorators that you use to define your application's behavior.
- **`@app.get("/")`**: This decorator is a specific method of the **`FastAPI`** class used to handle **GET** requests. The string `"/"` specifies the path or URL where this route will be accessible. In this case, `"/"` represents the root of your web application, meaning that when a user visits the base URL of your application, this route will be triggered.
    - **Decorators in Python**: A decorator is a way to modify or enhance the behavior of a function or method. When you use **`@app.get("/")`**, you are telling FastAPI to take the `read_root` function and register it as a handler for GET requests to the root URL `/`.
- **`read_root`**: The name of the function (**`read_root`**) is arbitrary and can be anything descriptive. The function name is not tied to the URL; it simply helps you (and others) understand what the function is doing.

2. **Understanding `@app.get` and `@app.post` Decorators**

Maybe the most obvious task concerning FastAPI is defining routes. Routes are the different endpoints of your API and hint at how your application will react to different types of HTTP requests. FastAPI uses decorators to make this quite intuitive and easy to do. Python decorators constitute a very powerful feature that allows you to modify the behavior of a function or method. In FastAPI, decorators are used to associate particular HTTP methods (such as GET, POST, and so on) with Python functions that are meant to handle those requests.

In FastAPI, the decorators define routes, which are the different endpoints of your API. The most common decorators used are **`@app.get`** and **`@app.post`**, which correspond to GET and POST HTTP methods, respectively.

- **`@app.get`**: It is a decorator to declare an endpoint that listens to GET requests. In most cases, GET requests are used to fetch data from servers. For example, whenever you open a webpage, your browser will send a GET request to the server to fetch its content. Typically, in an API, GET requests can be used for fetching information such as user details, listings of products, or any other thing that does not require modifications to the server's resources.

- **`@app.post`**: It is used to define an endpoint that responds to POST requests. A POST request is used when the client wants to send some data to the server. It is very often used for creating or updating a resource. Sending a form on a website, for example-to register for an account or publish a comment-is a good example of how a POST request is used. In an API, a POST request is frequently used for creating a new user, submitting a new order, or uploading a file.

Here is an example of a POST request handler:

```
@app.post("/items/")
async def create_item(item: dict):
    return {"item": item}
```

In this example, the **`create_item`** function accepts data as a dictionary and returns it as part of the response. This simple mechanism allows you to handle and respond to client requests effectively.

6. **Running the FastAPI Application**

After you have created the code for your FastAPI application, you then run it so that you are able to get in contact with your API. FastAPI is an ASGI web framework, which means it needs an ASGI server in order to be executed. Uvicorn is a lightweight but high-performance ASGI server, often used together with FastAPI for both developing and serving applications.

To run your FastAPI application, use the Uvicorn server:

```
uvicorn main:app --reload
```

- **`main:app`** tells Uvicorn to run the **`app`** object from the **`main.py`** file.
- **`--reload`** enables auto-reloading, meaning the server will restart whenever you make changes to your code.

After running the command, your FastAPI application will be accessible at `http://127.0.0.1:8000/`. You can open this URL in your browser to see your API in action. Then FastAPI also automatically provides an interactive API documentation interface at `http://127.0.0.1:8000/docs`, where you can test your API endpoints directly.

Explanation of the `@app.get` and `@app.post` Decorators

The various **`@app.get`** and other types of decorators used in FastAPI, such as for linking specific functions in your code to a list of HTTP methods, are pretty powerful ways that connect client requests with the best-fitting server-side logic. Decorators form a core component of FastAPI's routing and request processing procedures;

therefore, the dependency-injection framework is able to remove all boilerplate code for defining clear, intuitive APIs.

`@app.get` Decorator:

- The **`@app.get`** decorator is used to define endpoints that respond to HTTP GET requests. GET requests are one of the most common types of HTTP requests and are primarily used to retrieve data from the server. When you define an endpoint using **`@app.get`**, you are essentially creating a read-only access point in your API, where clients can request information without making any changes to the server's data.
- In the example above, **`@app.get("/")`** maps the root URL **`/`** to the **`read_root`** function. When a GET request is made to `/`, the function is executed, and its return value is sent back to the client as a JSON response.

`@app.post` Decorator:

- The `@app.post` decorator is used for defining endpoints that handle HTTP POST requests. Unlike GET requests, which are used to retrieve data, POST requests are typically used to send data to the server for processing. This could involve creating a new resource, submitting form data, or performing actions that modify the server's state.
- You might define a POST endpoint like this:

```
@app.post("/create-item")
def create_item(item: dict):
    return {"item": item}
```

- Here, when a POST request is made to **`/create-item`** with a JSON body, the **`create_item`** function is executed, processing the incoming data and returning a response.

Combining GET and POST:

A great strength of FastAPI is its ability to flexibly handle different HTTP methods for the same URL endpoint, which allows defining both GET and POST operations for a single URL:

- FastAPI allows you to combine different methods for the same endpoint. For example:

```
@app.get("/items/{item_id}")
@app.post("/items/{item_id}")
def manage_item(item_id: int, item: dict = None):
    if item:
        return {"item_id": item_id, "item": item}
    return {"item_id": item_id}
```

- This setup allows the same URL to handle both GET and POST requests, with different logic depending on the HTTP method.

This can prove to be very useful where you have the option of presenting a few ways of interacting with a resource. For example, you may request the current state of some resource using a GET request. Conversely, you may ask to update or create a new version of that same resource using a POST request. FastAPI, then, has great potential for building flexible and dynamic APIs because it makes minimal configurations possible in both operations.

Implementing Basic Route Handling and Returning Responses

Route handling in FastAPI is both intuitive and powerful, allowing developers to create robust APIs with minimal effort. In FastAPI, routes are defined using decorators such as **`@app.get()`**, **`@app.post()`**, **`@app.put()`**, and others, which correspond to HTTP methods. Each decorator specifies the path for the route, and can also include path parameters, query parameters, and request bodies.

Path parameters are embedded directly within the route path and are captured as variables within the function handling the request. For example, a route with a path parameter might look like **`@app.get("/items/{item_id}")`**, where **`item_id`** is a variable that the route will capture and pass to the function.

Query parameters, on the other hand, are included in the URL after a question mark (for example, **`?search=query`**). These parameters are automatically parsed and made available to the function as arguments.

FastAPI also allows returning different types of responses. The standard data types, such as dictionaries, can be returned: FastAPI will automatically convert them into JSON responses. You might also use Pydantic models, which not only do automatic validation and serialization of data but also ensure that responses are of the right structure and type.

More complex use cases can be achieved in FastAPI when you use models for custom responses, status codes, and headers, ensuring that there is full control over the format and contents of API responses. This allows you to build flexible, easy-to-maintain APIs using FastAPI routing and response functionalities.

Path Parameters:

- Path parameters allow you to capture dynamic parts of the URL. For example:

  ```
  @app.get("/users/{user_id}")
  def get_user(user_id: int):
      return {"user_id": user_id}
  ```

- Here, **`{user_id}`** is a path parameter. When a request is made to **`/users/42`**, the **`get_user`** function will receive **`42`** as the **`user_id`** argument.

Query Parameters:

- Query parameters are appended to the URL after a **?**. For example:

```
@app.get("/items/")
def read_item(skip: int = 0, limit: int = 10):
    return {"skip": skip, "limit": limit}
```

- Accessing **/items/?skip=20&limit=5** will pass **20** to **skip** and **5** to **limit** in the **read_item** function.

Returning JSON Responses:

- FastAPI automatically converts the return values of your functions into JSON. This makes it incredibly easy to build APIs that return structured data.
- For instance, returning a Python dictionary from a route automatically sends it as a JSON response to the client.

Customizing Responses:

- You can customize the response further by using FastAPI's `Response` class:

```
from fastapi import Response

@app.get("/custom-response")
def custom_response():
    return Response(content="Custom plain text response", media_
type="text/plain")
```

- Here, instead of JSON, a plain text response is sent back to the client.

Advanced Routing:

- FastAPI allows for more advanced routing options, such as including routers, creating sub-applications, and adding middleware. These topics will be covered in more detail in subsequent chapters.

With this solid foundation of core concepts under your belt—you have built a simple FastAPI application, used decorators to define routes, and returned responses—you are well-equipped to build much more complex APIs. As you move on throughout the book, you will find it helpful to keep in mind this foundation upon which the book builds upward.

This section, by its very detail, should lay a good foundation in how to create and understand a simple FastAPI application. Each step here builds on the previous one, so you will know what you need to develop even more complex APIs, when you get to that point in the book. A combination of practical examples and core concepts should leave you feeling confident in using FastAPI to create high-performance, asynchronous web APIs.

Handling Asynchronous Requests

Now, modern web applications need asynchronous programming for performance and scalability. FastAPI, like any other current web framework, exploits Python's asynchronous functionality for high-concurrency operations. Here, you will be able to process multiple requests at once without blocking the other requests' execution due to the asynchronous request handlers that FastAPI offers, which significantly boosts throughput and responsiveness in your API.

Understanding Python's `async` and `await` Keywords

Keywords in the center of asynchronous programming in Python are async and await. With them, it is possible to define and run coroutine functions that can pause their execution and hand over control back to the event loop so that other operations may proceed in the meantime. The async keyword can be used for the definition of a coroutine function, and the await keyword is used to suspend execution within a coroutine until its result is available. This mechanism helps in writing non-blocking code, which can handle I/O operations such as network requests or file operations better. This simplifies greatly building clean and maintainable asynchronous code while employing all concurrency features of Python.

Introduction to Asynchronous Programming

- Traditionally, Python code runs sequentially; that is to say, one thing after another. This model actually works great for many of the time-consuming operations that do not block, but the thing becomes a bottleneck, when dealing with I/O-bound operations such as database queries or requests against an API, where the program waits for external resources to yield before it can continue.
- It eliminates the limitation of the preceding by allowing certain functions to stop and resume their operation. This is achieved through the use of asynchronous functions as well as coroutines. It enables some function to yield control back to the event loop when it is waiting for I/O operations to complete. It will then continue with its other tasks instead of waiting idly for the I/O operations. Asynchronous programming, particularly for web applications that have multiple I/O operations, would be something developers must use in order to see significant performance boosts. It may lead to more responsive and scalable applications because it maximizes the efficiency of resource usage and reduces idle time.

The `async` Keyword

- In Python, the `async` keyword is used to define an asynchronous function, commonly referred to as a coroutine. By using **`async def`** to declare a function, you are not creating a regular function but rather a coroutine object. This coroutine object represents a function that will be executed asynchronously.
- When a function is defined with **`async def`**, it does not execute immediately. Instead, it returns a coroutine object that needs to be awaited. The **`await`** keyword is used to pause the execution of the coroutine until the awaited result is available, allowing other tasks to run concurrently in the meantime. This approach is particularly useful for I/O-bound operations where you want to avoid blocking the execution while waiting for external resources.
- Example:

```
async def fetch_data():
        # Simulate a delay
        await asyncio.sleep(1)
        return "Data fetched"
```

In this example, `fetch_data` is defined as an asynchronous function. When called, it returns a coroutine object that can be awaited. Inside the function, **`await asyncio.sleep(1)`** simulates a delay, representing a typical I/O-bound operation. During this delay, other tasks can be executed, making the code more efficient and responsive.

The `await` Keyword:

- The **`await`** keyword is an essential component of asynchronous programming in Python. It is used to pause the execution of an **`async`** function until the awaited task or coroutine completes. This mechanism allows an **`async`** function to be non-blocking, enabling other tasks to proceed, while waiting for the awaited operation to finish.
- When you use **`await`** in an `async` function, you effectively tell the program to wait for the result of the awaited coroutine before continuing with the execution of the remaining code. This is what makes the function asynchronous, allowing it to handle other operations concurrently without blocking the event loop.
- Example:

```
async def main():
    result = await fetch_data()
    print(result)
```

- In this example, the **`main`** function is an asynchronous function that awaits the result of **`fetch_data`**. The `await` **`fetch_data()`** line pauses the execution of `main` until **`fetch_data`** completes its execution, which involves a simulated delay of 1 second. During this delay, other tasks could be performed by the event loop. Once `fetch_data` finishes and returns its result, `main` resumes and prints the result.

Benefits of Asynchronous Programming:

Asynchronous programming offers several key benefits that can greatly enhance the performance and scalability of applications:

- **Concurrency**: Asynchronous programming executes many operations concurrently rather than in sequential order. This introduces the possibility for one operation to wait for an I/O-bound task to complete, while other operations continue running. Overlapped tasks improve the throughput of the application by allowing the application to accomplish more operations within the same time frame if executed in a synchronous way.
- **Efficiency**: Asynchronous programming really comes to bear on I/O-bound and high-latency operations. In synchronous code, there can be a lot of idle time sitting around for external resources: Databases or network responses, for instance. If you use asynchronous techniques, then you minimize such idle time and optimize the usage of system resources as well. The application is much better if you can start more I/O operations in parallel and wait only for completion if you need to.
- **Scalability**: Asynchronous programming also represents one of the most significant advantages in terms of scaling efficiency. Asynchronous code can handle a significantly greater number of simultaneous connections or requests than synchronous code. The scalability that this provides is very crucial in modern web applications and services, which must be able to accommodate an extremely large number of concurrent users or requests. Asynchronous programming handles multiple operations without blocking the flow and sustains performance levels as connections rise.

More responsive and efficient applications are provided by overall asynchronous programming techniques along with better scalability, especially in environments that inherently involve handling large concurrent tasks or highly-latency operations as a normal requirement.

Comparison with Synchronous Programming:

- In this type of synchronous programming, the programs run one by one in a sequenced way, and the program waits for the completion of each operation before doing the next. As you can guess, this often causes inefficiency when doing I/O-bound operations, such as reading from a file, making network requests, or querying a database. These I/O operations often tend to leave the CPU idle as it will wait for an answer from the external resource, hence wasting resources with reduced overall performance.

- In asynchronous programming, the use of resources is much more efficient. An asynchronous task that initiates an I/O operation does not block the execution of the program. Instead, while waiting for the I/O operation to complete, the program can continue performing other tasks. This non-blocking behavior allows the CPU to engage in other operations during wait time and, hence, makes better use of system resources. As such, asynchronous code can handle several tasks concurrently, which brings about improvements in responsiveness as well as throughput.
- For instance, an example of an application can be when a web server receives several requests. In this case, if it is a synchronous model, then the server has passed one request and after that another, which leads to queueing time and reduced capacity. However, an asynchronous server accepts multiple requests and processes them all concurrently by performing I/O operations on each request simultaneously, thus being able to minimize wait times as a whole. This factor is particularly important in areas such as high-traffic servers, which, if they do not function efficiently, will not be able to utilize the available resources resourcefully.

The asynchronous programming model may be generally more resource-consuming and harder to understand than the synchronous programming model; however, it has many merits regarding the utilization of resources as well as scalability in applications where there are repeated and/or long I/O operations.

How FastAPI Leverages Asynchronous Programming for Improved Performance

FastAPI is designed with asynchronous programming at its core, which is a significant factor behind its reputation as one of the fastest web frameworks available. By utilizing Python's **async** and **await** syntax, FastAPI efficiently handles a large number of concurrent requests, optimizing both performance and scalability.

Asynchronous Request Handling in FastAPI:

- FastAPI inherently supports asynchronous request handlers, enabling developers to define endpoints using **async def** functions. This integration allows FastAPI to harness Python's asynchronous capabilities directly.
- Example:

```
from fastapi import FastAPI

app = FastAPI()

@app.get("/data")
async def get_data():
```

```
        data = await fetch_data_from_db()
        return {"data": data}
```

In this example, **`get_data`** is an asynchronous function that retrieves data from a database using the **`await`** keyword. By awaiting the **`fetch_data_from_db`** function, FastAPI can perform other tasks while waiting for the database operation to complete. This approach ensures that the server remains responsive, and can process additional requests during I/O operations.

Concurrency in FastAPI:

- FastAPI is optimized for running multiple requests in parallel. It does so because of asynchronous functions as they are structured such that the server will begin to process new requests even as it waits for the other I/O-bound task, for example, a database query or call to an external API, to complete. Such a concurrency model that the server happens to follow is the most productive when used in real-time applications or in systems that have heavy user interactivity. Its primary advantages are the prevention of blocking of requests and, therefore, enhancement of throughput in general.
- For example, in a high-traffic environment, FastAPI allows for serving lots of users very efficiently while minimizing latency and maximizing responsiveness because it can serve multiple requests simultaneously without waiting for each I/O operation to complete.

Performance Benefits:

- The non-blocking nature of the asynchronous code in FastAPI leads to better CPU utilization and faster response times. In scenarios where high traffic is a priority, and small responses are required, asynchronous design in FastAPI may present quite an advantage. Benchmarks and performance tests have demonstrated that any well-optimized web application built in FastAPI tends to very effectively handle asynchronous operations in a non-blocking manner compared to many other web frameworks.
- This is because FastAPI minimizes wait times on I/O operations, leaving much more CPU resources to be used, hence, making responses faster and even much more reliable.

Scalability and Resource Management:

- As an asynchronous framework, FastAPI is scalable. It is quite effective in handling a higher number of concurrent users without an empirical increase in hardware resources, mainly because of the effective management of I/O-bound tasks. Efficient resource management makes FastAPI an excellent choice for building microservices and APIs that must scale with horizontal scaling across multiple servers.

- This makes it suitable for microservices and APIs that have to scale in multiple servers horizontally, since fast APIs can run I/O-bound tasks such as reading from databases very efficiently.

Real-World Applications:

- It is employed by many companies in projects that demand high performance and scalability. Examples include API gateways, microservices, and real-time data processing systems. Mainly, this is a result of the efficiency, when there are asynchronous requests. Performance characteristics of FastAPI are such that it makes for an excellent application, where concurrent tasks must be strongly handled and high throughput is required.

Practical Examples of Handling Asynchronous API Calls

But to understand how using asynchronous programming is beneficial in FastAPI really well, this needs to be demonstrated using real-world applications. The following examples are provided for you to implement asynchronous routes, along with how you should interact with databases or other external services without blocking the main thread.

Asynchronous Database Queries:

- When dealing with databases, asynchronous queries can significantly enhance performance by allowing other operations to proceed, while waiting for database responses. By using asynchronous database clients, such as `asyncpg` for PostgreSQL or `databases` for SQLAlchemy, you can perform non-blocking database operations.
- Here is an example using the **`databases`** library:

```
from fastapi import FastAPI
from databases import Database

app = FastAPI()
database = Database("postgresql://user:password@localhost/db-
name")

@app.on_event("startup")
async def startup():
    await database.connect()

@app.on_event("shutdown")
async def shutdown():
    await database.disconnect()
```

```
@app.get("/users")
async def get_users():
    query = "SELECT * FROM users"
    results = await database.fetch_all(query)
    return {"users": results}
```

In this example, the **get_users** route performs an asynchronous query to fetch user data from a PostgreSQL database. By using `await`, the server can handle other requests while waiting for the query to complete, improving overall responsiveness.

Asynchronous API Requests:

- FastAPI also supports making asynchronous requests to other APIs, which is useful for aggregating data from multiple sources. The `httpx` library provides an easy way to make asynchronous HTTP requests.
- Example using **httpx**:

```
import httpx
from fastapi import FastAPI

app = FastAPI()

@app.get("/external-data")
async def fetch_external_data():
    async with httpx.AsyncClient() as client:
        response = await client.get("https://api.example.com/
data")
        return response.json()
```

In this example, the **fetch_external_data** route makes an asynchronous HTTP request to an external API. By using **await** with **httpx.AsyncClient**, the server can process other requests while waiting for the external API response.

Long-Running Tasks:

- Handling long-running tasks asynchronously ensures that these operations do not block the server from handling incoming requests. For example, you might need to process large datasets or perform complex calculations.
- Here is how you can handle such tasks:

```
import asyncio
from fastapi import FastAPI

app = FastAPI()

@app.get("/process-data")
async def process_data():
    await asyncio.sleep(5)  # Simulate a long-running task
    return {"status": "Data processed"}
```

In this example, the **process_data** route simulates a long-running task using **await asyncio.sleep(5)**. The server remains responsive to other requests, while waiting for the simulated task to complete.

Combining Asynchronous Operations

- FastAPI allows you to combine multiple asynchronous operations within a single route. This is useful when you need to perform several I/O-bound tasks simultaneously, such as querying a database and making an external API call.
- Here is an example:

```
from fastapi import FastAPI
import asyncio

app = FastAPI()

async def query_database():
    await asyncio.sleep(2)
    return "database result"

async def fetch_api_data():
    await asyncio.sleep(3)
    return "api result"

@app.get("/combined")
async def get_combined_results():
    db_result, api_result = await asyncio.gather(query_data-
base(), fetch_api_data())
    return {"database": db_result, "api": api_result}
```

In this example, the **get_combined_results** route uses **await asyncio.gather** to run both **query_database** and **fetch_api_data** concurrently. The results are returned together, making efficient use of time by performing both operations in parallel.

In this section, we probe the basics of asynchronous programming in Python and how FastAPI exploits them to create highly efficient, non-blocking web applications. Understanding and applying asynchronous requests in FastAPI improves your performance and helps you build scalable applications that can easily cope with most of the demands on modern web services.

Path and Query Parameters

One aspect of creating your APIs is ensuring that you have endpoints to accept every type of input from your users. Then there are path and query parameters, which FastAPI equips you with in this regard to capture and further process the information from the URL to adapt your response to suit the client's specific needs.

Finally, knowing when to use path versus query parameters will really make an API intuitive and effective.

Path parameters are embedded within the URL itself, typically to identify specific resources. For example, in a URL such as **`/users/{user_id}`**, the **`{user_id}`** part is a path parameter. This parameter is required, meaning the client must provide a value for it in the request. Path parameters are ideal when you want to create endpoints that directly correspond to individual resources or entities, such as a specific user, product, or post.

On the other hand, query parameters are appended to the end of the URL and provide additional context or options for the request. These parameters are optional and are used to filter, sort, or customize the data returned by the API. For instance, in a URL like **`/users?sort=asc&limit=10`**, **`sort`** and **`limit`** are query parameters that allow the client to specify how the data should be presented. Query parameters are particularly useful when you want to provide flexible options for how data is retrieved or processed without altering the endpoint structure.

In FastAPI, handling path and query parameters is straightforward and integrates seamlessly with the framework's routing system. By leveraging these parameters, you can create dynamic and user-friendly APIs that cater to a wide range of client needs, enhancing the overall functionality and usability of your application.

Introduction to Path and Query Parameters in FastAPI

Path and query parameters are two very important aspects of web APIs that contribute a lot to the interaction of a client with your application. Such parameters offer a means to pass data directly in the URL so that, based upon that information, the server can dynamically process requests. Understanding and effectively using path and query parameters is crucial in making highly flexible, intuitive, and strong API endpoints that could meet varied clients' needs.

Path parameters are directly included in the URL structure. They are highly used to identify any specific resource that is contained in a larger collection. For example, imagine you have a list of items. Every item can be fetched using a unique path parameter. Under such circumstances, an API endpoint is both intelligible and inexpensive. Path parameters are always required: That is, the client has to provide a path parameter to get an endpoint to function properly. They are very good for scenarios when the API needs to reference a specific entity, say a user profile, a product page, or some specific order.

Query parameters are more versatile. This is the way by which clients can extend or alter their request without interfering with the composition of the base URL. Such parameters are located right after a ? appended to the URL and must be represented as key-value pairs. Query parameters are optional, meaning clients can apply the filtering, sorting, or pagination operations according to their needs. This is exactly where query parameters come into a handy role, especially for endpoints that are supposed to return and fulfill the most diverse range of responses, such as database queries, filter applications, or responses in a special output format.

FastAPI makes the definition and use of both path and query parameters very easy. Path parameters are simply added directly to the route definition; thus, the right data ends up going to the proper function. Query parameters mostly appear as arguments of a function but are allowed to have default values, making them optional and highly customizable by the client.

Path Parameters

- **Definition:** Path parameters are defined as parts of the URL path that help in identifying a specific resource from a larger set or collection. They are directly used in the route and become necessary for the endpoint to function properly.
- **Usage:** Path Parameters are specified by locating them inside the path of a route. This makes it such that FastAPI will automatically extract these parameters out of the URL, and pass them to the function it corresponds to. By doing so, the function becomes enabled to access and employ the said data.
- **Example**:

  ```
  from fastapi import FastAPI

  app = FastAPI()

  @app.get("/items/{item_id}")
  async def read_item(item_id: int):
      return {"item_id": item_id}
  ```

  In this example, **`item_id`** is a path parameter. When a client sends a request to **`/items/42`**, the value **`42`** is extracted from the URL and passed to the **`read_item`** function as the **`item_id`** argument. This allows the function to retrieve or process the specific item requested by the client.

Query Parameters

- **Definition:** Query parameters are additional data appended to the URL after the **?** symbol. They are used to pass optional information to the server, typically for filtering, sorting, or modifying the behavior of the API response. Unlike path parameters, query parameters are not part of the URL structure itself and can be added or omitted as needed.

- **Usage:** Query parameters in FastAPI are specified as function arguments with default values. This means that they are optional, and the client can choose whether or not to include them in the request. FastAPI automatically extracts these parameters from the URL and passes them to the endpoint function, where they can be used to modify the response.
- **Example**:

```
@app.get("/items/")
async def read_item(skip: int = 0, limit: int = 10):
    return {"skip": skip, "limit": limit}
```

In this example, **skip** and **limit** are query parameters. A client can make a request to **/items/?skip=10&limit=5**, which will pass the values **10** and **5** as arguments to the **read_item** function. These parameters can then be used to control the pagination of the items returned by the endpoint, allowing the client to retrieve a specific subset of the data.

Combining Path and Query Parameters

- One of the strengths of FastAPI is its ability to combine both path and query parameters in a single endpoint. This combination provides a powerful tool for creating versatile and dynamic API routes that can handle a wide range of requests. By using both types of parameters together, you can create endpoints that target specific resources, while also allowing clients to customize their requests.
- **Example:**

```
@app.get("/users/{user_id}/items/")
async def read_user_items(user_id: int, skip: int = 0, limit:
int = 10):
    return {"user_id": user_id, "skip": skip, "limit": limit}
```

In this example, **user_id** is a path parameter used to identify a specific user, while **skip** and **limit** are query parameters that allow the client to control the pagination of the items associated with that user. This endpoint provides a flexible way for the client to request items for a particular user while also specifying how the results should be displayed.

By combining path and query parameters, FastAPI enables you to build more complex and responsive APIs that can serve a variety of use cases, from simple data retrieval to more intricate operations involving multiple parameters.

Techniques for Capturing and Validating User Input

Any API captures and validates user input. Proper input validation allows you to ensure data is in the expected format when it is received from your API; this reduces the chances of errors, preserves data integrity, and enhances the level of security. Such robust tools for capturing and validating user input, such as FastAPI, make it easier to develop reliable and secure applications.

Automatic Validation with FastAPI

- One key benefit of using FastAPI is that it automatically verifies incoming data against Python's type annotations. For example, when you define a parameter in your endpoint with a certain type, FastAPI will check that the data passed into that parameter matches the expected type. However, if it cannot convert the data to that specific type, it will deny that request with an appropriate error response.
- For example, consider an endpoint designed to retrieve user information based on a user ID:

```
@app.get("/users/{user_id}")
async def read_user(user_id: int):
    return {"user_id": user_id}
```

In this example, **`user_id`** is expected to be an integer. If a client attempts to access the endpoint with a string value, such as **`/users/foo`**, FastAPI will automatically validate the input and return a **422 Unprocessable Entity** error, indicating that the value **foo** could not be converted to an integer. This built-in validation mechanism helps prevent common errors and simplifies the process of handling user input.

Using Pydantic Models for More Complex Validation

- Type annotations are very powerful as well, and in many instances, they may not cut it for more complex data validation requirements. Where you might need to enforce more complex data structures, FastAPI works fantastically with a library called Pydantic, which allows one to define complex models with really detailed validation rules and constraints.
- With Pydantic models, you can be precise about the type of data your API should accept; this includes specifying required fields, optional ones, data types, and also possibly custom validation logic. So, for example, here is a new item's endpoint; consider that a new item has several attributes.

```
from pydantic import BaseModel

class Item(BaseModel):
    name: str
    description: str = None
    price: float
    tax: float = None
```

```
@app.post("/items/")
async def create_item(item: Item):
    return item
```

In this example, the **`Item`** model ensures that any data sent to the **`/items/`** endpoint conforms to the specified schema. FastAPI will automatically validate the incoming request body against the `Item` model, checking that required fields are present and that the data types are correct. If the validation fails, FastAPI will return a clear and structured error message, allowing the client to understand what went wrong.

Custom Validation

- In addition to automatic and Pydantic-based validation, FastAPI allows you to define custom validation logic for parameters that require more specific rules. For example, you might want to ensure that a string query parameter meets certain length constraints or falls within a specific range of values.
- FastAPI's **`Query`** function provides an easy way to add custom validation rules to query parameters. Here is an example that enforces a minimum and maximum length for a query parameter:

```
from fastapi import Query

@app.get("/items/")
async def read_items(q: str = Query(..., min_length=3,
max_length=50)):
    return {"q": q}
```

In this case, the **`q`** parameter must be a string with a length between 3 and 50 characters. If a client provides a string that does not meet these criteria, FastAPI will automatically return a validation error.

Handling Validation Errors

- When FastAPI encounters validation errors—whether from automatic type checks, Pydantic models, or custom rules—it returns a structured JSON response detailing the errors. This response includes information about where the error occurred, the type of error, and a message describing the issue. This feature is invaluable for both developers and API consumers, as it provides clear feedback that can be used to correct the input.
- For example, if a query parameter is expected to be an integer but the client provides a string, FastAPI might return an error response like this:

```
{
    "detail": [
        {
            "loc": ["query", "q"],
            "msg": "value is not a valid integer",
            "type": "type_error.integer"
```

```
            }
        ]
    }
```

This structured response makes it easy to identify and fix the problem, leading to a better user experience and more robust API interactions.

Examples Demonstrating How to Use Parameters in API Endpoints

Understanding how to use path and query parameters is kind of the essence of creating flexible and dynamic endpoints in APIs with FastAPI. These enable giving a wide range of control over the data requested, especially getting more complex and personalized responses from an API. Here are a few practical examples that help illustrate the usage of path and query parameters in FastAPI, along with a better illustration of how these concepts work in practical application.

Filtering Data with Query Parameters

- Query parameters are very flexible. They might be used to filter data returned by an API endpoint in specific ways. An e-commerce application may, for instance, need to allow users to filter items by categories or price ranges. This capability is needed to provide users with the ability to narrow down search results and find exactly what they are after.
- **Example**:

```
@app.get("/items/")
async def read_items(category: str = None, min_price: float =
None, max_price: float = None):
    items = [{"item_id": 1, "category": "book", "price": 9.99},
             {"item_id": 2, "category": "electronics", "price":
99.99}]
    if category:
        items = [item for item in items if item["category"] ==
category]
    if min_price:
        items = [item for item in items if item["price"] >= min_
price]
    if max_price:
        items = [item for item in items if item["price"] <= max_
price]
    return items
```

In this example, the endpoint **`/items/`** supports filtering by **`category`**, **`min_price`**, and **`max_price`**. If a user requests **`/items/?category=book&min_price=5`**, the response will include only those items that belong to the "book" category and have a price greater than or equal to $5. This type of filtering is powerful in scenarios where users need to sift through large datasets based on specific conditions.

Pagination with Query Parameters

- Pagination is a common requirement in APIs that deal with large sets of data. It allows the client to request a specific subset of the data, such as a particular page of results. This is typically achieved by passing query parameters such as **`page`** and **`per_page`**, which dictate the range of data to be returned.
- **Example**:

```
@app.get("/items/")
async def read_items(page: int = 1, per_page: int = 10):
    items = [{"item_id": i} for i in range(100)]  # Simulate 100
items
    start = (page - 1) * per_page
    end = start + per_page
    return items[start:end]
```

Here, the **`/items/`** endpoint is designed to return a paginated list of items. The page parameter specifies which page of data to return, and **`per_page`** determines how many items each page should contain. For example, a request to **`/items/?page=2&per_page=5`** would return items 6 through 10. Pagination is essential for enhancing user experience in applications with extensive data, ensuring that clients do not have to load all items at once.

Path Parameters for Resource Identification

- Path parameters are embedded directly in the URL and are commonly used to uniquely identify resources. They are particularly useful in RESTful APIs, where each resource (such as a user, product, or article) has a unique identifier. This identifier can be passed as a path parameter to retrieve or manipulate a specific resource.
- **Example**:

```
@app.get("/users/{user_id}/items/{item_id}")
async def read_user_item(user_id: int, item_id: int):
    return {"user_id": user_id, "item_id": item_id}
```

In this example, the endpoint **`/users/{user_id}/items/{item_id}`** retrieves an item belonging to a specific user. The **`user_id`** and **`item_id`** are path parameters that identify which user and item to retrieve. If a client requests **`/users/1/items/42`**, the function will return data associated with user 1 and item 42. This use of path parameters is typical in APIs that need to operate on specific instances of a resource.

Combining Path and Query Parameters

- Often, API endpoints need to combine both path and query parameters to provide a more nuanced and flexible interface. This combination allows for specific resource identification while also enabling additional customization of the returned data through query parameters.
- **Example:**

```
@app.get("/users/{user_id}/items/")
async def read_user_items(user_id: int, skip: int = 0, limit: int
= 10):
    return {"user_id": user_id, "skip": skip, "limit": limit}
```

In this scenario, the endpoint **`/users/{user_id}/items/`** uses a path parameter (**`user_id`**) to identify the user, and query parameters (**`skip`** and **`limit`**) to control pagination. This setup is beneficial in cases where you want to retrieve a subset of a user's items, for instance, returning the first 10 items or skipping the first 5 items.

With a good understanding and effective usage of path and query parameters in FastAPI, you can develop dynamic, responsive, and user-friendly API endpoints to meet the immense variety of client needs. The examples below show how you can combine the parameters to build a more flexible yet powerful kind of API, making sure your applications are robust and powerful enough to handle all kinds of data requests.

Conclusion

With this chapter, you have opened up the core features that characterize FastAPI as a way forward powerful tool for modern development of APIs. You learned how to build a basic application, handle asynchronous requests efficiently, and benefit from path and query parameters to create dynamic and responsive APIs. These are fundamental skills that any developer needs with the intent to build a robust, scalable, and high-performance web application. Mastering these concepts ensures that you are prepared to face the challenges of real-world API development, and hence, how to design your applications in a manner that would be good enough for the varied demands of users with a good performance over changing conditions.

As you dive deeper into FastAPI, these skills will form the basis for bigger, more complex apps. Whether you are doing microservices or real-time processing of data, or complex interactions between users, this chapter will give you knowledge on how to construct elegant and efficient APIs.

In the following chapter, you will learn about "**Dependency Injection,**" an important feature by which you will be able to dependably manage and inject dependencies in your FastAPI applications. That is a feature by which you will become aware of building much more modular, maintainable, and testable code–a feature that will take your API development skills to a different level. You will master dependency injection well to produce even more advanced and scalable applications, further consolidating your expertise in FastAPI.

Multiple Choice Questions

1. **What is the main decorator used to define a GET endpoint in FastAPI?**
    a. `@app.route`
    b. `@app.get`
    c. `@app.http`
    d. `@app.endpoint`
2. **What is the key benefit of using FastAPI over other frameworks?**
    a. Easier handling of static files
    b. Speed and asynchronous support
    c. Built-in template engine
    d. Simplified HTML rendering
3. **Which Python keywords are essential for handling asynchronous requests in FastAPI?**
    a. `async` and `await`
    b. `yield` and `async`
    c. `async` and `yield`
    d. `await` and `yield`
4. **In FastAPI, which component is used to run the application?**
    a. Gunicorn
    b. uvicorn
    c. Flask
    d. Tornado
5. **Path parameters are defined:**
    a. In the request body
    b. In the URL path

   c. As query strings
   d. Using cookies
6. **FastAPI automatically validates data based on:**
   a. Type annotations
   b. Visual Studio Code
   c. HTML form fields
   d. File types
7. **What are query parameters typically used for in FastAPI?**
   a. Identifying resources
   b. Filtering and modifying the response
   c. Defining the API route
   d. Logging user sessions
8. **Which method is used to define a POST request in FastAPI?**
   a. `@app.route`
   b. `@app.post`
   c. `@app.create`
   d. `@app.get`
9. **How does FastAPI handle asynchronous API calls?**
   a. By default, using multithreading
   b. Through the `async` and `await` syntax
   c. With scheduled jobs
   d. By running background workers
10. **Path parameters are defined inside the:**
    a. Function signature
    b. HTTP headers
    c. Response body
    d. Query string

11. **Query parameters are typically appended:**
    a. To the request body
    b. As part of the URL path
    c. After a ? in the URL
    d. In the HTTP headers
12. **Which FastAPI decorator is used to create a DELETE endpoint?**
    a. `@app.delete`
    b. `@app.remove`
    c. `@app.del`
    d. `@app.clear`
13. **What type of object is returned by default from a FastAPI endpoint?**
    a. A dictionary (JSON-encoded)
    b. HTML response
    c. XML response
    d. Text-based response
14. **What feature of FastAPI ensures that documentation is automatically generated?**
    a. Swagger UI
    b. Blueprint integration
    c. HTML templates
    d. Tornado rendering engine
15. **FastAPI is built on top of which Python library for request handling?**
    a. Flask
    b. Pydantic
    c. Starlette
    d. Django

Answers

Question	Answer
1	b
2	b
3	a
4	b
5	b
6	a
7	b
8	b
9	b
10	a
11	c
12	a
13	a
14	a
15	c

Chapter 5
Dependency Injection

Introduction

Yet another pattern in the design used by modern web development, dependency injection leverages the construction of dependencies being separated from their use. So, because this method has got a system of dependency injection, FastAPI stands out for being quite efficient and simple–the approach taken is especially due to its use in the management of dependencies in the respective Python dynamic type hinting system. This system facilitates developers to inject any type of resources, such as database connections, authentication services, and third-party APIs, into specific routes or services, which causes less repetition of code and makes the code more modular.

Since most components of large applications rely on using similar types of resources such as databases, authentication layers, or caching mechanisms, resource management of such bulky things becomes harder to manage. Without a robust Dependency Injection (DI) system, these resources could end up being passed around or initialized repeatedly with possible errors and making any future maintenance even more painful. This is where FastAPI does its magic: it allows centering all shared resource management, hence simplifying the code and reducing the possibility of resource mismanagement.

What is more, the DI system of FastAPI is quite scalable. It means one could build deep dependency trees where a dependency depends on another. The whole structure will be automatically resolved by FastAPI at runtime so that every single route or component receives the resources it needs without boilerplate code. Furthermore, FastAPI's interaction with Python type hints simplifies the whole process of defining natural, Pythonic dependencies. Type hints help not only for resolving dependencies but also for auto-validation and documentation.

This chapter takes up a big part on creating reusable, scalable dependencies and discusses some pitfalls developers are likely to stumble into sooner or later, such as circular dependency or over-reliance on global states. So long as you adhere to best practice by avoiding mutable state in dependencies and by following the single responsibility principles, you can rest assured that FastAPI applications remain flexible, easy to test, and future-proof.

Throughout the chapter, you will also find practical examples ranging from basic utility functions to advanced ones such as injecting configuration settings, managing authentication and authorization flows, or handling database connections. Examples of this type will illustrate how to make use of FastAPI's capabilities for dependency injection in order to realize modular, maintainable applications in a testable fashion.

By the end of this chapter, you will know what the main principles of DI are and will feel confident in applying these techniques in your FastAPI projects, which will guide towards maintainable and scalable codebases capable of evolving with ease as project requirements increase.

Structure

- **Understanding Dependencies**
  - Introduction to Dependency Injection
  - Benefits of DI in FastAPI
  - How DI Promotes Modularity and Testability
  - Use cases of DI: Authentication, Database Connections, External APIs
- **Creating and Using Dependencies in FastAPI with Examples**
  - Defining Simple and Complex Dependencies
  - Using `Depends()` for Injection
  - Nested Dependencies
  - Managing State with Dependency Injection
  - Reusability and Best Practices for Building Maintainable Dependencies

Understanding Dependencies

A dependency in FastAPI refers to any resource or functionality that your route or function might need to be able to run. This could include database connections, third-party API clients, authentication mechanisms, or even utility functions that are shared by multiple pieces of code. Dependencies help to separate your concerns, allowing for the core logic to focus on its pure purpose while everything to do with external resources has to be injected and managed in a different way. This makes the system's dependency management very flexible and scalable, making it greatly effective for most large, complex applications where resources need to be shared and reused efficiently.

FastAPI's dependency injection system is engineered to make dependency management painless by automatically resolving based on Python's type hints, and returning the necessary resources to a function that requires them. This helps you in defining what your reusable dependencies are, which you inject into multiple routes to maintain consistency and avoid code duplication.

Introduction to Dependency Injection (DI):

Dependency Injection (DI) is a fundamental design pattern that addresses one of the most common issues in software development–tight coupling between components and their dependencies. Without DI, objects or services typically create instances of their dependencies internally. This approach leads to rigid and inflexible code because modifying or swapping dependencies requires changes to the original component logic. DI resolves this by decoupling instantiation from usage: the dependencies are not created within the object but are instead instantiated externally and then provided to the object. This process makes the code more modular, reusable, and easier to test.

In FastAPI, a dependency is therefore injected through **`Depends()`** to allow the framework to automatically handle and inject dependencies into route handlers or other functions. A dependency setup using **`Depends()`** will take care of resolving and injecting it whenever that route or function is invoked. This can be incredibly handy for shared resources such as database connections, authentication services, or any kind of external APIs. Such services might be created once, and FastAPI injects where the resource is needed; therefore, one has to spend much less time on resource management and less redundant code.

But the advantages of DI in FastAPI are not limited to the above. Separating resource management from the core logic of your routes improves a cleaner separation of concerns and maintainability of code over time. This pattern also brings with it an increase in flexibility where you can readily switch dependencies, such as changing a database driver or authentication mechanism, without rewriting large parts of your application. This also improves the testability, as in unit testing, the dependencies may be mocked or replaced with test-specific implementations. This results in more reliable and isolated tests. In a sense, a DI system like that of FastAPI has helped in saving development effort while creating a scalable and maintainable application.

Benefits of Dependency Injection in FastAPI

Dependency injection can be defined as the benefit that FastAPI offers because it will give you a specific critical set of benefits that make DI an important pattern for developing scalable applications that are maintainable and testable. This procedure will decouple the method of creating the dependencies from their usage, thereby allowing you to better manage shared resources such as databases, authentication mechanisms, and third-party services. Thus, it leads to more modular and cleaner code, while at the same time, it is much easier to update or replace the dependencies of the project in its evolution without disturbing other parts of the codebase.

FastAPI applies the `Depends()` function and takes in Python type hints fully for its built-in DI system, which makes it easy to inject resources into specific routes or functions. The DI pattern allows for components to be tested in isolation and really boosts the quality of the application at large. Some of the key benefits that DI offers to FastAPI development are:

- **Modular Code:** One of the major advantages of using dependency injection in FastAPI is the feature of modularization. In traditional approaches, database connections, authentication mechanisms, external API clients, and so on, are all instantiated directly in their usage places, with business logic being highly coupled to underlying dependencies. This results in slightly more rigid code since updates to these dependencies require changes to the entire codebase. DI, on the other hand, allows you to define these dependencies in a modular fashion and external to the components that depend on them. Using FastAPI's Depends() function lets you inject these modules easily into different parts of your application without requiring direct knowledge of how it is created. This separation between instantiation and usage also promotes better organization, where each component only needs to focus on the responsibility that it needs to fulfill. Modularized code, by its very nature, is more scalable: new features or services are simply created in the form of new modules and injected into the appropriate places in the application without the need to care about already established code structures. It leads to cleaner, better maintainable, and easier-to-understand codebases, especially in bigger applications where complexity over time gets the better of you.
- **Testability:** Another key advantage of DI in FastAPI is to make your codebase highly testable. When components are too tightly bound with their dependencies, testing becomes complex because now every component leans on actual implementations of services, such as those done by databases or external APIs. This makes it pretty complicated and slow to test in isolation. Testing will be much easier and efficient with DI, however. The reason it is easy to replace real services with mock objects, known as test doubles, during unit testing is due to the injection of dependencies from outside. FastAPI's DI system makes it possible for you to create mock dependencies and inject them into the routes or services you would wish to be tested, allowing you to isolate and test each component in isolation. This reduces the chance of errors in testing since the tests are now about the functionality of the component and not the behavior of its dependencies. More tests can be executed faster and with fewer side effects, which increases the reliability of continuous integration and deployment pipelines in this case, given the ability to mock and control dependencies. Put simply, DI allows developers to create testable applications because of the fine-grained control exercised over the dependencies each component depends upon.

- **Maintainability:** DI aids in keeping a large codebase simple because it favors resource management to be centralized. You will see that database connections, configuration settings, or third-party services are being used throughout the application in a complex application very often. Without DI, if you wanted to replace database connections, configuration, or even third-party services, this would become a hunt in the codebase for all the places they are being used and then update each of them manually. It is not only time-consuming but also risks missing instances, and therefore bugs or inconsistencies. In contrast, DI centralizes control over these resources. Defining and injecting dependencies in one location implies that changes to those resources only have to be made once, which makes them safer and more efficient. More importantly, the DI system of FastAPI gives clear and declarative management over dependency that decreases the cognitive load on developers. Whenever a component needs a different resource, say a new database driver or an upgraded API client, these can be done with minimal disruption to the rest of the application. That results in a more maintainable codebase where updates can be performed with increased confidence, and the risk of regressions will be very low. Further, maintenance is improved because DI fosters a natural separation of concerns, thereby making it easier to refactor or replace individual parts as the application evolves.
- **Scalability:** The others include maintainability and scalability. DI is known to contribute more to the scalability of your application. With the growth of your projects in terms of code complexity and user demands, the architecture should mature accordingly to fit new requirements. DI is considered a tool for management of growth through encouragement of service-oriented architecture, where dependencies are treated as interchangeable modules. In this way, scaling the application from adding new features to integrating new services or optimizing the existing ones will not lead to a tangled web of tightly coupled components. Injecting dependencies in a way that the application could easily adapt to the changes in its environment is totally doable: it allows it to connect to multiple databases, integrate new authentication providers, or migrate from one external API to another. The good thing about DI is that these changes may be achieved readily without necessarily having to redesign the entire code base. In this manner, it supports horizontal scaling and vertical scaling of an application.
- **Security and Flexibility:** Dependency injection becomes an important feature for making apps built with FastAPI more secure and flexible. For example, in operations that make up sensitive actions such as authentication or authorization, it is vital to ensure that such resources are handled appropriately and consistently in a secure way. This ability gives you the chance to inject security dependency types, such as authentication schemes for users, JWT token validation, or even role-based access controls, into endpoints where

they might be needed. You can centralize these mechanisms as well, and apply them uniformly across the relevant routes. Also, DI provides flexibility when it comes to the integration of third-party services or external APIs that tend to change with time. This is because dependencies can easily be swapped or reconfigured, and thus it becomes uncomplicated to introduce new services or replace outdated ones without really disturbing the core application logic.

In short, FastAPI's dependency injection system employs modularity, testability, maintainability, and scalability in web application development. Clean and organized codebases based on the reuse and testability of components are encouraged through decoupling the instantiation of resources from their usage. Centralized management of dependencies simplifies and streamlines updates for easier maintenance and extension of applications over time. All of this flexibility provided by DI also makes FastAPI applications adapt to changes in their resource requirements, security needs, and external integrations of services, leading to more robust and future-proof applications.

How Dependency Injection Works in FastAPI

Dependency Injection in FastAPI Dependency injection is a powerful and flexible mechanism used to manage resources and share functionality across your application. Technically, it works with the Depends function, which is used to define and inject dependencies into your route handlers, background tasks, or any other callable. Whether you are injecting a trivial utility function, or a shared resource such as database connections, or something more complex because it has dependencies itself upon which it relies, FastAPI's DI makes the process seamless.

Callables as Dependencies

Anything that can be called, whether it is a function, class, or coroutine, can be treated as a dependency in FastAPI. This means that FastAPI can automatically call the dependencies, resolve their return values, and inject them into routes or other callable items. The `Depends()` function automatically determines the dependencies needed, creates them, reuses them, and injects them whenever necessary. This is very helpful for reusable components that one might need in multiple routes, such as a connection to a database, an API client, or an authentication service.

Here is a simple example of how to use a dependency in FastAPI:

from fastapi import FastAPI, Depends

```
app = FastAPI()

def get_api_key():
    return "supersecretapikey"
```

```
@app.get("/items/")
async def read_items(api_key: str = Depends(get_api_key)):
    return {"api_key": api_key}
```

In this example, the **get_api_key()** function is used as a dependency and injected into the **read_items()** route. FastAPI handles the invocation of **get_api_key()** and ensures that its result (**supersecretapikey**) is passed into the **api_key** parameter of the route handler. You did not need to explicitly call the dependency or manage its lifecycle–FastAPI did that for you.

Nested Dependencies

A very powerful aspect of the DI system of FastAPI is resolving nested dependencies. Most often in larger applications, one can see that a dependency depends on other dependencies. FastAPI automatically handles the situation where it resolves the whole chain of dependencies and ensures that all resources required are injected correctly without considering how deep the dependency tree goes.

Let us consider a more complex example with nested dependencies:

```
from fastapi import Depends, FastAPI

app = FastAPI()

def get_db():
    # Here you'd typically return a database session
    return "database_connection"

def get_user(db: str = Depends(get_db)):
    # This function depends on the database connection
    return {"username": "John", "db": db}

@app.get("/user/")
async def read_user(user: dict = Depends(get_user)):
    return user
```

In this example, the get_user() function depends on another function, **get_db()**, to retrieve a database connection. FastAPI automatically resolves this nested dependency chain: first, it calls **get_db()** to get the database connection, and then it calls **get_user()** with the database connection as its argument. Finally, it injects the **user** object into the **read_user()** route. This cascading resolution of dependencies ensures that each function or component gets exactly the resources it needs without manual intervention.

Dependency Lifecycle and Management

FastAPI's DI system also handles the lifecycle of dependencies intelligently. For example, FastAPI can create dependencies that are only needed for the duration of a single request, ensuring that resources are managed efficiently. In cases where you need to manage the state of a dependency—such as initializing a database connection, performing operations within a transaction, and then closing the connection—FastAPI's DI system can handle that as well. The lifecycle of such dependencies can be controlled using **yield** within the dependency functions.

Here is an example of managing the lifecycle of a database connection using **yield**:

```
from fastapi import Depends, FastAPI


app = FastAPI()


def get_db():

    db_connection = "database_connection"

    try:

        yield db_connection  # Use the connection within this scope

    finally:

        print("Closing database connection")


@app.get("/items/")

async def read_items(db: str = Depends(get_db)):

    return {"db": db}
```

In this example, **get_db()** is a dependency that uses **yield** to return the database connection. The lifecycle of the database connection is managed automatically by FastAPI—when the request is completed, FastAPI ensures that the **finally** block is executed, where the database connection is closed. This is crucial for ensuring that resources such as database connections are properly cleaned up, reducing the risk of memory leaks or dangling connections.

Dependency Overriding

FastAPI also allows you to override dependencies, which is particularly useful for testing or for swapping out implementations in different environments (for example, production versus development). Dependency overriding enables you to change the behavior of a dependency without modifying the code that uses it, keeping your application flexible and maintainable.

Here is how you can override a dependency in FastAPI:

```
from fastapi import FastAPI, Depends

app = FastAPI()

def get_db():
    return "production_db_connection"

def override_get_db():
    return "test_db_connection"

@app.get("/items/")
async def read_items(db: str = Depends(get_db)):
    return {"db": db}

# Override the dependency
app.dependency_overrides[get_db] = override_get_db
```

In this example, the **`get_db()`** dependency is overridden by **`override_get_db()`** during testing or other special scenarios. This allows you to inject a mock or test database connection into your route without changing the actual route code. Overriding dependencies is a powerful technique that promotes flexibility and simplifies testing, especially when dealing with external services or resources that are difficult to replicate in a testing environment.

Security and Authorization Dependencies

Another common use case for FastAPI's DI system is managing security and authorization. In many applications, access to certain routes or resources is restricted based on user authentication or specific roles. FastAPI makes it easy to inject security dependencies that validate user credentials, tokens, or permissions before allowing access to a route.

For example, you might have a security dependency that validates a user's token and injects the authenticated user into your route:

```
from fastapi import Depends, HTTPException, status, FastAPI

app = FastAPI()

def get_current_user(token: str):
    if token != "valid_token":
        raise HTTPException(status_code=status.HTTP_401_UNAUTHO-
RIZED)
    return {"username": "John"}
```

```
@app.get("/secure-data/")
async def secure_data(user: dict = Depends(get_current_user)):
    return {"user": user}
```

In this case, **`get_current_user()`** checks if the token provided by the client is valid. If it is not, it raises an **HTTP 401 error**. If the token is valid, the user information is injected into the route. This pattern allows you to encapsulate security logic into reusable dependencies that can be easily applied to different routes.

Dependency Trees

FastAPI will handle resolving dependencies, but while doing so, it can also build out a dependency tree for deciding the order of execution, which would be correct and not do anything interesting by default, but just in case there are circular dependencies, the dependency tree will ensure that the dependencies are called in the right order. FastAPI works on that dependency tree at runtime, ensuring everything gets resolved optimally.

Suppose you have several nested dependencies, where the resolution of one dependency depends on another, which may depend on another. FastAPI constructs a tree that determines the optimal resolution order. The developer does not need to manually manage those relationships. This not only makes development easier but can also handle complex dependency structures in large-scale applications more efficiently.

Dependency injection, one of the many powerful features of FastAPI, handles the multiple resource requirements in a sophisticated manner. FastAPI decouples both the creation and usage of resources. The applications that this framework develops are flexible, modular, and maintainable at a more excellent level even when scaled up. Whether it is simple utility functions or nested dependencies, complex authorization flows, FastAPI's DI system will be able to support it, to keep the adaptations clean, testable, and possible in the future. FastAPI developers can develop powerful and production-ready applications with minimal effort by enabling lifecycle management, dependency overriding, and nested dependency resolution.

Use Cases of Dependency Injection in FastAPI

Dependency Injection, or DI, in FastAPI is not just a design pattern for organizing code but a very practical solution for managing great sophisticated resources with a coherent reuse of the code within such applications. Databases, authentication systems, and many more external services are nowadays part of shared resources within modern web applications; they might be distributed across multiple routes. DI makes it pretty easy to inject these resources into appropriate routes for making your application modular, maintainable, and testable. In this way, utilizing DI, you make authentication management as well as database connection management easier, besides making additions of remote services relatively simple.

- **Authentication**: In many applications, one has to authenticate a user for certain routes, meaning that only the legitimate users should get access to some resources. FastAPI also enables one to use DI in order to inject authentication logic into routes without repeating any code. This way, all secured endpoints have uniform validation for users. For example, you can establish a dependency to validate a token of the user, retrieve the user's data, and then inject the authenticated user object into your route. Such an approach centralizes your authentication logic; thus, it is easy to manage and update if needed, yet it is still safe against unauthorized access in a reusable way.
- **Database Connections**: Managing database connections wisely in any web application is always important. FastAPI DI makes this task much more straightforward because a database connection could be shared by many routes using just one connection. Here is how you can inject the database connection created by the database connection dependency into any route where the route needs to interact with the database. This, of course, advocates the reuse of code and further ensures proper handling of connection lifecycle events, for example, opening and closing connections or even managing transactions. Switching databases or simply changing the logic in your connections also becomes much easier with the use of DI in this manner.
- **External Services**: FastAPI's DI system is also ideal for integrating external services, such as third-party APIs, messaging services, or payment gateways. Instead of hardcoding API clients into each route, you can define these clients as dependencies and inject them where needed. This modular approach makes it easy to swap out or reconfigure external services without having to refactor your entire codebase. It also enables better error handling and testing since you can mock external services during testing, ensuring that your application remains reliable even when these services are unavailable or changed.

Example 1: Simple Dependency Injection

```
from fastapi import Depends, FastAPI

app = FastAPI()

def log_request():
    print("Request logged")
    return "Request Logged"

@app.get("/")
def read_root(log: str = Depends(log_request)):
    return {"log": log}
```

Here, **log_request()** is a simple dependency injected into the **read_root** route. Each time the route is accessed, the dependency will be resolved and executed.

Example 2: Complex Dependency Injection

```
from fastapi import Depends, FastAPI

class DatabaseConnection:
    def __init__(self):
        self.connection = "Connected to DB"

def get_db():
    return DatabaseConnection()

@app.get("/items")
def read_items(db: DatabaseConnection = Depends(get_db)):
    return {"db_status": db.connection}
```

This example shows how to inject more complex dependencies such as a database connection.

Creating and Using Dependencies in FastAPI with Examples

FastAPI's dependency injection system is flexible and powerful for managing a set of resources and sharing functionality throughout your application. Once you define dependencies, you can use them everywhere–from different routes, middleware, or background tasks, thereby ensuring that code stays clean and maintainable. Whether it is injecting a database connection, authenticating users, or passing configuration settings, the `Depends()` function in FastAPI will handle resolution and injection. It ends here, but let us start with the real use of dependencies in FastAPI.

Defining and Injecting Dependencies in FastAPI

An important feature of FastAPI are the dependencies, through which a developer could inject functionality or resources into their routes in a modular and reusable way. Dependence can be a one-liner function doing a quick utility job or a more complex class interaction with third parties' services–databases, APIs, or authentication systems. Encapsulate the logic or resources commonly used into a standalone component that could then be injected into any route or function where they would be needed. This makes your code much more maintainable, easier to test, and modular.

For example, define a simple dependency by having it return a configuration value or shared resource, such as a connection to a database. The dependency can then be reused over any number of routes. This means that code or the precise logic does not need to be repeated in every instance, keeping your code DRY, or Don't Repeat Yourself, which will also make changes easier because any update of the dependency will automatically be reflected throughout in the other locations it is used.

The `Depends()` Function

FastAPI uses the **`Depends()`** function to inject dependencies into your routes or other functions. The **`Depends()`** function allows you to declare that a specific callable (such as a function or class) should be injected at runtime into the route handler. This means that the actual dependency does not need to be manually invoked within your route; FastAPI automatically resolves and injects it, based on the context of the request. This approach brings greater flexibility and decouples the dependency logic from the route itself.

Here is an example that demonstrates how the **`Depends()`** function is used in practice:

```
from fastapi import FastAPI, Depends

app = FastAPI()

def get_current_user():
    # Simulate fetching user details from a token or session
    return {"username": "JohnDoe"}

@app.get("/profile/")
async def get_profile(user: dict = Depends(get_current_user)):
    return {"user": user}
```

In this example, the **`get_current_user()`** function is defined as a dependency. By using the **`Depends()`** function inside the **`get_profile`** route, FastAPI will call **`get_current_user()`** automatically and pass its return value (**`user`**) into the route. The route itself remains clean and focused on handling the business logic, while the user authentication process is encapsulated within the dependency.

The power of **`Depends()`** becomes evident in more complex applications where multiple routes or functions rely on the same functionality. Instead of copying and pasting the same logic across different parts of your application, you simply define the dependency once and inject it wherever necessary. This modular approach makes it much easier to maintain and scale your application, as dependencies are centralized and can be modified in one place.

Additionally, dependencies in FastAPI are not limited to single functions. You can use classes, external services, or even asynchronous operations as dependencies. For instance, if you are managing a database connection or an external API client, these can be encapsulated within a class or async function and injected using **`Depends()`**.

By decoupling dependency logic from routes, FastAPI's DI system improves code organization, testability, and scalability, ensuring that your web application remains maintainable and flexible as it grows in complexity.

Example of Using `Depends()`

```
from fastapi import FastAPI, Depends

app = FastAPI()

def get_config():
    return {"version": "1.0", "app_name": "FastAPI Example"}

@app.get("/config")
def read_config(config: dict = Depends(get_config)):
    return config
```

Nested Dependencies

Nested dependencies are one of the most powerful features of FastAPI's dependency injection system. In real-world applications, many have a case where dependencies are based on other dependencies for proper function. For example, a method designed to retrieve user data could depend on accessing a database connection, or an authenticating mechanism could depend on an external service for the validation of tokens. FastAPI elegantly handles such complex scenarios through automatic full resolution of chains of dependencies and injection into suitable routes or functions without any added complexity for the developer.

Nested dependencies compose more complex systems by stacking simple dependencies on top of each other. With FastAPI's DI system, you can be sure that all dependencies evaluate correctly regardless of the complexity of their internal dependency graphs. This also promotes a clean separation of concerns and simplifies resource management because developers can define each component in isolation and let FastAPI do the rest of the wiring together.

Example of Nested Dependencies

Let us consider an example to illustrate the concept of nested dependencies. Suppose you have a scenario where a route requires user information, and to fetch this user information, you need access to a database connection. Both the user retrieval function and the database connection function are dependencies, and FastAPI will resolve them in a nested manner.

```
from fastapi import FastAPI, Depends

app = FastAPI()

# First dependency: Provides a database connection
def get_db():
    db = "database_connection"
    try:
        yield db
    finally:
        print("Closing database connection")

# Second dependency: Fetches user data, relies on the database
connection
def get_user(db: str = Depends(get_db)):
    return {"username": "johndoe", "db": db}

@app.get("/user/")
async def read_user(user: dict = Depends(get_user)):
    return user
```

In this example, the **get_user()** function depends on the **get_db()** function to retrieve a database connection. FastAPI will first resolve the **get_db()** dependency to establish the connection and then pass that connection as an argument to the **get_user()** function. Finally, the **get_user()** function is injected into the route, allowing the user data to be returned.

This nested structure allows you to manage each layer of logic independently, yet still make them accessible to any route that requires them. The developer does not need to manually manage the order of dependency resolution–FastAPI builds a **dependency tree** and ensures that everything is resolved in the correct sequence.

Advantages of Nested Dependencies

- **Clean and Modular Code:** Breaking up long and complex operations into small, independent dependencies would make the code maintainable. Dependencies are kind of responsible for just one thing–they might connect to something, fetch something, or authenticate something. That separation makes maintenance and extension so much easier since a change in how you handle your database connectivity, for example, does not necessarily entail that you have to change everything else.
- **Flexibility and Reusability:** Nested dependencies promote reusability. For example, the **get_db()** function in the above example can be reused across multiple routes, not just for user-related queries but also for product

data, orders, or any other database interaction. Similarly, the **get_user()** dependency can be injected into any route that requires user information, without needing to repeatedly write the same logic.

- **Simplified Dependency Management:** FastAPI automatically resolves the whole dependency chain, so there is no need for manual orchestration. For example, if a dependency depends on some other resource, FastAPI will first resolve that resource. That can be very helpful in those scenarios where you have rather complex resource requirements, such as transactions or services that talk to many external systems. Here, you focus on the business logic since FastAPI will handle the dependency graph for you.
- **Testing and Mocking Dependencies:** Nested dependencies make testing much easier, as each dependency can be mocked independently. For instance, you can mock the **get_db()** dependency to return a test database or even mock **get_user()** to simulate authenticated users in a testing environment. This allows for unit testing of routes and services in isolation, without needing to bring up actual database connections or external services.

Asynchronous Nested Dependencies

FastAPI also supports asynchronous nested dependencies, which is particularly useful when your dependencies perform IO-bound tasks, such as making network requests, reading from disk, or querying a database. You can define async dependencies that rely on other async dependencies, and FastAPI will handle the async resolution seamlessly.

```
from fastapi import FastAPI, Depends

app = FastAPI()

# Async dependency: Provides an async database connection
async def get_async_db():
    db = "async_database_connection"
    try:
        yield db
    finally:
        print("Closing async database connection")

# Second dependency: Fetches user data asynchronously, relies on
the async database connection
async def get_async_user(db: str = Depends(get_async_db)):
    return {"username": "johndoe", "db": db}

@app.get("/async-user/")
async def read_async_user(user: dict = Depends(get_async_user)):
    return user
```

In this example, both **`get_async_db()`** and **`get_async_user()`** are asynchronous. FastAPI will automatically resolve the dependencies, ensuring that each async operation is awaited properly. This is crucial for performance optimization in applications that rely heavily on IO-bound operations, allowing them to handle multiple requests efficiently.

Nested dependencies in FastAPI are a fantastic way to build modular, maintainable, and reusable code. The developer takes advantage of automatic resolution of dependency chains to write each resource or functionality without caring about the internal wiring, which is left up to FastAPI. This applies whether you are dealing with utilities, database connections, or other external services; nested dependencies ensure your application stays scalable and easy to test. You can have robust applications, yet ensure that the code is clean, structured, and open to future variations by using a method of complicated operations that actually break down the application into layered dependencies.

State Management with Dependency Injection

State management is as important as having avoided a resource leak, concurrency problems, or performance bottlenecks in high-traffic sites to ensure that a web application is properly managed in connection with a database, session, or other shared resources. Dependency injection is provided by FastAPI to manage state without cluttering the code process; hence, it ensures the sharing of resources across requests when needed or proper instantiation and disposal in a request lifecycle.

Using DI, FastAPI manages state in a predictable way without requiring the developer to keep a manual count of resource allocation and cleanup. This can come in handy where the application needs to manage a pool of database connections, manage user sessions, or cache expensive computations. FastAPI's DI system lets you make just such a dependency to make sure that resources, such as database connections, are opened and closed properly for each request or connection–it promotes modular code, makes testing easier, and wastes fewer resources.

The lifecycle of dependency injection will take care of dependencies for you, so you do not have to worry about initializing and cleaning up state; instead, you are left with focusing on business logic. Let us see an example so we know how state management looks with DI, but mainly now for database connections.

Example: Managing Database Connections with DI

One of the most common examples of state management in web applications is managing database connections. FastAPI uses its dependency injection system to have very efficient management of database connections, from when the connection is just created to when it is not being used. This would ensure proper closure once not in use. Such an approach would help prevent the problem of connection leaks or having excessive database connections, which could eventually overwhelm the database server and degrade its performance.

The following is an example of how to manage a database connection using a dependency:

```
from fastapi import FastAPI, Depends

app = FastAPI()

# Simulating a database connection class
class DatabaseConnection:
    def __init__(self):
        print("Opening database connection")
    def close(self):
        print("Closing database connection")

# Dependency to manage the database connection lifecycle
def get_db():
    db = DatabaseConnection()
    try:
        yield db  # Yielding the connection object to be used in
the route
    finally:
        db.close()  # Ensures that the connection is closed after
the request is handled

# Route that uses the database connection
@app.get("/items/")
async def read_items(db: DatabaseConnection = Depends(get_db)):
    # Interact with the database
    return {"message": "Database connection active"}
```

Breakdown of the Example:

- **`DatabaseConnection` Class:** This class simulates a database connection. In a real-world application, this could be a connection to a SQL or NoSQL database. The **`__init__`** method initializes the connection, and the **`close()`** method closes the connection.
- **`get_db()` Dependency:** The `get_db()` function is responsible for managing the lifecycle of the database connection. It instantiates the **`DatabaseConnection`** class and then uses the **`yield`** keyword to allow the route handler to use the connection. After the request is processed, FastAPI ensures that the **`finally`** block is executed, closing the database connection.
- **Using the Dependency in a Route:** The `read_items` route uses the **`Depends()`** function to inject the **`get_db()`** dependency. FastAPI automatically handles

the initialization and cleanup of the database connection, allowing the route to focus purely on the business logic without worrying about resource management.

This pattern ensures that the database connection is created only when needed and is closed after the request is completed, preventing connection leaks or other issues related to improper resource management.

Sharing State across Requests

That is to say, you might need to share state across several requests. Suppose you are working with a connection pool; it is much more efficient to reuse database connections rather than opening and closing a connection for every single request. FastAPI's Dependency Injection system supports this: it can create global or shared dependencies that are persisted across multiple requests.

Here is an example using a database connection pool:

```
from fastapi import FastAPI, Depends
app = FastAPI()
# Simulating a database connection pool
class DatabaseConnectionPool:
    def __init__(self):
        self.pool = ["Connection1", "Connection2", "Connection3"]
        print("Creating a database connection pool")

    def get_connection(self):
        return self.pool.pop()

    def release_connection(self, connection):
        self.pool.append(connection)
        print(f"Connection {connection} released back to the
pool")

# Creating a global instance of the connection pool
db_pool = DatabaseConnectionPool()

# Dependency to get a connection from the pool
def get_db_from_pool():
    connection = db_pool.get_connection()
    try:
        yield connection
    finally:
        db_pool.release_connection(connection)

# Route that uses a database connection from the pool
@app.get("/pools/")
```

```
async def read_pools(connection: str = Depends(get_db_from_
pool)):
    return {"db_connection": connection}
```

Explanation:

- **`DatabaseConnectionPool` Class:** This class simulates a connection pool where a set of connections is available, and each request can borrow a connection and return it after use.
- **Global `db_pool`:** The **`db_pool`** object is instantiated globally and persists for the lifetime of the application. This allows multiple requests to reuse connections from the pool instead of creating new ones.
- **`get_db_from_pool()` Dependency:** This dependency manages obtaining a connection from the pool using **`get_connection()`**, and after the request is processed, it releases the connection back into the pool.

By using this approach, your application can efficiently manage a limited set of database connections, optimizing performance while maintaining state across multiple requests.

Advantages of State Management with DI

- **Efficient Resource Utilization:** Using DI to manage resources such as database connections or external services ensures that they are only created when needed and are properly disposed of afterward. This prevents resource leakage, improves performance, and reduces the likelihood of exhausting critical resources such as database connections.
- **Cleaner Code:** By separating resource management from business logic, your routes remain clean and focused. You do not need to worry about when or how to create or close connections, as this is handled by the dependency itself.
- **Modular and Reusable:** Dependencies that manage resources can be reused across multiple routes. For instance, a single database connection dependency can be injected into any route that requires database access, making the code more modular and reducing duplication.
- **Scalable:** As the application grows, managing resources becomes more complex. FastAPI's DI system makes scaling easier by allowing you to define how and when resources are created, shared, or cleaned up. This helps in building large-scale applications that handle resources efficiently under high loads.

Resource management–such as handling database connections, external APIs, or other services–is crucial for building robust web applications. FastAPI's dependency injection system provides a simple yet powerful mechanism to manage these resources: you can define dependencies with their own lifecycle and let FastAPI handle their creation and cleanup. This ensures optimal resource management, clean code, and modularity. Whether you are dealing with individual database connections or pooling shared services, FastAPI's DI system provides a flexible solution that grows with your application.

Reusability and Best Practices for Building Maintainable Dependencies

Reusability is probably one of the greatest advantages of FastAPI's DI system. It ensures that when you define a dependency, be it a database connection, an authentication mechanism, or a logging utility, you can use the same dependency across several routes or functions, which is essentially how you must manage shared logic and resources for scalability, modularity, and maintainability. Shared dependence reduces redundancy and makes the code DRY - Don't Repeat Yourself. Developers can focus more on business logic instead of re-creating the same services or utilities in every endpoint.

Utilizing reusable dependencies makes FastAPI lightweight while developing modular components consistent throughout an application. For example, the authentication check can be declared as a dependency and then utilized within several routes that demand the validation of users. Similar shared dependencies, such as database sessions, API clients, and middleware, would probably be easier to manage when the tendency to leak resources, to improve performance, and to keep the codebase more maintainable is being mitigated.

In this section, let us dive deeper into best practices for building maintainable dependencies on FastAPI. Remembering these best practices will save you from writing code that is efficiently modular, reusable, and ultimately maintainable in the long run. Lastly, we will also walk through the dangers of ill-structured dependencies and how to avoid them.

Best Practices for Building Maintainable Dependencies

- **Keep Dependencies Modular**

  The first and foremost best practice, when designing dependencies in FastAPI is to keep them modular. This principle emphasizes that each dependency should serve a single responsibility or task. By ensuring that dependencies are small and focused, they become easier to test, debug, modify, and reuse.

  For example, if you are managing a database connection, create a single dependency to handle the lifecycle of that connection. If you are managing user authentication, encapsulate that logic in a separate dependency. Each of these modules can then be reused across multiple routes, keeping the code organized and maintaining separation of concerns.

Example:

```
from fastapi import Depends, FastAPI
app = FastAPI()
# Dependency to handle a database connection
def get_db():
    db = DatabaseConnection()
    try:
        yield db
    finally:
        db.close()

# Dependency to handle user authentication
def get_current_user(db=Depends(get_db)):
    user = db.get_user_from_token(token="user_token")
    if user is None:
        raise HTTPException(status_code=401, detail="Invalid
token")
    return user

# Reusing both dependencies in a route
@app.get("/items/")
async def read_items(user=Depends(get_current_user), db=De-
pends(get_db)):
    return {"message": f"Hello, {user.username}"}
```

In this example, both **`get_db`** and **`get_current_user`** are modular dependencies with distinct responsibilities. They can be easily reused in other routes, ensuring that database access and authentication remain consistent and maintainable.

- **Use Dependency Classes for Complex Logic**

  While functions are excellent for simple dependencies, more complex scenarios may require managing state or multiple steps in a sequence. In such cases, using a class as a dependency is a better approach. Dependency classes allow you to encapsulate logic, manage internal state, and break down complex processes into smaller, manageable methods.

  For example, if your dependency involves multiple operations, such as connecting to an external API, validating responses, and caching results, encapsulating that logic into a class helps keep the code organized and ensures that state is managed correctly.

Example:

```
class APIClient:
    def __init__(self, api_key: str):
        self.api_key = api_key
        self.base_url = "https://external-api.com"
```

```
    def get_data(self, endpoint: str):
        # Logic to make a request to the external API
        response = requests.get(f"{self.base_url}/{endpoint}",
headers={"Authorization": f"Bearer {self.api_key}"})
        if response.status_code != 200:
            raise HTTPException(status_code=500, detail="API
request failed")
        return response.json()
# Dependency to inject the API client
def get_api_client():
    return APIClient(api_key="your_api_key")
@app.get("/external-data/")
async def read_external_data(api_client: APIClient = Depends
(get_api_client)):
    data = api_client.get_data(endpoint="data")
    return data
```

By using a class for the **`APIClient`**, we encapsulate the logic of connecting to the API, managing state, and handling failures. The dependency class is reusable, maintainable, and scales well as the logic grows in complexity.

- **Handle Exceptions in Dependencies**

  When building dependencies, it is important to ensure that errors and exceptions are handled gracefully. This is especially crucial when dealing with shared resources such as databases, external APIs, or file systems that can fail due to various reasons, such as network issues or timeouts.

  Handling exceptions within dependencies helps make routes more robust, as it prevents unhandled exceptions from propagating and causing unexpected crashes. Dependencies should catch, log, and appropriately manage exceptions, returning meaningful error messages to the client while ensuring resources are properly cleaned up.

Example:

```
from fastapi import HTTPException, Depends

# Dependency for fetching data from an external service
def fetch_data_from_service():
    try:
        response = requests.get("https://service.com/data")
        response.raise_for_status()
    except requests.exceptions.HTTPError as e:
        raise HTTPException(status_code=500, detail=f"Service
request failed: {str(e)}")
    return response.json()
```

```
@app.get("/service-data/")
async def get_service_data(data=Depends(fetch_data_from_service)):
    return data
```

In this example, if the request to the external service fails, the dependency catches the exception, logs it, and raises an appropriate **HTTPException**. This ensures that the route remains stable, and handles errors gracefully.

- **Avoid Deep Nesting**

  While FastAPI supports nested dependencies, too many levels of nested dependencies can introduce unnecessary complexity. Deep nesting can make it difficult to understand the flow of dependencies, and managing errors or state across many layers becomes cumbersome. It is important to strike a balance between using nested dependencies for modularity and avoiding over-complicating the dependency chain.

  When faced with deep nesting, consider refactoring your dependencies. Break down complex chains into smaller, more manageable units, and limit the depth of nesting to only what is absolutely necessary.

Example of deep nesting:

```
# This is a scenario to avoid: too many levels of nested
dependencies
def dep1():
    return "data1"
def dep2(data1=Depends(dep1)):
    return f"data2 {data1}"
def dep3(data2=Depends(dep2)):
    return f"data3 {data2}"
@app.get("/deep-nesting/")
async def read_data(data3=Depends(dep3)):
    return data3
```

This example shows deep nesting across three dependencies (**dep1, dep2, dep3**). While technically correct, the dependency chain is harder to follow. To simplify, consider flattening the logic or refactoring to reduce unnecessary levels of dependencies.

- **Document Your Dependencies**

  Clear documentation is essential when working with shared dependencies, especially when other developers need to understand or modify your code. It is important to document what each dependency does, what resources it manages, and how it interacts with other components.

  This becomes increasingly important in larger teams or when the codebase grows over time. A well-documented dependency will help future developers understand its purpose, potential side effects, and usage without diving into the implementation details.

Example:

```
# Dependency that manages a database connection
def get_db():
    """
    This dependency provides a database connection for the
duration of the request.
    The connection is automatically closed after the request is
processed.
    """
    db = DatabaseConnection()
    try:
        yield db
    finally:
        db.close()
```

This can be attained by including clear docstrings or comments such that the developer understands the purpose of the dependency and the underlying logic in interaction with other components.

Another core strength of FastAPI's dependency injection is its reusability, and you will find it really helpful in managing shared logic and resources, while working with multiple routes and services. Best practices include keeping dependencies modular, classes for complex logic, error handling not too deep, and documenting your dependency so that you maintain a maintainable and scalable code.

Well-structured dependencies can make your application easier to maintain, as well as improve the process of testing and minimize redundancy. Therefore, if developers work on creating well-designed and reusable dependencies, then developers can focus on implementing business logic and scaling the application without any doubt.

Conclusion

Dependency injection is one of the most powerful tools available in FastAPI, which helps you write clean, modular, and maintainable code. Separation of concerns to manage shared resources and even make them easily reusable improves your application's structure and scalability.

The next chapter is *Request and Response Models*, in which you will be guided to design robust APIs by defining request and response schemas using Pydantic models. The need for data validation and consistency is reached with this step by validating the FastAPI application's data.

Multiple Choice Questions

1. **What is Dependency Injection in FastAPI?**
    a. A method to handle HTTP requests.
    b. A way to manage external services like databases.
    c. A design pattern for managing dependencies.
    d. A way to create routes in FastAPI.
2. **Which of the following is a key benefit of using Dependency Injection in FastAPI?**
    a. Improved maintainability of code
    b. Slower execution time
    c. Less modular code
    d. Harder to test components
3. **In FastAPI, dependencies are declared using**
    a. `Query` and `Path`
    b. `Depends` function
    c. `BackgroundTasks`
    d. `HTTPException`
4. **Which of the following can be used as dependencies in FastAPI?**
    a. Functions
    b. Classes
    c. Other dependencies
    d. All of the above
5. **What is the purpose of Depends in FastAPI?**
    a. It handles database connections.
    b. It defines routes.
    c. It injects dependencies into path operations.
    d. It validates user inputs.

6. **Which of the following best describes FastAPI's handling of asynchronous dependencies?**
   a. FastAPI does not support asynchronous dependencies.
   b. FastAPI automatically handles asynchronous dependencies without needing any additional code.
   c. Asynchronous dependencies must be managed manually in FastAPI.
   d. Asynchronous dependencies make FastAPI applications slower.
7. **How can you reuse a dependency in multiple routes in FastAPI?**
   a. By declaring the dependency in every route separately
   b. By wrapping the dependency in the **`Depends()`** function
   c. By using global variables
   d. By writing new code for each route
8. **What happens if a required dependency fails in FastAPI?**
   a. FastAPI continues without it.
   b. FastAPI returns an appropriate error response.
   c. The app crashes.
   d. It defaults to a placeholder value.
9. **How does FastAPI handle asynchronous API calls?**
   a. By default using multithreading
   b. Through the `async` and `await` syntax
   c. With scheduled jobs
   d. By running background workers
10. **Which of the following is NOT a recommended best practice when managing dependencies in FastAPI?**
    a. Documenting the dependencies
    b. Nesting dependencies excessively
    c. Keeping dependencies modular
    d. Handling exceptions in dependencies

Answers

Question	Answer
1	c
2	a
3	b
4	d
5	c
6	b
7	b
8	b
9	b
10	a

Chapter 6
Request and Response Models with Pydantic

Introduction

In any modern web application, data is constantly flowing between a client and a server. Correct and accurate data makes all the difference in having robust APIs. FastAPI with Pydantic, therefore, provides an intuitive way to declare, validate, and serialize data models. Pydantic helps developers define classes that would describe the structure of incoming as well as outgoing data. So, Pydantic ensures there is less chance of inconsistency and that both requests, as well as responses, follow the requested format.

Pydantic helps to create models at the heart of FastAPI data management for validating incoming API request data and formatting outgoing responses. These models ensure that the requests given to an API meet certain requirements to prevent applications from getting malformed or incorrect information. It uses models for the request and response body in FastAPI auto-validated input data, while always giving neat output as formatted JSON. It perfectly deals with the developer in handling big, complex data structures to clean, well-structured, and safe code.

FastAPI, using Pydantic for the validation of data, makes it nearly effortless. Developers do not have to write custom validation functions or manually handle edge cases; they can instead define the structure of the expected data using Pydantic models. Models are easy to implement and highly customizable, with an extremely high degree of control over data types, constraints, and validation rules. This allows developers to either enforce strict data requirements or accommodate a wide variety of input types, depending on what the application requires.

Pydantic models are not only used for request validation but also for defining the structure of the responses sent back to the client. Developers can thus ensure that their API consistently returns well-formed data by controlling the output format. Clients will then predictively interact with the API, and errors or misinterpretations when handling data are reduced to a minimum. Developers can also filter out unwanted data before sending it back to the client through response models, thus enhancing security and performance.

Data validation does not stop at simple type-checking. Pydantic supports features such as custom validators, complex nested data structures, and conditional field requirements. This helps developers build sophisticated models that can handle many different scenarios. Whether it is dealing with user input, validating external API data, or transforming complex objects, the robust validation mechanisms in Pydantic ensure data integrity throughout your application.

Another related importance is serialization and deserialization. FastAPI manages its serialization and deserialization pretty efficiently with Pydantic. It parses all raw JSON data directly and converts it into its most convenient Python object structures suitable for internal use in the opposite direction to build a data structure so that both sides of your application, be it API serving or the client doing the request, can consume the same data structures that are always predictable. Knowing about its use of Pydantic for serialization and deserialization is where making scalable and maintainable APIs lies.

In this chapter, we are going to cover the entire process of defining, validating, and serializing data using Pydantic models in FastAPI. From simple model declarations to handling complex scenarios, we will cover everything in this chapter.

For data validation scenarios, we will provide a comprehensive guide to managing data in your FastAPI application.

Structure

In this chapter, we will cover the following topics:

- **Declaring Request Models**
  - Defining Pydantic Models for Incoming API Requests
  - Validating Fields and Handling Required/Optional Data
  - Example: Creating a Basic Request Model for User Input
- **Response Models in FastAPI**
  - Defining a Response Model
  - Field Aliases and Transforming Response Data
  - Customizing and Optimizing Responses
- **Data Validation and Serialization**
  - Data Validation with Pydantic
  - Serialization fo Data

- Custom Serialization
- Handling Complex Data Types
- Security Considerations in Data Serialization

- **Introduction to the Real-World Scenarios and Solutions**

Declaring Request Models

The core aspect of building APIs with FastAPI is handling incoming requests efficiently, securely, and accurately. FastAPI allows you to have a robust mechanism for validating and parsing request data using Pydantic models. These models ensure that the incoming data conforms to the expected structure, type, and validation rules so that errors or unexpected behavior can be avoided. In this section, we will discuss how to declare and use Pydantic models for incoming API requests in detail.

Defining Pydantic Models for Incoming API Requests

At the core of FastAPI's request validation is **Pydantic's `BaseModel`**. A Pydantic model defines the schema for the data your API expects. By subclassing `BaseModel`, you define fields and their types, and Pydantic automatically ensures that incoming data matches the specified structure.

```
from pydantic import BaseModel

class User(BaseModel):
    name: str
    age: int
    email: str
```

This model ensures that any incoming request data representing a **User** must contain:

- **name**: a string
- **age**: an integer
- **email**: a string

If the incoming request data fails to meet these criteria, FastAPI will generate a detailed error message, specifying what went wrong. This automatic validation ensures that invalid data never reaches the core application logic.

Example Breakdown:

- **Subclassing BaseModel**: The **`User`** model subclasses Pydantic's **`BaseModel`**. All models must inherit from **`BaseModel`** to enable Pydantic's powerful validation features.

- **Field Definitions**: Each field in the model represents a key in the request body. Pydantic checks the incoming request to ensure these fields exist and have the correct types.

Validating Fields and Handling Required/Optional Data

By default, Pydantic treats all fields without a default value as **required**. However, you can declare fields as **optional** using Python's **`Optional`** type from the **`typing`** module or by assigning a default value (None or otherwise) to the field. This flexibility allows you to handle optional data and set default values when necessary.

Example of Required vs. Optional Fields:

```
from typing import Optional

class User(BaseModel):
    name: str  # Required field
    age: Optional[int] = None  # Optional field with a default of
None
    email: str  # Required field
```

In this model:

- The **`name`** and **`email`** fields are required.
- The **age** field is optional. If not provided by the client, it will default to **`None`**.

If a client omits the **age** field or sends an invalid value, FastAPI will not raise an error, since the field is not required. However, if the client omits a required field such as **`name`** or provides the wrong data type, FastAPI will automatically raise a **validation error**.

Using Default Values

You can also specify default values for fields in your Pydantic models. If a client omits a field that has a default value, the model will automatically use that default when processing the request.

Example of Using Default Values:

```
class User(BaseModel):
    name: str
    age: int = 18  # Default value of 18 if age is not provided
    email: str
```

In this model:

- If the **age** field is not provided, it will default to `18`.

- The **name** and **email** fields remain required.

This allows your API to be flexible and offer fallback values for fields that are not always mandatory.

Nesting Pydantic Models

Pydantic also allows for **nested models**, which is useful when dealing with more complex request structures. For instance, if a **User** has an **Address**, the **Address** can be modeled separately and referenced within the **User** model.

Example of Nested Models:

```
from typing import List

class Address(BaseModel):
    street: str
    city: str
    country: str

class User(BaseModel):
    name: str
    age: int
    email: str
    addresses: List[Address]  # Nested list of Address models
```

Here, the `User` model contains a list of `Address` models. FastAPI automatically validates that each item in the `addresses` field is a valid `Address` object, ensuring consistency and correctness in more complex data structures.

Field Validation with Constraints

Pydantic also supports **field validation with constraints**. You can specify additional constraints on fields, such as minimum/maximum lengths, regex patterns, or value ranges.

Example of Field Constraints:

```
from pydantic import BaseModel, Field
class User(BaseModel):
    name: str = Field(..., min_length=3, max_length=50)
    age: int = Field(..., ge=18, le=100)  # Age must be between
18 and 100
    email: str
```

In this model:

- The **name** field must be between **3** and **50** characters long.

- The **age** field must be between **18** and **100**.
- FastAPI automatically enforces these constraints and returns an error if they are not met.

Example: Creating a Basic Request Model for User Input

Let us consider an example of creating an API endpoint that accepts user information and validates it using Pydantic models. Here is a simple FastAPI application with a route to accept user data:

```
from fastapi import FastAPI
from pydantic import BaseModel

app = FastAPI()

class User(BaseModel):
    name: str
    age: int
    email: str

@app.post("/user/")
def create_user(user: User):
    return {"message": f"User {user.name} with email {user.email}
added!"}
```

In this example:

- **User Model**: The `User` model defines the expected structure of the request data.
- **POST Endpoint**: The **/user/** endpoint accepts POST requests and expects the request body to conform to the `User` model.
- **Data Validation**: FastAPI automatically validates the incoming request, ensuring it matches the `User` model. If the requested data contains invalid fields (for example, missing required fields or wrong data types), FastAPI will return a detailed error message.

Custom Error Messages and Validation

Pydantic allows you to define **custom error messages** and complex validation rules by using validators.

Example with Custom Validation:

```
from pydantic import BaseModel, validator, EmailStr

class User(BaseModel):
    name: str
    age: int
    email: EmailStr  # Validates email format

    @validator('age')
    def check_age(cls, value):
        if value < 18:
            raise ValueError('Age must be 18 or older')
        return value
```

This model adds:

- **EmailStr**: A built-in field type for validating email formats.
- **Custom Validator**: A custom validator for the **age** field to ensure that the user is at least 18 years old.

By using Pydantic models in FastAPI, developers can:

- **Ensure Data Integrity**: Validate incoming data against predefined schemas, reducing errors.
- **Handle Complex Data**: Use nested models to manage complex request structures.
- **Enforce Constraints**: Define custom validation rules and constraints to ensure that data meets specific criteria.

FastAPI, combined with Pydantic, streamlines the process of declaring, validating, and handling request data, enabling developers to build secure, efficient, and maintainable APIs.

Response Models in FastAPI

In FastAPI, response models form an important feature whereby a developer can define and enforce the structure of the data returned by API endpoints. Just like request models, response models use Pydantic to validate and ensure consistency in outgoing data that should give well-structured and predictable responses to the client. It is an essential feature that will be maintained in terms of integrity and clarity, especially when creating scalable APIs that demand defined contracts between the client and server.

Response models help filter and transform data so that only the information required is returned to the client, thus optimizing performance, and maintaining security by excluding sensitive data. By the end of this section, you will know how to define, customize, and optimize response models in FastAPI.

Defining a Response Model

A response model defines the format of data the API endpoint should return; in FastAPI, we use the `response_model` attribute in the route decorator for this purpose. So, essentially, when defining a response model, you ensure data returned by an API endpoint is validated against and meets the schema definition specified by the model, thus it can be handled by the FastAPI itself through any data transformation or filtering based on the definition of your model.

Example: Basic Response Model

```
from pydantic import BaseModel
from fastapi import FastAPI

app = FastAPI()

class UserOut(BaseModel):
    name: str
    age: int

@app.get("/user/", response_model=UserOut)
def read_user():
    return {"name": "Alice", "age": 25, "email": "alice@example.
com"}
```

In this example:

- **Defining the Response Model**: The **`UserOut`** model is defined as a Pydantic model with two fields: **name (string) and age (integer)**.
- **Specifying the Response Model**: In the **`read_user`** route, the **`response_model`** parameter is set to **`UserOut`**, which tells FastAPI to expect responses to conform to this model.
- **Response Filtering**: Even though the function returns a dictionary that includes the **`email`** field, FastAPI automatically filters out the **email** field because it is not part of the **`UserOut`** model. Only the **name** and **age** fields are returned to the client.

This behavior ensures that the API responses are concise and only include the fields that are necessary for the client, even if the internal data contains additional fields. It also hides sensitive or irrelevant information from the client without the need for manual filtering.

Field Aliases and Transforming Response Data

One powerful feature of Pydantic is the ability to define **field aliases**. This allows you to map internal field names to different names in the API response. Aliases are particularly useful when the internal naming conventions of your data structures (for example, from a database) differ from the naming conventions you want to expose to the clients via your API.

Example: Using Field Aliases

```
class UserOut(BaseModel):
    name: str = Field(alias="first_name")
    age: int
```

In this example:

- **Alias Definition**: The **name** field in the **`UserOut`** model has an alias **`first_name`**. This means that when the response is generated, FastAPI will use the field **`first_name`** from the returned data, but expose it as **`name`** in the API response.
- **Data Transformation**: If your internal data uses a field called **`first_name`**, but you want to present it as **`name`** in the API response, Pydantic's **`Field`** with the **`alias`** argument provides an elegant solution.

This feature gives developers flexibility in how data is presented, allowing you to tailor API responses to match client expectations or public-facing standards without needing to modify your internal data models or database schemas.

Customizing and Optimizing Responses

FastAPI also allows for **granular control** over the response models. This control is especially useful when you need to modify the structure of the response dynamically or handle multiple scenarios with varying requirements. You can use the **`response_model_include`** and **`response_model_exclude`** parameters to include or exclude specific fields from the response on a per-route basis.

Example: Excluding Fields from the Response

```
@app.get("/user/", response_model=UserOut, response_model_exclude
={"age"})
def read_user():
    return {"name": "Alice", "age": 25}
```

In this example:

- **Excluding Fields**: The **`response_model_exclude`** parameter is used to exclude the **age** field from the response. Even though the function returns the **age** field, FastAPI will exclude it from the response because of this parameter.

- **Dynamic Control**: This allows you to return different subsets of the data based on the route or user role, ensuring that sensitive or unnecessary data is not exposed.

Similarly, you can use **response_model_include** to selectively include only certain fields in the response. These features are particularly useful, when building APIs with multiple user roles, where different levels of detail may be required for different types of users.

Example: Including Specific Fields in the Response

```
@app.get("/admin/user/", response_model=UserOut,
response_model_include={"name"})
def read_user():
    return {"name": "Alice", "age": 25}
```

In this case, only the name field is included in the response, even though both name and age are returned by the function. This feature allows the API to expose different data structures depending on the context, such as returning full user profiles to administrators and limited data to regular users.

Controlling Response Formats and Data Validation

One of the most powerful aspects of using response models in FastAPI is the ability to **validate and transform** the data before it is sent to the client. FastAPI ensures that the response matches the specified model before returning it, preventing incorrect or improperly formatted data from being sent.

Example: Enforcing Response Validation

```
class ProductOut(BaseModel):
    name: str
    price: float
    in_stock: bool

@app.get("/product/", response_model=ProductOut)
def get_product():
    return {"name": "Laptop", "price": "1000", "in_stock": True}
```

In this example:

- The **ProductOut** model specifies that the **price** field must be a float.
- If the endpoint returns the price as a string (as shown), FastAPI will automatically raise a validation error because the **price** field is not of the correct type. This prevents the API from returning invalid data to the client.
- This validation happens automatically without the need for manual checks in the code.

By enforcing response validation, FastAPI helps ensure that your API always returns data in the expected format, reducing the risk of bugs, and improving data consistency.

Nested Response Models

In many cases, API responses will involve nested data structures, such as returning a user along with a list of their addresses or orders. FastAPI and Pydantic make it easy to define and validate **nested response models**.

Example: Nested Response Models

```
from typing import List

class Address(BaseModel):
    street: str
    city: str
    zip_code: str

class UserOut(BaseModel):
    name: str
    age: int
    addresses: List[Address]

@app.get("/user/", response_model=UserOut)
def read_user():
    return {
        "name": "Alice",
        "age": 30,
        "addresses": [
            {"street": "123 Main St", "city": "New York",
"zip_code": "10001"},
            {"street": "456 Maple Ave", "city": "Boston",
"zip_code": "02118"}
        ]
    }
```

In this example:

- **Defining Nested Models**: The Address model represents a single address, and the UserOut model includes a list of addresses. This allows FastAPI to validate the nested structure of the data, ensuring that each address is properly formatted.
- **Returning Nested Data**: The read_user endpoint returns a user with a list of addresses, and FastAPI validates both the user data and the nested addresses, ensuring that the entire response structure adheres to the models.

Nested response models are particularly useful when working with relational data, such as a user and their associated entities (for example, addresses, orders, or roles). This feature allows FastAPI to handle complex data structures with ease.

Custom Responses with `Response` and `JSONResponse`

While FastAPI's `response_model` is a powerful tool for returning validated and structured data, there may be situations where you need more control over the response, such as returning custom headers or modifying the response format (for example, returning raw JSON, HTML, or a file). In such cases, FastAPI provides the **`Response`** and **`JSONResponse`** classes to customize the response.

Example: Customizing Responses with `JSONResponse`

```
from fastapi import FastAPI
from fastapi.responses import JSONResponse

app = FastAPI()

@app.get("/custom-response/")
def custom_response():
    content = {"message": "Hello, World!"}
    return JSONResponse(content=content, status_code=200)
```

In this example:

- **Custom Response**: The **`JSONResponse`** class is used to create a custom JSON response. You can specify the response content and status code directly.
- **Flexibility**: This approach gives you more control over the response, such as adding custom headers or modifying the status code dynamically.

You can also use the **`Response`** class for returning other types of content, such as plain text, HTML, or binary data.

FastAPI's response models provide a flexible, efficient, and secure way to define the structure of API responses. By leveraging Pydantic models for response validation, developers can ensure that API responses are consistent, well-structured, and free from invalid data. The ability to customize responses with field aliases, inclusion/exclusion parameters, and nested models makes FastAPI an excellent choice for building scalable, maintainable APIs.

Key takeaways include:

- **Consistency and Validation**: Response models ensure that the data returned by the API adheres to a well-defined structure.
- **Field Transformation**: Use field aliases to map internal data structures to client-facing responses.

- **Granular Control**: Dynamically include or exclude fields from the response based on the endpoint or user role.
- **Nested Models**: Handle complex data structures with nested models, ensuring data integrity across the entire response.
- **Custom Responses**: Use `Response` and `JSONResponse` for advanced customization when the default response model is not sufficient.

By defining response models, FastAPI helps developers build robust, scalable APIs that are both easy to use and maintain while ensuring data integrity and security at every step.

Data Validation and Serialization

Among all other vital aspects, ensuring web APIs' reliability and security with the help of necessary data validation and serialization makes an essential contribution. Working hand-in-glove, along with the power that comes through using Pydantic, much is accomplished within FastAPI in automation work concerning both the above-mentioned data-related functions: as such, it can now safely say both the outgoing as well as incoming data must inevitably appear in valid forms that preclude much if any, more room for mistakes or breaches to potentially be realized.

Data Validation with Pydantic

Data validation forms one of the major parts of an API, which ensures that the data provided to the server comes with respect to the specified format while it is going for some processing. In the case of FastAPI, such has taken place automatically by checking validity by Pydantic across requests for bodies, query parameters, and path parameters as well as its headers. Once again, while defining Pydantic models, FastAPI keeps providing the correct formatted information and data, entering the applications into your application to create those detailed validation errors regarding this if any particular point concerning the request becomes incorrect.

Example:

```
from pydantic import BaseModel, EmailStr
from fastapi import FastAPI

app = FastAPI()

class UserIn(BaseModel):
    name: str
    email: EmailStr
    age: int
```

```
@app.post("/users/")
def create_user(user: UserIn):
    return user
```

In this example:

- The **UserIn** model defines the expected structure for a user input: a **name** as a string, an **email** as a valid email using the **EmailStr** type, and an **age** as an integer.
- FastAPI automatically checks the incoming data for each field. For example, the **EmailStr** field ensures that the input for **email** is formatted correctly, returning an error if it's not.
- If the validation fails (for example, the **email** field contains an invalid email address or the **age** is not an integer), FastAPI will return a clear and structured error response with a 422 status code (Unprocessable Entity).

Custom Validation

While FastAPI's built-in validation is powerful, there are times when custom validation logic is required. Pydantic supports custom validation with the **@validator** decorator, allowing you to define fine-grained rules for validating individual fields.

Example: Custom Age Validation

```
from pydantic import BaseModel, validator
class UserIn(BaseModel):
    name: str
    age: int

    @validator("age")
    def check_age(cls, value):
        if value < 18:
            raise ValueError("Age must be at least 18")
        return value
```

In this example:

- A custom validator is added to the **age** field to enforce that the user's age must be at least 18. If the provided value is below 18, a **ValueError** is raised with a descriptive message.
- This level of validation allows for more specific checks on incoming data beyond simple type validation.

Error Handling in Data Validation

The clear and explicit way of error response by FastAPI, if the data fails the validation process, for instance, is about presenting the error in the most standard form:

describing which location has encountered an error–for example, within the body, query, or path–and then highlighting what exactly triggered this failure.

Example: Validation Error Response

```
{
  "detail": [
    {
      "loc": ["body", "age"],
      "msg": "Age must be at least 18",
      "type": "value_error"
    }
  ]
}
```

This error message helps both developers and API consumers understand the nature of the error and how to correct it. FastAPI also automatically returns these validation errors with a `422 Unprocessable Entity` HTTP status code.

Serialization of Data

Serialization is converting Python objects, such as Pydantic models, to data formats that can be transferred over the network in general, usually JSON. FastAPI's tight coupling with Pydantic allows you to automatically serialize data with the guarantee that API responses will be in the proper format without having to define any conversion logic.

Example: Basic Serialization

```
from pydantic import BaseModel
class UserOut(BaseModel):
    name: str
    age: int
@app.get("/user/", response_model=UserOut)
def get_user():
    return {"name": "Alice", "age": 25, "email": "alice@example.
com"}
```

In this example:

- The **`UserOut`** model defines the structure of the outgoing data. Although the actual return value from the function includes an **`email`** field, only the **`name`** and **`age`** fields are included in the response because of the **`response_model`** parameter.
- FastAPI handles this filtering and serialization automatically, ensuring that the API only returns the fields specified in the model.

This automated serialization ensures consistency in the responses, and the exclusion of unnecessary or sensitive fields simplifies the data and protects sensitive information.

Custom Serialization

Pydantic provides the ability to customize the serialization process, allowing developers to control how the data is formatted before being returned in the response. For example, you can override the **`json()`** method in a Pydantic model to modify the default serialization behavior.

Example: Custom Serialization with `json()` Method

```
class UserOut(BaseModel):
    name: str
    age: int

    def json(self, *args, **kwargs):
        return super().json(by_alias=True)
```

In this example:

- By overriding the **`json()`** method, you can customize the serialization logic. For instance, you could choose to return field aliases instead of the actual field names or alter how nested models are serialized.
- This gives you full control over how your data is formatted and presented to clients, especially in cases where a standard JSON serialization might not meet your needs.

Handling Complex Data Types

FastAPI, through Pydantic, excels at handling **complex data structures**, such as lists, dictionaries, and nested objects. This feature is essential for building APIs that work with hierarchical or relational data, such as returning a user and their associated addresses or orders.

Example: Nested Models in Serialization

```
from typing import List

class Address(BaseModel):
    city: str
    zip_code: str

class UserOut(BaseModel):
    name: str
```

```
        addresses: List[Address]

    @app.get("/user/")
    def get_user():
        return {
            "name": "Alice",
            "addresses": [
                {"city": "New York", "zip_code": "10001"},
                {"city": "Los Angeles", "zip_code": "90001"}
            ]
        }
```

In this example:

- The **UserOut** model includes a list of **Address** objects. FastAPI automatically serializes this complex data structure, ensuring that both the user and their list of addresses are returned in the correct format.
- Nested models like this allow for clean, organized, and easily extendable APIs, especially when dealing with relational data.

Security Considerations in Data Serialization

One important aspect of serialization is ensuring that sensitive information, such as passwords, API keys, or personal identifiers, is not exposed in the API response. FastAPI and Pydantic allow you to exclude sensitive fields from being serialized, ensuring that only safe and necessary data is returned to the client.

Example: Excluding Fields for Security

```
class UserOut(BaseModel):
    name: str
    email: str

    class Config:
        orm_mode = True
        exclude = {"email"}
```

In this example:

- The **Config** class inside **UserOut** specifies that the **email** field should be excluded from serialization, even though it is part of the internal data structure.
- This is particularly useful when you need to return user data but want to hide sensitive information such as email addresses, payment details, or authentication tokens.

It prevents your sensitive information from falling into the wrong hands while at the same time protecting your API responses to the world.

It is directly built into FastAPI, powered by Pydantic, and natively supports data serialization and validation. It does this by making sure the input and output data are always proper and validated. Pydantic models help in defining strict validation rules, enabling custom validations, complex handling of data types, as well as safe serialization of data for responses during API calls.

Key points to remember:

- **Data Validation**: FastAPI validates incoming data automatically, using Pydantic models to enforce type safety and structure.
- **Custom Validation**: You can extend FastAPI's validation with custom logic to handle more complex scenarios, such as age restrictions or field-specific checks.
- **Serialization**: FastAPI seamlessly serializes Python objects into JSON responses, allowing for easy and consistent data transfer between the server and clients.
- **Security**: By excluding sensitive fields during serialization, you can protect your API from exposing confidential data.

By leveraging these features, you can build robust, secure, and highly maintainable APIs with FastAPI, ensuring that your data remains accurate and your API responses are consistent and safe.

Introduction to the Real-World Scenarios and Solutions

Real-world problems that API development usually involves are complex data handling, strict validation requirements, and dynamic customization of responses. With APIs scaling and dealing with sensitive data or complex nested structures, ensuring smooth and secure interactions between the client and server becomes critical.

FastAPI is a modern, fast (high-performance) web framework for building APIs with Python 3.7+ based on standard Python-type hints. It uses Pydantic for data validation and serialization, so all incoming and outgoing data will be in a strict format and type. This will remove common sources of bugs, ensure data security, and streamline the development process through automatic and efficient error handling.

Further, we discuss three concrete problems developers could face with APIs and walk through their complete solutions using FastAPI, each trying to encapsulate the Request Models, Response Models, Data Validation, and Serialization concerns for real-world applications. We present the technical solution as well as code structuring techniques for handling issues to optimize performance.

Problem 1: Ensuring Consistency and Security in API Request and Response Models

Problem Statement:

You will implement an API that accepts a user's registration details, including name, email, and password, and returns a confirmation response, excluding sensitive information such as the password. The API should also validate the email by checking if it is well-formatted and return structured error messages if validation fails.

Solution:

To solve this problem, we will:

- Define a **Pydantic request model** to validate the incoming data.
- Use **custom validation** to enforce constraints on the email and password fields.
- Define a **response model** to control which fields are returned to the client, ensuring the password is never exposed.

Step-by-step Solution:

1. **Request Model**:
    a. Define a Pydantic model to validate the request data. We will use `EmailStr` from Pydantic to enforce a valid email format.
    b. Add a custom validator for the password field to ensure it meets the length requirements.
2. **Response Model**:
    a. Use a separate Pydantic model to define what data should be returned in the response. The password field will be excluded.
3. **Custom Error Handling**:
    a. FastAPI will automatically return a 422 error if any of the validations fail, providing detailed feedback to the client.

Code Implementation:

```
from pydantic import BaseModel, EmailStr, validator
from fastapi import FastAPI, HTTPException

app = FastAPI()

# Request Model with Validation
class UserCreate(BaseModel):
    name: str
```

```
    email: EmailStr
    password: str

    # Custom validation to ensure password length
    @validator("password")
    def password_min_length(cls, value):
        if len(value) < 8:
            raise ValueError("Password must be at least 8
characters long")
        return value

# Response Model to exclude sensitive data
class UserResponse(BaseModel):
    name: str
    email: str

# Endpoint for user registration
@app.post("/register", response_model=UserResponse)
def register_user(user: UserCreate):
    # In a real application, save the user to a database
    return user
```

Explanation:

- **UserCreate**: This is the request model where we enforce data validation. The `email` field must be a valid email, and the password is checked for a minimum length of 8 characters.
- **UserResponse**: The response model excludes the password, ensuring sensitive information is not returned to the client.
- **Automatic Validation**: If any validation fails, FastAPI will return a 422 error with a structured error message indicating what went wrong.

Sample Request and Response:

- **Request:**

```
{
  "name": "John Doe",
  "email": "johndoe@example.com",
  "password": "secret123"
}
```

- **Response:**

```
{
  "name": "John Doe",
  "email": "johndoe@example.com"
}
```

- **Error (Invalid Password):**

```
{
  "detail": [
    {
      "loc": ["body", "password"],
      "msg": "Password must be at least 8 characters long",
      "type": "value_error"
    }
  ]
}
```

Problem 2: Managing Complex Nested Data in API Requests and Responses

Problem Statement:

In a user registration API, sensitive information such as passwords must be handled securely. The API should validate user input (such as email and password), ensure that no sensitive information (such as passwords) is exposed in the response, and handle validation errors gracefully.

Challenges:

- Validating that the email is in the correct format.
- Ensuring the password meets security requirements (for example, length, complexity).
- Excluding sensitive information such as passwords from the response.
- Providing detailed and informative error messages.

Solution:

This problem is addressed by developing a Request Model for registration of users, which verifies all the input fields: name, email, password, and a Response Model ensuring the API response contains only the non-sensitive data (name, email). Built-in validation in FastAPI would ensure data consistency, raising detailed error messages when incorrect data is passed.

Step-by-step Solution:

1. **Define a Request Model**: This model will handle input validation, ensuring that email addresses are correctly formatted and passwords meet specific criteria (for example, minimum length).
2. **Define a Response Model**: This model ensures that only non-sensitive data is included in the response to avoid security risks.

3. **Handle Validation**: FastAPI automatically raises 422 errors when validation fails, and a clear error message is returned to the user.
4. **Return Only Required Fields**: In the response, sensitive fields such as passwords are excluded to ensure data security.

Code Implementation:

```
from pydantic import BaseModel, EmailStr, conint
from typing import List
from fastapi import FastAPI
app = FastAPI()

# Model for an ordered item
class Item(BaseModel):
    name: str
    quantity: conint(gt=0)  # Ensure quantity is greater than 0

# Model for user details
class User(BaseModel):
    name: str
    email: EmailStr

# Request model for placing an order
class OrderCreate(BaseModel):
    user: User
    items: List[Item]

# Response model for the order summary
class OrderResponse(BaseModel):
    user: User
    total_items: int

# Endpoint for placing an order
@app.post("/orders", response_model=OrderResponse)
def create_order(order: OrderCreate):
    total_items = sum(item.quantity for item in order.items)
    return {"user": order.user, "total_items": total_items}
```

Explanation:

- **Request Model (`UserIn`)**:
    - `name`: A required field (string).
    - `email`: Validated using `EmailStr` to ensure it is a properly formatted email.
    - `password`: Must be a string with a minimum length of 8 characters.

- **Response Model** (`UserOut`):
  - Only the **`name`** and **`email`** fields are returned, ensuring sensitive data (such as the password) is never exposed.
- **API Logic**: Upon successful registration, the API returns only the user's name and email, while validation failures automatically return 422 errors with details about what went wrong.

Sample Request and Response:

- **Valid Request:**
  - **Input:**

```
{
  "name": "Alice",
  "email": "alice@example.com",
  "password": "supersecret"
}
```

  - **Response:**

```
{
  "name": "Alice",
  "email": "alice@example.com"
}
```

- **Invalid Request (e.g., short password):**
  - **Input:**

```
{
  "name": "Alice",
  "email": "alice@example.com",
  "password": "short"
}
```

  - **Response:**

```
{
  "detail": [
    {
      "loc": ["body", "password"],
      "msg": "ensure this value has at least 8 characters",
      "type": "value_error.any_str.min_length"
    }
  ]
}
```

This response clearly indicates that the quantity field is invalid because it is less than 1, providing users with detailed feedback on what caused the validation error.

Time and Space Complexity:

- **Time Complexity:**
  - **O(n)**, where **n** is the number of items in the order. The total number of items is calculated by iterating over the list of items and summing their quantities, so the time taken grows linearly with the number of items.
- **Space Complexity:**
  - **O(n)**, where **n** is the number of items in the order. The space required is proportional to the number of items in the request, as each item is stored in memory for validation and processing.

Best and Worst-Case Conditions:

- **Best Case**: The user submits valid data with well-formatted items and quantities. In this case, the API will simply process the data, compute the total, and return a successful response.
- **Worst Case**: The user submits invalid data, such as an empty list of items or a negative quantity for an item. In this case, the API will return a detailed error message specifying what went wrong.

Noob-to-Expert Approach:

- **Noob Approach**: A beginner might handle this problem by writing manual validation code inside the API route, which could lead to bugs, inefficiency, or inconsistent error handling.
- **Expert Approach**: An experienced developer would use Pydantic's built-in validation capabilities, which are integrated with FastAPI, to handle data validation automatically. They would also structure the code to separate request and response models, ensuring only the necessary data is exposed in the response.

Problem 3: Customizing and Controlling API Responses Based on User Role

Problem Statement:

You are building an API that is supposed to return user profile data, but the client is expecting that this API response should strictly use the camelCase naming convention, whereas your backend models only accept **snake_case**. In addition, this API has to work with the nested fields, for example, user addresses, so that even the nested fields use camelCase.

The problem involves:

- Transforming field names from the backend's snake_case naming convention to the client's camelCase naming convention.
- Handling nested data (such as addresses) where each field, including nested ones, must be transformed to the required format.
- Ensuring that data serialization and validation are handled efficiently.

Challenges:

- **Field Name Transformation**: The backend uses **snake_case** (for example, **`first_name`**, **`last_name`**), while the client expects **`camelCase`** (for example, **`firstName`**, **`lastName`**). You need to transform all the field names in the response.
- **Handling Nested Structures**: If the user has an address, each field within the address must also follow the **`camelCase`** naming convention (for example, **`cityName`**, **`zipCode`**).
- **Efficient Data Serialization**: The solution needs to ensure that the API response is optimized in terms of performance while correctly transforming the field names without redundant code.

Solution:

The solution to this problem is with the help of field aliases from Pydantic. It allows you to have an internal name for your model and map it into other names in a serialized output. You can, in this case, have the **snake_case** names inside, and you can then use **camelCase** aliases in an API response.

Additionally, FastAPI supports easy handling of nested models so that the field alias can also be applied to transform nested fields, such as an address.

Step-by-step Solution:

1. **Define Pydantic Models with Aliases**: Use Pydantic's **`Field`** function to specify the alias for each field. The alias will be used in the API response, ensuring that the field names follow the required camelCase format.

2. **Handle Nested Data**: Ensure that nested fields, such as addresses, are also given aliases that follow the camelCase convention.

3. **Enable Alias Population**: Pydantic's `Config` class has a configuration option called **`allow_population_by_field_name`**. This allows the API to recognize and transform field names during serialization.

4. **Customize Serialization**: Use Pydantic's built-in JSON serialization to transform the model fields into the camelCase format automatically.

Code Implementation:

```
from fastapi import FastAPI
from pydantic import BaseModel, Field

app = FastAPI()

# Defining the nested Address model
class Address(BaseModel):
    city: str = Field(alias="cityName")
    zip_code: str = Field(alias="zipCode")

# Defining the UserProfile model
class UserProfile(BaseModel):
    first_name: str = Field(alias="firstName")
    last_name: str = Field(alias="lastName")
    address: Address

    class Config:
        allow_population_by_field_name = True  # Ensures aliases
are used in the response

# API route that returns the user profile
@app.get("/user-profile/", response_model=UserProfile)
def get_user_profile():
    # Example user profile data with snake_case field names
    user_profile = {
        "first_name": "John",
        "last_name": "Doe",
        "address": {
            "city": "New York",
            "zip_code": "10001"
        }
    }
    return user_profile
```

Explanation:

- **Alias Configuration:**
    a. The **`Field`** function is used to set an alias for each field. For instance, the **`first_name`** field in the backend is aliased as **`firstName`** for the API response, and **`zip_code`** is aliased as `zipCode`.
- **Nested Models:** The **`Address`** model defines an alias for its fields (**`city`** becomes **`cityName`**, and **`zip_code`** becomes **`zipCode`**). This ensures that nested fields are also transformed correctly.

- **Config Class:** By setting `allow_population_by_field_name = True`, we ensure that Pydantic uses the aliases in the serialized response. This configuration allows the backend to work with **snake_case**, while the client sees **camelCase**.
- **API Route:** In the route `/user-profile/`, we return the user profile in **snake_case**, but thanks to the Pydantic configuration, the response is automatically transformed into **camelCase**.

Sample Request and Response:

- **Request**: This is a `GET` request, so no request body is needed.
- **Response**: The response will return the profile with **camelCase** field names, as expected by the client.

```
{
  "firstName": "John",
  "lastName": "Doe",
  "address": {
    "cityName": "New York",
    "zipCode": "10001"
  }
}
```

- **Regular User Request:**
  - GET `/profile/user`
- **Regular User Response:**

```
{
  "name": "John Doe"
}
```

Time and Space Complexity:

- **Time Complexity:**
  - **O(1)** for each field since the transformation of field names via aliases occurs during serialization. The overall time complexity depends on the number of fields being transformed, but it remains constant per field.
  - For nested models, the time complexity grows linearly with the depth and size of the nested structure, so **O(n)** where **n** is the depth and number of nested fields.
- **Space Complexity:**
  - **O(n)** where **n** is the total number of fields, including nested fields, that need to be stored and serialized.

Best and Worst-Case Conditions:

- **Best Case:**
  - The API handles small data with simple structures, where the transformation of field names is minimal and occurs quickly.
- **Worst Case:**
  - The API handles large, deeply nested structures with many fields to transform. In such cases, the time and space complexity increase with the number of fields and depth of nesting.

Noob-to-Expert Approach:

- **Noob Approach:**
  - A beginner might attempt to manually map the field names inside the route handler using dictionary manipulations. This approach would be inefficient and prone to errors, especially when dealing with nested structures.
- **Expert Approach:**
  - An experienced developer leverages Pydantic's alias feature to handle field name transformations automatically. By defining aliases directly in the model, the code remains clean and maintainable, while FastAPI and Pydantic take care of serialization.

This problem illustrates how to deal with one of the common problems in developing an API: the transformation of field names from one naming convention to another. FastAPI and Pydantic make this really easy using aliases, which gives developers a chance to maintain their backend code consistent with client requirements on camelCase naming. We have handled the transformation of both flat and nested data effectively while maintaining the API flexible and scalable using the Field aliases of Pydantic and response modeling in FastAPI.

Each style, from noob to expert, demonstrates how one can use Pydantic features to automate the hard part of serialization so that developers may focus on application logic rather than the transformation of the data.

With strong integration to Pydantic, FastAPI enables the developer to handle complex, real-world scenarios, such as validation of requests, customized responses, and secure data. The following examples of using FastAPI functionalities apply to solving common API problems with robust, clean, and efficient code. In fact, using Pydantic models for requests as well as responses helps to make the data strongly consistent while securing it, thus allowing more flexible APIs that scale for real-world applications.

Conclusion

In this chapter, we investigate the role of Pydantic in FastAPI and, in particular, in validation and serialization. The use of Pydantic models would automatically cut down errors in the developed API since a good number of incoming data validations, as well as required constraints in outgoing data, depend on using Pydantic models. We discussed how request models can be declared together with response models, validation efficiencies, as well as serialization of data into formats, say JSON. It has further demonstrated how Pydantic's error handling, custom validation, and support for complex data structures can be used to simplify development, making the API work robustly and consistently.

The bottom line is that Pydantic simplifies the management of data in FastAPI, as well as enhancing the reliability of applications with structured error messages and the prevention of invalid data input. Such aspects are foundational for scalable, secure, and high-performing APIs.

The next chapter goes through one of the most critical aspects of API development: **Authentication and Authorization**. FastAPI supports several built-in mechanisms to manage user access, namely OAuth2, JWT, and session-based authentication. This chapter explains the differences between authentication and authorization (which verify identity and grant permissions, respectively) and guides the reader in setting up secure authentication flows within a FastAPI application. You will learn the best practices for securing and managing endpoint protection, roles, and permissions in such a way that ensures that your API is both secure and resilient.

Multiple Choice Questions

1. **What is the primary use of Pydantic in FastAPI?**
   a. Handling HTTP routing
   b. Data validation and serialization
   c. Managing database connections
   d. Monitoring API performance
2. **Which of the following is a feature of Pydantic models?**
   a. Implicit type coercion
   b. Dynamic route generation
   c. Strict type validation
   d. Built-in SQL database support

3. **Which keyword is used to define a Pydantic model?**
   a. class
   b. def
   c. model
   d. schema
4. **What happens if invalid data is provided to a Pydantic model?**
   a. The server automatically corrects it.
   b. An error is raised with detailed messages.
   c. The invalid data is ignored silently.
   d. It passes but logs a warning.
5. **What is the primary function of a request model in FastAPI?**
   a. To format outgoing responses
   b. To validate incoming data
   c. To define API routes
   d. To handle server errors
6. **Which HTTP method is associated with creating a resource in FastAPI?**
   a. GET
   b. POST
   c. PUT
   d. DELETE
7. **In Pydantic, what is the correct way to define a field as optional?**
   a. **`Field(None)`**
   b. **Optional[str]**
   c. **Nullable[str]**
   d. **OptionalField[str]**
8. **What does the `@app.post` decorator indicate in FastAPI?**
   a. It defines a new resource.
   b. It sends data to the client.

   c. It specifies a POST endpoint.
   d. It deletes a resource.

9. **Which serialization format does FastAPI use by default for responses?**
   a. XML
   b. YAML
   c. JSON
   d. CSV
10. **What is the role of response models in FastAPI?**
    a. To filter and validate the outgoing data
    b. To authenticate users
    c. To encrypt request payloads
    d. To monitor server performance
11. **How can you exclude a specific field from a response model?**
    a. Set it as `None`
    b. Use **`@exclude_field`** decorator
    c. Use **`response_model_exclude`** parameter
    d. Define it outside the Pydantic model
12. **Which Pydantic method converts a model instance to a dictionary?**
    a. **`model.dict()`**
    b. **`model.serialize()`**
    c. **`model.to_json()`**
    d. **`model.export()`**
13. **What is a key benefit of reusing request models in FastAPI?**
    a. Reduces HTTP latency
    b. Simplifies code maintenance
    c. Increases server load
    d. Improves response time

14. **Which field type is recommended to handle date and time inputs in Pydantic?**
    a. `datetime`
    b. `str`
    c. `timestamp`
    d. `time`
15. **How does FastAPI handle nested models within Pydantic?**
    a. Using inheritance
    b. Through nested dictionaries
    c. With recursive model references
    d. Via relational database joins

Answers

Question	Answer
1	b
2	c
3	a
4	b
5	b
6	b
7	b
8	c
9	c
10	a
11	c
12	a
13	b
14	a
15	c

CHAPTER 7
Authentication and Authorization

Introduction

In the modern digital world, protection of data and prevention from unauthorized use are not only technical issues, but the basis of user trust. Contemporary APIs constantly exchange data between endpoints, and thus, security remains an ongoing issue. FastAPI, a high-speed Python web framework, has intrinsic tools for securing applications by means of authentication and authorization. Although they are mistakenly used interchangeably, authentication confirms the identity of the user, and authorization specifies what a user can do. There are two very popular strategies in FastAPI, which are JWT (JSON Web Tokens) and OAuth2. JWT is a lightweight, low-overhead token format that is perfect for authentication of users and authorization with minimal overhead, whereas OAuth2 is an industry-wide standard used extensively in third-party sign-in use cases such as "Login with Google."

Protection of FastAPI endpoints is all about finding a trade-off between security and user experience. Proper role and permission management enables developers to limit access to sensitive data without compromising the smooth user experience. This chapter offers hands-on examples on how to initialize sessions, create and validate tokens, and regulate resource access based on user roles. These implementations play an important part in creating secure and scalable APIs. By the time they finish, developers will have both conceptual knowledge and hands-on experience in creating solid, user-conscious applications that mature securely with time.

Structure

In this chapter, we will discuss the following topics:

- **JWT (JSON Web Token) Tokens**
    - Introduction to JWT and Token-Based Authentication
    - Generating and Validating JWT Tokens for FastAPI

    - Refresh Tokens and Token Expiration Handling
- **OAuth2 Implementation**
    - Overview of OAuth2 and Its Working
    - Implementing OAuth2 Login Flows in FastAPI
    - Handling Scopes and Permissions with OAuth2
- **Securing API Endpoints**
    - Protecting Endpoints with Role-Based Access Control
    - Middleware for Authentication and Authorization
    - Error Handling and Response Formatting for Secure Endpoints
- **Cross-Origin Resource Sharing**
    - Understanding CORS
    - Working of CORS
    - Implementing CORS in FastAPI
    - Best Practices for CORS
- **Mini Project**

JWT (JSON Web Token) Tokens

JWT refers to JSON Web Tokens – a lightweight and simple way to securely transmit information between parties in a compact, self-contained JSON object. As one of the most widely adopted choices for stateless authentication, it places relevant data, from user IDs to session information, all right within the token itself. This self-contained nature allows for fast, scalable authentication and authorization of users without the requirement for ongoing server-side sessions, making JWT especially well-suited for modern API-driven applications like those built with FastAPI.

Introduction to JWT and Token-based Authentication

JWT stands for JSON Web Tokens; it is a compact serialized security token intended for quick, stateless authorization. It is used for such purposes because all the needed information, including user ID and session information, is embedded in the token itself. JWT allows for the possibility of fast user authorization with a scalable approach without holding continuous server-side sessions and is, therefore, a perfect match for modern APIs such as FastAPI.

A typical JWT is divided into three components: Header, Payload, and Signature. These parts make up a compact, self-contained token that can be used securely to transmit user data from one party to another.

- **Header**: The header is the first component of a JWT and carries metadata about the token. This usually consists of two fields, the typ field, indicating the type of token–which in most cases will be JWT–and the alg field, which defines what algorithm has been used for signing, such as HS256, which is short for HMAC using SHA-256. This information will aid the server in decoding and understanding how the integrity of the token could be verified once it is received.
- **Payload**: That is where the core data or "claims" of the JWT reside, meaning meaningful content of the JWT. Claims can be standard fields such as sub (subject or user ID), exp (expiration time), and iat (issued at time), as well as custom fields that are relevant to the application, such as user roles or permissions. This information can enable the server to promptly identify the token holder with his permissions, among other data that might be required quickly. Since the payload is not encrypted but instead encoded, confidential information should be avoided in this portion.
- **Signature:** The last bit is the signature, responsible for token verification for being authentic and complete. The signature is generated through the encoded header and payload, combined, and then signed with a secret key (or a private key in asymmetric algorithms such as RS256). Once the token reaches the server, that server can recompute the signature to ensure that nothing has been tampered with in the token. This makes it impossible for unauthorized alterations of the header or payload to occur since any change will yield a mismatched signature.

JWTs are really pervasive access tokens that allow an application to remove any burden of session handling by continuous server-side, which makes them light and fully scalable. The technique particularly gains value in the newest forms of modern stateless API, wherein the authenticity of client requests can be granted without necessarily relying on any server memory for every individual session. As such, the method increases speed as well as scalability.

Generating and Validating JWT Tokens for FastAPI

For an efficient application of JWT to FastAPI for authentication purposes, it needs to be used the right way. Firstly, one needs to create a JWT after successful login, which then needs to be checked with every request made, so that a user can remain authorized at all times. This process typically includes creating an authentication endpoint, which upon successful validation of the user's credentials will provide a

JWT; implementing dependencies for validating the token on each protected route; and token expiration management to further ensure security.

1. **Installing Dependencies**

   Install the required packages:

   ```
   pip install fastapi pyjwt passlib[bcrypt] uvicorn
   ```

   - **`pyjwt`**: Handles token creation and validation.
   - **`passlib`**: Manages password hashing for secure storage.

2. **Generating a JWT Token** Create an endpoint to issue a JWT token upon user login:

   ```
   from fastapi import FastAPI, Depends, HTTPException
   from datetime import datetime, timedelta
   import jwt

   SECRET_KEY = "mysecretkey"
   ALGORITHM = "HS256"

   def create_jwt(data: dict, expires_delta: timedelta = timedel-
   ta(minutes=30)):
       data.update({"exp": datetime.utcnow() + expires_delta})
       return jwt.encode(data, SECRET_KEY, algorithm=ALGORITHM)
   ```

3. **Validating JWT Tokens**

   Use middleware or dependencies to verify tokens for each request:

   ```
   from jwt import PyJWTError

   def verify_jwt(token: str):
       try:
           payload = jwt.decode(token, SECRET_KEY,
   algorithms=[ALGORITHM])
           return payload
       except PyJWTError:
           raise HTTPException(status_code=401, detail="Invalid
   token")
   ```

4. **Endpoint Example**

   Create a simple login route to issue JWT tokens:

   ```
   @app.post("/login")
   async def login(username: str):
       token = create_jwt({"sub": username})
       return {"access_token": token, "token_type": "bearer"}
   ```

Refresh Tokens and Token Expiration Handling

JWT tokens are typically issued with a limited lifetime to also establish a limited usage period while minimizing the attack window should the token have been stolen. This limitation causes the user to log in again once the token has timed out, so that it has recent access. However, in order to be convenient and not sacrifice security, an access token can be sent with a refresh token. A **refresh token** lives longer and is stored safely. Therefore, after the expiration of the access token, a user does not need to re-enter their credentials but rather use the refresh token to obtain a new access token.

A refresh token can maintain a secure yet smooth flow of sessions using the refresh token. Access as well as refresh tokens, issued upon user login: Since an access token grants direct access, access, as well as refresh tokens, are issued simultaneously. Now that an access token automatically expires, using refresh tokens generates a new access token at that point. This will allow applications to provide uninterrupted access while reducing the number of times sensitive credentials are exchanged, especially useful for applications requiring high security, such as banking or e-commerce platforms.

- **Creating a Refresh Token**

  Modify the login endpoint to return both access and refresh tokens:

  ```
  refresh_token = create_jwt({"sub": username}, timedelta(days=7))
  return {"access_token": token, "refresh_token": refresh_token}
  ```

- **Using the Refresh Token**

  Implement an endpoint to allow users to refresh their access token:

  ```
  @app.post("/refresh")
  async def refresh_token(refresh_token: str):
      payload = verify_jwt(refresh_token)
      new_access_token = create_jwt({"sub": payload["sub"]})
      return {"access_token": new_access_token}
  ```

Best Practices for JWT Usage

- **Utilize Secure Secret Keys**: As the security of JWT relies heavily on the secret used for signing it, your secret key also should be long, generated randomly, and kept secure in order not to fall into any unknown hands. Do not utilize predictable or short keys. These are highly susceptible to brute-force attacks. Implement rotation of your secret key periodically and maintain it at a secure location, like in the secrets manager.

- **Set Short Expirations:** Since the JWT can only be active for so long–and this can be short depending on the typical lifespan of access tokens–it offers some protection if one does steal the token, for any time a token gets compromised. For instance, one could set the access token's exp to expire 15-30 minutes into a user session, where access then must be retrieved either from a refresh token or forced re-authentication of that user. This method of implementing security while keeping a tight balance between security and user experience is good.
- **Implement Refresh Tokens:** You might want to implement refresh tokens in order not to force people to log in again continuously, without limiting the lifetime of every access token. You implement refresh tokens with an expiry period longer than an access token and store the tokens more securely, either as HTTP-only cookies, and when an access token expires, the application would use the refresh token to obtain a new access token that would allow for continuation, uninterrupted user sessions with credentials not re-entered again.
- **Restrict Token Scope:** JWTs should be scoped carefully so that they only contain the permissions and data necessary for the intended use. For example, tokens used to access read-only resources should not include permissions for sensitive write operations. By limiting the token's scope, you reduce the risk of privilege escalation if a token is compromised. Defining specific scopes or roles within tokens and careful selection of each endpoint requirement must be maintained to adhere strictly to principle-of-least-privilege security with API-driven applications.

Using these practices will help you create a safe and efficient JWT-based authentication scheme that is user-friendly, ensuring sensitive information is better protected while maintaining a smooth user experience.

JWT tokens are an excellent way to handle user sessions and API authentication in a scalable and efficient manner, especially suited for FastAPI's asynchronous, high-performance framework. Unlike traditional session-based authentication, JWTs are stateless, meaning all the necessary information about the user session–such as user ID, permissions, and token expiration–is stored within the token itself. This statelessness removes the need for server-side session storage, which means that applications can scale much more easily because they do not need to keep track of every single user's session. JWT tokens are also lightweight, consisting of a compact header, payload, and signature components, making them perfect for fast transmission and ideal for the performance needs of microservices and modern web applications.

JWTs can support the utilization of access and refresh tokens to keep a user's experience secure and uninterrupted, using an access token immediately for a short-lived life and a **refresh token** good for a longer duration, making it possible to renew his session without asking him again to log in. Thus, this dual-token system strikes a balance between usability with security so that the resource may be accessed by users without too frequent login procedures and, simultaneously, less risk in case a token is compromised. All these factors make JWT tokens a pretty good candidate for FastAPI applications that need security, speed, and scalability.

Following **OAuth2**, we will continue with the other **industry standards for authentication and authorization management**. Here, we learn how to implement secure login flows, how to handle scopes in order to limit permissions on tokens, and finally, control resource access within FastAPI applications. It will give you a rich insight into what OAuth2 does and how it should be implemented, helping you produce **secure applications** according to the best practices in API security.

OAuth2 Implementation

OAuth2 is the most widely accepted authorization framework that permits applications to obtain **secure access** to resources without exposing the user's credentials. It issues access tokens, issued by third-party services that can, in turn, trade such tokens on behalf of a user, granting the latter minimal access to information without their having to give away passwords. This is especially beneficial for modern applications that add features such as "Sign in with Google" or "Log in with Facebook." These features improve the user's experience and increase security for the modern application. It works by allowing steps consisting of authorization requests, exchange of tokens, and accessing of resources while allowing every aspect to work with secure interactivity and efficiency.

Overview of OAuth2 and Its Working

OAuth2 is an authorization framework that enables applications to access resources securely on behalf of a user. It is often used in APIs to enable third-party applications to access the data of users without exposing credentials. The **token-based** approach in OAuth2 increases security as authentication and authorization are separated. This makes OAuth2 ideal for modern API security.

OAuth2 provides endpoint securing and permission management in FastAPI. Further, this is even highly efficient while implementing OAuth2 due to the simplicity associated with its scope management.

Implementing OAuth2 Login Flows in FastAPI

1. **Installing Dependencies**

   To get started with OAuth2 in FastAPI, ensure you have FastAPI installed, along with the additional `passlib` library for hashing:

   ```
   pip install fastapi passlib[bcrypt] uvicorn
   ```

2. **Using `OAuth2PasswordBearer`**

   FastAPI provides `OAuth2PasswordBearer` for managing password-based OAuth2 flow. This utility extracts the token from the request header and verifies it:

   ```
   from fastapi.security import OAuth2PasswordBearer
   oauth2_scheme = OAuth2PasswordBearer(tokenUrl="token")
   ```

3. **Creating a Token Endpoint**

   The token endpoint accepts the user's credentials, verifies them, and returns a token if they are correct. This is the core authentication endpoint in OAuth2:

   from fastapi import Depends, HTTPException

   ```
   from pydantic import BaseModel
   import jwt

   class Token(BaseModel):
       access_token: str
       token_type: str

   @app.post("/token", response_model=Token)
   async def login(username: str, password: str):
       # Verify credentials here (e.g., check database)
       access_token = create_jwt({"sub": username})
       return {"access_token": access_token, "token_type": "bearer"}
   ```

4. **Securing Endpoints with OAuth2**

   With OAuth2 enabled, secure any endpoint by adding **`Depends(oauth2_scheme)`**, which checks for the token in the request header and validates it:

   ```
   @app.get("/protected")
   async def protected_route(token: str = Depends(oauth2_scheme)):
       payload = verify_jwt(token)
       return {"status": "You are authorized!"}
   ```

Managing Scopes for Granular Access Control

Scopes in OAuth2 define levels of access granted by the token. FastAPI's **`OAuth2PasswordBearer`** lets you specify and enforce these scopes in your endpoints:

- **Declaring Scopes**

  Define the required scope for each route to ensure only users with specific permissions can access it:

  ```
  oauth2_scheme = OAuth2PasswordBearer(tokenUrl="token", scopes
  ={"admin": "Access admin area", "user": "Access user area"})
  ```

- **Enforcing Scopes in Endpoints**

  Use scopes to restrict access, such as an admin-only area:

```
from fastapi import Security
@app.get("/admin", dependencies=[Security(oauth2_scheme,
scopes=["admin"])])
async def admin_area():
    return {"status": "Admin access granted!"}
```

- **Using Scopes in Tokens**

  When generating the JWT, include the user's scopes:

```
def create_jwt(data: dict, scope: list):
    data.update({"scope": " ".join(scope)})
    return jwt.encode(data, SECRET_KEY, algorithm=ALGORITHM)
```

Handling Scopes and Permissions with OAuth2

Token expiration, together with revocation, forms one of the most important approaches towards the management of strong security in OAuth2 implementations. The problem with access tokens is the direct mapping of users to the resources in question. The lifespan of a token tends to be short; chances are minimized if one occurs there during the lifetime process. The following are some critical strategies that can be embraced:

- **Token Expiration:** The life of an access token needs to be set short, several minutes to an hour at most. This reduces damage from a stolen token. When an access token is about to expire, you can get a new access token using a refresh token without re-authenticating. To do this, you need to implement a refresh token endpoint in your OAuth2 workflow. This endpoint will request new access tokens, which will verify the refresh token and issue a new access token if the refresh token is still valid. This approach will not only improve security in terms of token lifespan but also enhance user experience because users can continue accessing with no need for repeated logins.
- **Revoking Tokens:** Although using expiration policies, there are scenarios where tokens need to be revoked before they would expire naturally, such as when a user logs out or suspicious activity is noticed. To handle token revocation efficiently, consider keeping a record of token usage and maintaining a mechanism that is usually called a **blacklist**, which maintains a list of **revoked tokens**. If the token is revoked, then it goes into the blacklist, which means subsequent requests using that particular token will not pass through a check against the list. It allows the system to respond in real-time to potential security breaches. A different type of whitelisting strategy could be

controlling which tokens are even permitted to issue new access tokens, thus providing whitelisting over refresh tokens.

Combining such strategies as short-lived access tokens, robust refresh mechanisms, and revocation algorithms allows you to greatly enhance security around your OAuth2. Not only is this beneficial to the user's sensitive information, but it also helps users to ensure their data safety behind this application, thereby generating a safe place for human interactions.

OAuth2 implementation in FastAPI provides applications with a robust and **scalable** means of managing the **security** of APIs. Applications can protect endpoints, set levels of access, and make user data privacy stronger without lowering usability. FastAPI applications are significantly more robust with scopes, tokens, and endpoint security.

In the next section, we will add to these concepts, discussing how to keep API resources safe from improper access and best practices in API security.

Securing API Endpoints

Securing API endpoints is a strong building block of trust in fast and robust FastAPI applications. This section details steps that you can use to provide strong protection to your API so that only legitimate users can access the data while the API behaves exactly as expected in all situations. In this section, we shall discuss role-based access control, authentication and authorization middleware, and how errors and responses should be managed to have a smooth experience of interacting with an API safely.

Protecting Endpoints with Role-Based Access Control

This role-based access control (RBAC) is one of the security models that actually defines permissions based on what their roles are within the system; for example, this might be **admin, user, and guest**. Its implementation ensures that every user will only have access to or the ability to modify data within the bounds of permissions by their role, thereby minimizing data exposure while enforcing data integrity.

Defining User Roles and Permissions

In FastAPI, one would generally use dependency injection to implement roles in their application, linking specific permissions to the respective roles, and validating the role of a user before proceeding to grant him access to an endpoint.

Example

```
def get_current_user_role(role: str):
    # Retrieve user's role from token and verify access level
    pass
```

Role Verification in Endpoints

Each endpoint can then restrict access based on roles. Here is how an endpoint might be secured:

```
@app.get("/admin-dashboard")
async def admin_dashboard(current_user=Depends(get_current_user_
role)):
    if current_user.role != "admin":
        raise HTTPException(status_code=403, detail="Access
forbidden")
    return {"status": "Welcome, Admin"}
```

Benefits of RBAC:

- RBAC reduces risk as it provides a certain structure to permissions and tends to reduce accidental exposure to sensitive data. It simply streamlines audits and ensures compliance since access privileges get centralized and defined.

Middleware for Authentication and Authorization

Middleware in FastAPI is used to manage requests based on the application level, which can be very useful before any endpoint is reached, since it can perform tasks that include authentication and authorization for a request.

Setting Up Authentication Middleware

Authentication Middleware verifies user credentials for any incoming request. It blocks invalid access attempts early through interception.

Example Middleware:

```
        from starlette.middleware.base import BaseHTTPMiddleware

class AuthMiddleware(BaseHTTPMiddleware):
    async def dispatch(self, request, call_next):
        # Perform token validation here
        response = await call_next(request)
        return response

app.add_middleware(AuthMiddleware)
```

Using Authorization Middleware for Access Control

The access control middleware inspects the authenticated user to ensure they meet the RBAC or other policies for accessing the application.

In FastAPI, authorization checks are usually made through dependencies, but in more complicated systems, middleware can further centralize things.

Advantages of Middleware-Based Security:

- Middleware centralizes access control, which ensures consistency across endpoints. It reduces code duplication by handling common security tasks in a single place.

Error Handling and Response Formatting for Secure Endpoints

Handling errors elegantly is crucial to giving the end user useful feedback while keeping sensitive implementation details confidential. FastAPI's built-in exception handling, along with structured responses, adds to your API's security and professional touch.

Custom Error Messages for Authentication Failures

Customize errors, such as unauthorized access or invalid tokens, to avoid exposing backend details while providing users with useful guidance.

Example:

```
raise HTTPException(status_code=401, detail="Invalid token.
Please re-authenticate.")
```

Unified Response Format

By structuring error responses uniformly, you can enhance the API's usability while preventing the leakage of sensitive details. FastAPI allows for custom responses using JSON schema.

Example response model:

```
from pydantic import BaseModel

class ErrorResponse(BaseModel):
    error: str
    message: str
    code: int

@app.exception_handler(HTTPException)
async def custom_error_handler(request, exc):
    return JSONResponse(
        status_code=exc.status_code,
        content={"error": "Unauthorized", "message": exc.detail,
"code": exc.status_code}
    )
```

Logging and Auditing for Enhanced Security

Implement logging to record unauthorized access attempts and other relevant actions. Auditing can help track unusual access patterns and quickly identify potential security threats.

Benefits of Structured Error Handling:

- Error handling provides a streamlined experience for users and clients by delivering consistent feedback. This approach also limits potential vectors for attacks that exploit unhandled errors or poorly formatted responses.

The most critical thing about ensuring the security and integrity of any application is securing API endpoints. With FastAPI, RBAC, middleware, and full error handling compatibility, the developer has flexible tools with which to protect his endpoints from unauthorized access. This overall security framework is built using RBAC, authentication, and authorization middleware that ensures only authorized users access the API in specified ways. This makes the API resistant to unauthorized access and helps keep the answers clean and consistent.

Cross-Origin Resource Sharing

Cross-Origin Resource Sharing (CORS) is a browser-enforced security feature that prohibits web pages from requesting a different domain than the one on which the web page was served. This is necessary to guard users from attacks by malicious websites that attempt to access data on another origin without authorization. But it introduces challenges for legitimate use cases, too—a frontend app hosted on one domain needs to communicate with an API on another. Developers need to explicitly configure their servers to allow such cross-origin requests.

Knowing CORS is important for developers to enable safe cross-origin communication by correctly setting the HTTP headers as in Access-Control-Allow-Origin, ensuring security while still supporting valid client-server interactions.

Understanding CORS

It is an intrinsic security feature of web browsers that helps avoid cross-site request forgery attacks. It will prevent sites with malicious intent from requesting things on other domains without permission. It also secures the user's data and allows only specific sources to access resources on a server. Whenever a web application attempts to access resources on another origin, be it a domain, protocol, or port, the browser verifies if the server allows cross-origin requests.

A web browser, by default, enforces the Same-Origin Policy, which denies a web page permission to make requests to a different domain than that from where the web page was actually served. This is why CORS is meant to allow certain domains access to resources on a server.

Working of CORS

When a browser makes a cross-origin request, it sends an HTTP request to the server that includes an `Origin` header, which indicates the origin of the request. The server can respond with specific headers to indicate whether the request is allowed:

- **Access-Control-Allow-Origin:** This header specifies which origins are permitted to access the resource. It can be set to a specific origin, a comma-separated list of origins, or the wildcard character *, which allows all origins.
- **Access-Control-Allow-Methods:** This header specifies which HTTP methods (for example, GET, POST, PUT, DELETE) are allowed when accessing the resource.
- **Access-Control-Allow-Headers:** This header lists the headers that can be included in the request.
- **Access-Control-Allow-Credentials:** This header indicates whether credentials (such as cookies or HTTP authentication) can be included in the request.

When a server responds to a preflight request (a CORS request that uses the OPTIONS method to check permissions), it must include these headers to allow the actual request to proceed.

Implementing CORS in FastAPI

FastAPI makes it easy to enable CORS in your application using the **`CORSMiddleware`**. The following is an example of how to implement CORS in a FastAPI application:

```
from fastapi import FastAPI
from fastapi.middleware.cors import CORSMiddleware

app = FastAPI()

# Add CORS middleware
app.add_middleware(
    CORSMiddleware,
    allow_origins=["https://example.com"],  # Specify allowed
origins
    allow_credentials=True,
    allow_methods=["GET", "POST"],  # Specify allowed methods
    allow_headers=["*"],  # Allow all headers
)
```

```
@app.get("/items/")
async def read_items():
    return [{"item": "Item 1"}, {"item": "Item 2"}]
```

In this example, the **`CORSMiddleware`** is added to the FastAPI application. The **`allow_origins`** parameter specifies which origins are allowed to access the resources. In this case, only requests coming from https://example.com will be permitted. The **`allow_methods`** and **`allow_headers`** parameters further define what is allowed in cross-origin requests.

Best Practices for CORS

To ensure secure and reliable cross-origin communication, developers should follow key CORS best practices that balance flexibility with protection against unauthorized access.

- **Limit Origins:** While configuring CORS settings for OAuth2, you should identify trusted origins. Instead of using a wildcard (*) to allow requests from any origin, you should define clearly the domains allowed to interact with your API. This prevents unauthorized access, as only legitimate applications are allowed to make requests to your resources. Restricting the sources narrows your attack surface via which bad people can take advantage of vulnerabilities or even continue cross-site request forgery attacks.
- **Use HTTPS:** This entails ensuring that an application uses HTTPs when operating so that it can fully protect the sensitivities being transferred between the clients and server. HTTP uses encryption, thus preventing snooping, man-in-the-middle attacks, and finally, tampering. It becomes more critical in OAuth2 workflows because access tokens, refresh tokens, and user credentials are exchanged. So when you enforce HTTPS throughout your application, you secure not only the data but also improve the trust that comes from a commitment to a user's security, with users being more likely to interact with applications that do the same.
- **Regular Audits:** The security process is dynamic; therefore, it is essential to undertake regular audits of your CORS policies and OAuth2 implementation to be abreast with current security requirements. Regular auditing will enable you to trace some of the outdated configurations or weaknesses in your settings. With changes in time, your application might require the addition of new features, services, or even users' requests for amendments to your existing security policies. Keeping your CORS configurations and OAuth2 configurations abreast with one another helps you design a security application that will never stop getting better in the fight against emerging threats but certainly comply with some best practices in security management.

An understanding of the proper procedure to work with CORS facilitates the securing of the FastAPI with cross-origin interaction that is needed, thus requiring proper configuration in how you secure your applications. It hence improves the user interface with regard to experience, since multiple clients from different origins are likely to access your API if set right using these principles. Thus, securing your resources becomes much simpler while maintaining flexibility in your need for application functionalities for the modern web application.

Mini Project

Project: Simple Task Management API

Overview:

This project builds a basic **Task Management API** using FastAPI. It involves setting up the environment, creating models, implementing authentication, handling dependencies, and uploading files (such as attachments).

Step-by-Step Implementation:

1. **Setting Up the Development Environment**

   a. Install Python and create a virtual environment:

   ```
   python -m venv env
   source env/bin/activate    # On Linux/macOS
   .\env\Scripts\activate     # On Windows
   ```

   o Install dependencies:

   ```
   pip install fastapi uvicorn python-jose[cryptography] pydantic
   email-validator
   ```

2. **Creating the Project Structure**

   ```
   /task_manager/
   │
   ├── main.py             # FastAPI app entry point
   ├── models.py           # Pydantic models for request/response
   ├── auth.py             # JWT and authentication logic
   ├── routers/            # API routes for tasks and users
   │   ├── tasks.py
   │   └── users.py
   └── requirements.txt    # List of dependencies
   ```

3. **Building the FastAPI Application**

   `main.py`: **FastAPI App Setup**

   ```
   from fastapi import FastAPI
   from routers import tasks, users
   ```

```
app = FastAPI()

app.include_router(tasks.router, prefix="/tasks", tags=["Tasks"])
app.include_router(users.router, prefix="/users", tags=["Users"])

@app.get("/")
def read_root():
    return {"message": "Welcome to the Task Management API"}
```

4. **Creating Models Using Pydantic**

   `models.py`: **Request and Response Models**

```
from pydantic import BaseModel, EmailStr
from typing import Optional

class Task(BaseModel):
    id: int
    title: str
    description: Optional[str] = None
    is_completed: bool = False

class User(BaseModel):
    username: str
    email: EmailStr
    password: str
```

5. **Implementing Authentication**

   `auth.py`: **JWT Token Logic**

```
from fastapi.security import OAuth2PasswordBearer
from jose import JWTError, jwt

SECRET_KEY = "mysecretkey"
ALGORITHM = "HS256"

oauth2_scheme = OAuth2PasswordBearer(tokenUrl="token")

def create_access_token(data: dict):
    return jwt.encode(data, SECRET_KEY, algorithm=ALGORITHM)
```

6. **Creating API Routes with Dependencies**

   `routers/tasks.py`: **Task Routes**

```
from fastapi import APIRouter, Depends
from models import Task
from typing import List

router = APIRouter()
```

```
tasks_db = []

@router.post("/", response_model=Task)
def create_task(task: Task):
    tasks_db.append(task)
    return task
@router.get("/", response_model=List[Task])
def get_tasks():
    return tasks_db
```

`routers/users.py`: **User Routes with JWT Authentication**

```
from fastapi import APIRouter, HTTPException, Depends
from auth import create_access_token
from models import User

router = APIRouter()

@router.post("/register")
def register_user(user: User):
    return {"message": f"User {user.username} registered!"}

@router.post("/token")
def login(user: User):
    token = create_access_token(data={"sub": user.username})
    return {"access_token": token, "token_type": "bearer"}
```

7. **Adding File Upload Feature**

   `routers/tasks.py`: **File Upload Endpoint**

```
from fastapi import File, UploadFile

@router.post("/upload/")
def upload_file(file: UploadFile = File(...)):
    return {"filename": file.filename}
```

8. **Running the Application**

   Start the FastAPI server using Uvicorn:

```
uvicorn main:app --reload
```

9. **Testing the API**

   Use Postman or Curl to Test Endpoints:

   - **Create a task:**
     `POST /tasks/`
   - **Get all tasks:**
     `GET /tasks/`

- **Register user:**
  `POST /users/register`
- **Generate token:**
  `POST /users/token`
- **Upload file:**
  `POST /tasks/upload/`

This project puts together how to handle dependencies, authentication with JWT, validation with Pydantic, and file upload, gathering together all the concepts developed across the previous chapters. It is pretty fundamental but already leaves space for many further extensions: on roles for users, on a task deadline, or even for complex filtering using queries.

This wraps up Task Management API – a simple, practical case that combines core FastAPI concepts.

Conclusion

In this chapter, we explored essential techniques to secure FastAPI applications through robust authentication and authorization strategies. Topics such as JWT tokens and OAuth2 implementation demonstrate how to manage user sessions effectively and protect resources from unauthorized access. We also covered best practices for securing API endpoints, ensuring a seamless and safe user experience while maintaining flexibility.

The next chapter, ***File Uploading***, builds on this foundation by demonstrating how to handle file transfers securely in FastAPI. It will introduce efficient ways to upload, validate, and manage files within APIs, further enhancing the capabilities of your application.

Multiple Choice Questions

1. **What does JWT stand for?**
   a. JSON Web Tokens
   b. Java Web Tokens
   c. JavaScript Wide Tokens
   d. JSON Wide Tokens

2. **Which algorithm is commonly used to sign JWTs?**
   a. SHA-512
   b. RSA
   c. HS256
   d. MD5
3. **What is the primary purpose of OAuth2?**
   a. Data encryption
   b. Delegated access
   c. Logging errors
   d. Authentication servers
4. **How can a JWT token be invalidated?**
   a. By modifying the payload
   b. By logging out
   c. Changing the secret key
   d. Changing the username
5. **Which HTTP header is typically used to send JWTs?**
   a. Content-Type
   b. Authorization
   c. Cookie
   d. X-JWT
6. **What is the main benefit of OAuth2 over OAuth1?**
   a. Enhanced encryption
   b. Simpler token structure
   c. No need for a digital signature
   d. Multiple tokens per user
7. **How does FastAPI simplify authentication implementation?**
   a. Using async functions
   b. Dependency injection

   c. Middleware chaining
   d. Database triggers
8. **Which FastAPI dependency manages OAuth2 token authentication?**
   a. OAuth2PasswordBearer
   b. OAuth2Authenticator
   c. JWTHandler
   d. TokenMiddleware
9. **What is the purpose of the scopes parameter in OAuth2?**
   a. To determine token expiration
   b. To specify user roles
   c. To define access permissions
   d. To log API calls
10. **What is CORS, and why is it important?**
   a. A token management system
   b. A security policy for cross-origin requests
   c. A database encryption technique
   d. A token serialization format

Answers

Question	Answer
1	a
2	c
3	b
4	c
5	b
6	c
7	b
8	a
9	c
10	b

CHAPTER 8
File Uploading

Introduction

This chapter covers the details about uploading files in FastAPI—an important topic for applications dealing with user-generated content. Whether it is a social network application that provides user profile images, a document management system, or an analytics platform dealing with large datasets, uploading files is essentially crucial in many modern applications. It allows you to create an easy and high-performance framework that can handle uploads efficiently with minimal effort, ensuring a seamless user experience. You really can do much better than that on improving the functionality and security of your application if you can understand the inner mechanics behind handling file uploads.

Now, let us focus on how to accept and process files in FastAPI. Handling uploads is mainly done in API endpoints where it gets the file data to its configuration and verifies whether file types and sizes have exceeded the limits for the possible misuse. FastAPI also makes it very simple: it offers some easily implemented tools for accepting files, allowing users to upload images or PDFs as part of their requests. In addition, we will discuss how to handle different file types and structures so that your application can support all kinds of upload requirements with data integrity.

Once files are uploaded, you need to have a safe storage solution. Files can be stored locally on the server, within a network drive, or in cloud storage services, depending on your application's requirements and scalability needs. The most excellent practices in choosing the proper storage solution will be presented. We will cover the usage of server-side storage on smaller applications and the usage of cloud storage, such as AWS S3, to store large-scale systems without being insecure. Security is foremost in this process: to defend files appropriately to protect sensitive files, then implement access control, including encryption, when necessary, so that user data is protected end-to-end throughout its cycle.

FastAPI's efficient file handling is capable of improving both the users' experience as well as the scalability of your application. With the ability to perform asynchronous file handling, regulate the size of the uploaded files, and server resources, you are much more likely to see to it that large quantities of data do not break your application. This chapter will give you a holistic approach to handling file uploads in FastAPI, from the initial setup to storage and security considerations, so you can build applications that can handle user uploads with ease and reliability.

Structure

In this chapter, we will cover the following topics:

- **Handling File Uploads in FastAPI**
  - Overview of `File` and `UploadFile` in FastAPI
  - Creating Endpoints for File Uploads
  - Supporting Multiple File Uploads
  - Handling Different File Types
  - Validating File Size and Type
  - Error Handling During Uploads
- **Storing and Processing Uploaded Files**
  - Saving Files Locally or on Cloud Storage
  - Directory Management and File Organization
  - Processing Uploaded Files: Parsing CSV and Image Resizing
  - Security Considerations for File Storage
  - Practical Examples and Use Cases

Handling File Uploads in FastAPI

Handling file uploads is one of the essential features in many web applications, allowing users to interact with the system using images, documents, and other types of file uploads. FastAPI makes this easy for you with intuitive tools to handle file uploads, which allow you to receive, validate, and process files in your API endpoints. FastAPI supports form-data requests, which makes it flexible for common file types; this is handy for the most varied needs of an application, from uploading profile pictures to document management systems.

Beyond the basics, there are best practices to be adopted in terms of security and error management when handling files. This section will take you step by step through the setting up of file upload endpoints to validate file sizes and format, along with mechanisms in place for error handling, towards a smooth user experience. We will also discuss what can be done to prevent an overload on the server to ensure that uploaded files go through a secure process within the local storage or those in cloud services. This will make sure that your application is responsive, secure, and user-friendly even with a large number of file uploads.

Overview of `File` and `UploadFile` in FastAPI

The **`File`** and **`UploadFile`** classes in FastAPI are used to handle file uploads efficiently. While **`File`** reads the entire file content into memory, **`UploadFile`** processes large files more efficiently by providing a file-like interface and support for streaming.

- In FastAPI, built-in classes **`File and UploadFile`** are used for efficient file management. These classes can handle incoming files according to their size, format, and purpose, thus being handled efficiently and easily in web applications.
- **`File`**: The File class is designed to accept smaller, less complex files as part of an API request. It is best suited for light inputs such as text, JSON, or configuration files. With File, you read and process the data directly; hence, it is great to use when dealing with very small text files or only a minimum level of file handling is needed. This is a synchronous implementation which reads the content of an entire file all at once, suitable where the size of the file fits well within a single operation that does not overload the memory.
- **`Fileupload`** : This class is specifically recommended for larger or even binary files. These include multimedia files, such as videos and images. Similar to the case of a file, reading in small chunks helps you avoid problems such as a memory overrun in processing large files with the UploadFile class compared to File. It also includes the metadata of a file, such as filename or content type, and an interface to read, write, or save files in a non-blocking fashion that is very beneficial for asynchronous processing. UploadFile lets FastAPI handle numerous large files at once, making the user experience sweet even in data-heavy uploads.
- Together, **`File`** and **`UploadFile`** provide a powerful toolkit to handle all types of files and sizes. FastAPI applications can thus support everything from simple file inputs to the most complex, large-scale uploads.

Example: Basic File Endpoint

```
from fastapi import FastAPI, File, UploadFile

app = FastAPI()

@app.post("/upload/")
async def upload_file(file: UploadFile = File(...)):
    return {"filename": file.filename}
```

Creating Endpoints for File Uploads

Creating endpoints for file uploads in FastAPI involves using the **`File`** or **`UploadFile`** class in the request body. These classes enable seamless handling of file data, making it easy to process and store uploaded files.

- **Endpoints** in FastAPI handle file uploads like other HTTP requests.
- Use **`@app.post`** to define endpoints receiving **`multipart/form-data`**, which browsers use for file uploads.
- Each endpoint accepts one or more files and returns responses based on the application's needs.
- Adding validations ensures that only authorized or valid content gets uploaded.

Supporting Multiple File Uploads

FastAPI supports multiple file uploads by accepting a list of **`UploadFile`** objects in the request body. This allows users to upload multiple files simultaneously, which can be processed iteratively within the endpoint.

- FastAPI allows multiple files to be uploaded through a single request by using Python's List type.

Example: Uploading Multiple Files

```
from typing import List
from fastapi import FastAPI, UploadFile, File

app = FastAPI()

@app.post("/upload/")
async def upload_files(files: List[UploadFile] = File(...)):
    return {"filenames": [file.filename for file in files]}
```

- In the frontend, this can be achieved with an **`<input type="file" multiple>`** element. The API can loop through and process each file individually.

Handling Different File Types

FastAPI allows you to handle different file types by validating the uploaded files' content types using the **`content_type`** attribute of **`UploadFile`**. This ensures that only files matching the expected MIME types, such as images, PDFs, or text files, are accepted for processing.

- Validating file types ensures security and performance since only trusted and expected formats will be allowed to the application. This procedure helps protect your system from probably malicious files that would seek to exploit vulnerabilities in such files. It further enhances the performance by reducing processing on unnecessary formats. You create a more robust and reliable environment for your application through strict validation checks on the types of files. The platform, therefore, enhances trust because it reassures users that data is handled in a safe and efficient way, such that there is no possibility of abusive content.

- You can use the **content_type** attribute of **UploadFile** to check the MIME type of the uploaded files.
- Example: Restrict uploads to only images by checking **image/png or image/jpeg**.

```
@app.post("/upload-image/")
async def upload_image(file: UploadFile = File(...)):
    if file.content_type not in ["image/png", "image/jpeg"]:
        return {"error": "Invalid file type"}
    return {"filename": file.filename}
```

Validating File Size and Type

FastAPI supports file validation by checking both size and type during upload processing. File size can be validated by inspecting the file content's length as it is read, while the type is verified using the **content_type** attribute of **UploadFile**. Combining these checks ensures that uploads meet the application's requirements for security and functionality.

- **File size and type validation** would be an important step during the development of a safe and robust file upload system. The limitation of files uploaded will protect your server from **potential overloads or denial-of-service (DoS)** attacks; an overly large file could possibly be uploaded to strain server resources. You can always ensure that your application will perform well, and is always responsive under load by making sure the sizes of the files are restricted to acceptable limits.
- There are several ways to validate file size. One of the first is through checking the Content-Length header inside the **HTTP request**; it contains the file size before the file is even processed. This way, you will be immediately rejecting oversized files and cut down on unneeded server load. It is possible to validate a file size while reading a byte stream, especially when **working with UploadFile**. Reading a file in chunks helps keep track of the size of your file in real-time, and then enables you to quit when the size exceeds whatever set limits you have on those files.
- You may **advance security** even further, as you would do on the frontend and backend levels, by validating both. **Front-end validations** would be through JavaScript in enforcing size limits placed upon the files uploaded in most cases. This has stopped users from selecting those whose sizes are larger than whatever preset size, thus increasing further protection before the servers come into play, and an instantaneous feedback to the user as well. Frontend

checks can sometimes be bypassed, meaning that they alone are not sufficient and, therefore, need to be complemented by backend validation so that only files that fall into reasonable ranges of size and type can be accepted. This strategy, on multiple levels of validation, protects your application against dangerous data attacks on file uploads.

Error Handling During Uploads

FastAPI provides robust error-handling mechanisms for file uploads to ensure a smooth user experience. You can use exception handling to catch issues such as unsupported file types, exceeding size limits, or corrupted files. Custom error messages and HTTP status codes such as **400 Bad Request,** can inform users about specific issues during the upload process.

- Network issues or incomplete files are common errors that need handling.
- FastAPI's **HTTPException** can return custom error messages.

One of the main things to be taken care of while creating a reliable and user-friendly application is the error handling in file uploads. Some common issues may arise while uploading files due to network interruption, incomplete transfer of files, or even unsupported file formats. This can really impact the user experience if not handled properly. It will guide the users in getting proper feedback, and how to solve their problems.

FastAPI offers a seamless way to deal with such errors by using its **HTTPException** class, which allows you to return custom error messages along with the corresponding HTTP status codes. For instance, if there is a network problem while uploading a file, you can recognize the incomplete file and then return an informative 400-series error, such as **HTTP_400_BAD_REQUEST**, with a message saying the upload failed due to a connection problem. This means if the user is uploading a file of an unsupported type, you can raise an HTTPException that will give 415 Unsupported Media Type status, indicating with a message about accepted file types. It tells the user what the problem is, but also what he should do to correct this: Upload again or upload in some other file format.

Robust error handling during an upload will prevent any unexpected behavior by the application, while boosting the user experience. Catching errors early and providing good, actionable messages leads toward a resilient file upload system that can elegantly control any form of disruption without requiring the support of most users.

Example: Handling Upload Errors

```
from fastapi import HTTPException

@app.post("/upload/")
async def upload_file(file: UploadFile = File(...)):
```

```
    try:
        content = await file.read()
    except Exception as e:
        raise HTTPException(status_code=500, detail="File upload
failed")
    return {"filename": file.filename}
```

- Implement **logging** to record failed uploads and notify users gracefully.

Storing and Processing Uploaded Files

Having a reliable storage solution, as well as an organizational strategy, is what uploading files effectively is all about, in terms of security. You can use FastAPI to store files locally on the server or on cloud storage services such as AWS S3, Google Cloud Storage, and Azure Blob Storage, whichever fits your application's needs best. For smaller projects, local storage is simple and inexpensive. However, for large-scale applications with high storage demands and access, cloud storage works perfectly. Whichever you select, organizing directories by user or date ensures that files are accessible and manageable over time.

The processing of uploaded files may require efficient and secure management of different formats. Although parsing and extracting data can be simple for text-based files, it may require resizing or encoding for multimedia files, such as images or videos, before processing. This is where FastAPI is at an advantage, with support for asynchronous functions that enable a smooth handling of large and complex files so that their tasks do not slow down your application. It would help in setting up secure storage and efficient workflows in processing so that files uploaded are kept in order, processed, and safely stored in your application in an effort to improve functionality as well as user experience.

Saving Files Locally or on Cloud Storage

FastAPI allows saving uploaded files either locally or on cloud storage, based on application needs. For local storage, files can be written to the filesystem using Python's `os` or `pathlib` modules. For cloud storage, integration with services such as AWS S3, Google Cloud Storage, or Azure Blob Storage can be implemented using their respective SDKs, enabling scalable and secure file management.

- **Local Storage:**
  - Files are saved directly to a server's filesystem.
  - Useful for small-scale applications or temporary file handling.
  - Example: Using Python's **`open()`** method to write a file locally.

    ```
    @app.post("/upload/")
    async def save_file(file: UploadFile = File(...)):
    ```

```
        with open(f"uploads/{file.filename}", "wb") as f:
            f.write(await file.read())
        return {"filename": file.filename}
```

- **Cloud Storage:**
  - For scalability, storing files on services such as **Amazon S3, Google Cloud Storage, or Azure Blob Storage** is recommended.
  - Libraries such as **`boto3`** (AWS) or **`google-cloud-storage`** facilitate interaction with cloud platforms.
  - Cloud storage ensures redundancy and better file access across different regions.

Directory Management and File Organization

FastAPI facilitates efficient directory management and file organization by allowing developers to structure file storage based on application requirements. You can create subdirectories for specific file types, users, or upload timestamps using Python's **`os`** or **`pathlib`** modules. Proper organization not only simplifies retrieval but also improves scalability and maintainability in projects handling large numbers of uploaded files.

- The directory's organized maintenance will speed the computer's search operations so that it and the users of the files can retrieve them much faster. With properly categorized files by either user or date, or other types of categories, it makes them search much easier and also quicker than if the directory were disorganized. Again, even more time gets saved in search operations due to its easy search properties. This structured approach will enhance both user satisfaction and system performance because it minimizes loads on the server when performing requests for specific files, thereby improving the system performance. Besides, a proper directory structure can also help in better data management, such as automated backups and ease in compliance with any data retention policies.
- **Strategies include:**
  - **Date-based directories:** Save files in folders named by year/month/day. Using date-based directories for holding files is very efficient in terms of organization due to the fact that it also increases accessibility as well as manageability. This is because you would have saved your files in folders labeled by year, month, and day, which gives an easy structure to trace where exactly your file is based on its upload date. This would not only make it easier to look for files but also tend to keep the system clean, especially applications that handle massive uploads over time. Additionally, it might allow cleaner automated processes to find which files are old enough to qualify for archiving or deletion.

- **User-based directories:** Store user-specific files separately for better tracking. It is best to maintain user-specific files in unique, designated directories for enhanced tracking and organization in your application. Files for a user can therefore be managed in a less complicated manner within an application, since their uploads or documents can also be retrieved easily without going through other related documents. This approach not only makes the user's experience better with access but also ensures ease of permissions management in the sense that you can set up access controls based on user directories. In addition, user-based directories facilitate auditing and compliance efforts by allowing easier monitoring of how users engage with their files.
- **File versioning:** Maintain different versions of the same file using version numbers in filenames (for example, **`report_v2.pdf`**). Maintaining different versions of the same file using version numbers in filenames is an effective strategy for document management and tracking changes over time. Users can easily identify the most recent version of a file while preserving previous iterations for reference or rollback if needed by appending version numbers to filenames, such as **`report_v2.pdf`**. This approach not only offers clarity in organising your file but also guards against possible overwrites; your important information cannot easily disappear. A further version of usability would be offered within your application when incorporating version history; here, users may view, compare, or probably restore previous versions of those files.

Example: Date-based File Saving

```
import os
from datetime import datetime

@app.post("/upload/")
async def save_file(file: UploadFile = File(...)):
    today = datetime.today().strftime('%Y-%m-%d')
    os.makedirs(f"uploads/{today}", exist_ok=True)
    with open(f"uploads/{today}/{file.filename}", "wb") as f:
        f.write(await file.read())
    return {"filename": file.filename}
```

Processing Uploaded Files: Parsing CSV and Image Resizing

FastAPI supports processing uploaded files by providing functionalities such as parsing CSV files and resizing images directly within endpoints. For CSV files, you can parse data using libraries such as **`pandas`** to read and manipulate the content. For image resizing, using libraries such as **`Pillow`** allows you to manipulate uploaded images on the fly, ensuring they meet application requirements before storage or display.

- **CSV Parsing:** Read and process CSV files using libraries such as **pandas** to store data in structured formats.

```
import pandas as pd
@app.post("/upload-csv/")
async def process_csv(file: UploadFile = File(...)):
    df = pd.read_csv(file.file)
    return {"columns": df.columns.tolist()}
```

- **Image Resizing:** Resize uploaded images with libraries such as **Pillow** to optimize them for storage and display.

```
from PIL import Image
@app.post("/upload-image/")
async def resize_image(file: UploadFile = File(...)):
    image = Image.open(file.file)
    resized = image.resize((300, 300))
    resized.save(f"uploads/{file.filename}")
    return {"message": "Image resized successfully"}
```

Security Considerations for File Storage

When dealing with uploaded files, it is very necessary to include high security to prevent exposing them to potential vulnerabilities. One step is in sanitizing the filenames such that path traversal attacks do not occur, whereby malicious users try to play with the file paths and access those restricted directories. You lessen the risk by removing the special characters, restricting to safe formats of filenames, and ensuring secure file paths.

- **Sanitizing Filenames:** Sanitization of filenames is an important security measure for protecting your application from potentially malicious threats. This prevents special characters and restricts safe characters in filenames, hence denying the possibility of path-traversal attacks, where attackers maneuver file paths to try to access restricted areas. This can also be done through the renaming of files upon uploading, for example, by appending a timestamp or generating a unique identifier. This would further reduce security risks and ensure that filenames are consistent and avoid conflicts or overwrites in the storage system.
- **File Size Limits:** One of the must-do items in maintaining performance and security within your application is to limit file sizes. This limits the upload of an unnecessarily large file from either the frontend or the backend, preventing server overload and denial-of-service attacks. Front-end validation can give immediate feedback to the users, thereby enriching their experience with the invalid upload before it actually reaches the server. Backend checks should

be in place to ensure that if a user is able to bypass frontend restrictions, the application will not accept files of size greater than the specified limits. This will ensure that the server remains intact and stable. Attempts to upload oversized files can also be logged to monitor potential abuse and improve overall security measures.

- **Content Type Validation:** Such uploaded content type into your application has to be validated in a way that only allows trusted file types. By checking the `content_type` of files meant to be uploaded, you will have prevented users from uploading files intended for exploitation or destruction of your system. It will set up a whitelist of accepted MIME types, that can be images such as **`image/jpeg`** and **`image/png`**, documents such as **`application/pdf`**, and any other format which you consider trusted; therefore, only files that can match those MIME types can be processed. Further verification of file types, say file signatures, or making use of libraries that parse the content of files, can validate if the uploaded files match their expected type and therefore not end up being malicious files masquerading with incorrect extensions. Thus, this comprehensive approach secures the application while making sure that your application does not betray the trust the user has placed in your application by handling their files.
- **Temporary Files:** The prudence of this strategy, however, lies in the approach of storing sensitive files as temporary files. This increases the security and protection of the user's data because only for the time required for processing or analysis are files stored, thus reducing the risks of unauthorized access or breach of data. It is very important to delete such temporary files securely after accomplishing the required operations to prevent malicious actors from retrieving them. Automated cleanup operations could be scheduled tasks or deletion event-driven; thus, it would keep the storage very clean and lessen the potential chances of having left-in sensitive data. Activities created in temporary files also enhance auditing and monitoring, identifying suspicious behavior in the interest of your application.

Example: Filename Sanitization

```
from fastapi import HTTPException

@app.post("/upload/")
async def upload_file(file: UploadFile = File(...)):
    filename = file.filename.replace("../", "")  # Basic
sanitization
    if not filename:
        raise HTTPException(status_code=400, detail="Invalid filename")
    with open(f"uploads/{filename}", "wb") as f:
        f.write(await file.read())
    return {"filename": filename}
```

Practical Examples and Use Cases

FastAPI's file upload and processing capabilities can be effectively utilized across a wide range of applications. For instance, a web application may require users to upload CSV files containing large datasets for processing, such as data analytics or importing into a database. FastAPI's integration with `pandas` enables seamless parsing and manipulation of these files directly on the server. Another use case is handling image uploads, where the ability to resize and compress images using `Pillow` ensures optimal performance and quality for web displays or storage. Additionally, integrating with cloud services such as AWS S3 allows for scalable and secure storage solutions, making it easier to manage and access uploaded files from any location. These features make FastAPI an excellent choice for applications requiring flexible and efficient file handling.

- **Profile Picture Uploads:** Uploading the profile picture is a basic feature of most applications in which users can upload avatars or images into their accounts to personalize the same. It is effortless to develop a system with the images that will be held in user-specific directories in order to easily retrieve the same. It will enable better user engagement and help handle user data more securely through an organized file structure.
- **CSV Data Import:** Another practical application of the system is the uploading and parsing of CSVs. Here, administrators will import huge data into the system using upload. The entry processes were streamlined because now users could upload large datasets one at a time, hence highly minimizing manual input time errors and thus errors. The robust validation checks released will ascertain that only well-constructed files are accepted. As such, integrity with the import process will not be compromised for the data.
- **Document Management Systems:** File upload capabilities are very handy for document management systems that enable users to upload, manage, and update any document type, including PDFs or Word files. This feature, including the use of versioning, will help track document history, so if it is needed, previous iterations will be accessible. It adds more value to user-to-user collaboration and creates an even more reliable structure that handles sensitive documents safely in the right manner.

Conclusion

Handling file uploads is an essential aspect of building robust web applications, and FastAPI provides a seamless way to manage this process. This chapter covered the practicalities of working with file uploads, from saving them locally to leveraging cloud storage solutions for scalability. We also explored directory management techniques and security measures, such as sanitizing filenames and setting file size limits, to ensure safe file handling. Furthermore, by walking through examples such as CSV parsing and image resizing, developers gain practical insight into processing files efficiently. This knowledge equips developers to implement file handling features confidently, ensuring optimal storage practices, while maintaining the security of uploaded content. With these skills in hand, readers are better prepared to meet the file management demands of modern web applications, creating systems that are both functional and scalable.

The next chapter delves into one of the most critical elements of web development: **integrating databases with FastAPI**. As applications grow, handling persistent data becomes necessary, and this is where databases come into play. The chapter will explore both SQL and NoSQL databases, explaining their differences and guiding developers on when and how to use each. Readers will learn to configure popular databases such as PostgreSQL and MongoDB, establish database connections, and manage query execution efficiently within FastAPI applications. Special attention will be given to ORM tools such as SQLAlchemy and Tortoise ORM, which simplify database interaction through Python models. Additionally, topics such as connection pooling, data migrations, and query optimization will ensure developers build scalable and performance-oriented systems. With a solid foundation in database connectivity, readers will be ready to handle complex data interactions, empowering them to create dynamic, data-driven applications with ease.

Multiple Choice Questions

1. **What decorator is used in FastAPI to handle file uploads?**
   a. `@app.upload`
   b. `@app.post`
   c. `@app.file`
   d. `@app.get`
2. **Which FastAPI class is used for handling file uploads?**
   a. UploadFile
   b. FileInput
   c. InputFile
   d. UploadedData
3. **Which method reads the entire content of an uploaded file in FastAPI?**
   a. `read_content()`
   b. `read()`

   c. `content()`

   d. `get_content()`

4. **What parameter defines the maximum size of a file in FastAPI uploads?**

   a. `max_file_size`

   b. `file_limit`

   c. `max_content_length`

   d. `size_limit`

5. **Which cloud storage service is commonly used with FastAPI for uploading files?**

   a. Google Drive

   b. AWS S3

   c. Dropbox

   d. OneDrive

6. **What should you sanitize to prevent malicious file uploads?**

   a. File content

   b. File size

   c. Filename

   d. File format

7. **Which HTTP status code indicates a successful file upload?**

   a. 200

   b. 201

   c. 204

   d. 404

8. **Which type of attack can occur if files are not validated correctly?**

   a. SQL injection

   b. XSS attack

   c. File inclusion attack

   d. CSRF attack

9. **Which of the following is an example of processing uploaded files?**
   a. Resizing images
   b. Changing metadata
   c. Encrypting files
   d. All of the above
10. **What is a common security practice, when storing uploaded files?**
    a. Store with public access.
    b. Encrypt sensitive files.
    c. Allow unrestricted file types.
    d. Store in the root directory.

Answers

Question	Answer
1	b
2	a
3	b
4	c
5	b
6	c
7	b
8	c
9	d
10	b

CHAPTER 9
Connecting to Databases

Introduction

Databases form the backbones of any backend service by storing essentials whose power validates applications and user interactions. In this chapter, we discuss how databases are integrated with FastAPI, which is an end web framework that couples well with both traditional and asynchronous databases. Using the powerful capabilities of FastAPI in conjunction with robust database management tools, developers can create reliable, scalable applications that fit real-world use cases.

We will consider two popular approaches to integrating the database: SQLAlchemy and Tortoise ORM. It is a very flexible ORM tool, famous for complex relational database queries, merging the best of ORM capabilities, and the ability to write raw SQL. This flexibility makes it suitable for developers requiring fine-grained control over their queries and database interactions. It is also designed for asynchronous frameworks such as FastAPI. The ORM is lightweight, less complex, and has been built specifically with the goal of handling asynchronous operations while working on non-blocking code.

This chapter will take the reader through establishing connections to popular databases such as SQLite, PostgreSQL, and MySQL. Detailed, step-by-step instructions on how to configure database connections, define data models, and perform CRUD (create, read, update, and delete) operations in an organized and efficient way are what developers will learn through these examples. With this book, readers will have robust data layers that are easy to maintain and expand as their applications grow.

What follows are broader benefits of using ORMs in API development: better scalability and maintainability. Proper database management is critical for production-ready applications, and this chapter covers techniques for managing database connections and organizing code to optimize both performance and readability. After reading it, people will be able to learn how to combine the FastAPI framework with databases, as well as know which tools are more appropriate for particular projects.

Structure

In this chapter, we will cover the following topics:

- **SQLAlchemy Integration**
    - Introduction to SQLAlchemy and ORM Models
    - Installing and Setting Up SQLAlchemy with FastAPI
    - Defining Models and Performing CRUD Operations
    - Managing Database Sessions and Connections
- **Working with SQLite, PostgreSQL, and MySQL**
    - Setting Up SQLite for Development
    - Connecting to PostgreSQL and MySQL in FastAPI
    - Handling Migrations with Alembic
    - Performing CRUD Operations on these Databases
- **Using Tortoise ORM with FastAPI**
    - Introduction to Tortoise ORM and async Support
    - Defining Models using Tortoise ORM
    - Handling Database Operations Asynchronously
    - Practical Examples of Using Tortoise ORM
- **Real-World Scenarios and Solutions**

SQLAlchemy Integration

This is a combination of the advantage of an ORM with the flexibility of using raw SQL, hence an extremely powerful tool to manipulate SQL-based databases in web applications. It is therefore possible to map Python classes to database tables to make CRUD operations look straightforward and turn database records into manageable Python objects. Using this ORM approach supports complex relationships between tables. This makes the code clean and more maintainable by data-driven applications. However, the real strength of SQLAlchemy lies in its hybrid model, allowing developers to mix ORM functionality with raw SQL queries for better control over performance. This is quite valuable in FastAPI because high-performance APIs require efficient management of databases. This section guides you on how to use SQLAlchemy together with FastAPI to construct scalable, production-ready applications able to connect to SQLite, PostgreSQL, MySQL, and other popular SQL databases, with examples of setup, configuration, and CRUD operations.

Introduction to SQLAlchemy and ORM Models

SQLAlchemy is a powerful Python library that provides full support for SQL databases and allows both simple and complex data interactions. The features also included are Object Relational Mapping (ORM) and SQL Expression Language. This means developers can either work with data as objects or through raw SQL queries. ORM helps developers map database tables directly to classes in Python so that one can transform rows into easy-to-manipulate data pieces in terms of Python objects. Using this object-based approach, not just the CRUD operations but even complex relational data structures will come under management since the relationship between tables is handled by Python syntax, which is familiar to developers.

This abstraction allows for a much more readable and maintainable code base where developers can understand what database interactions are being done by reading object-oriented code. When using it within a FastAPI application, SQLAlchemy's ORM really shines when working with relational databases such as PostgreSQL, MySQL, and SQLite. SQLAlchemy models are representations of the database tables, and provide the developer with the ability to interact with data in Python classes and methods instead of raw SQL statements. Another interesting property of SQLAlchemy's ORM is the built-in support for validating and managing relationships between tables. This makes it a good tool for developing and scaling more complex applications that rely on relational data.

Installing and Setting Up SQLAlchemy with FastAPI

Starting with SQLAlchemy in FastAPI will require installing a couple of necessary packages and a database connection. First off, you will need to install SQLAlchemy along with psycopg2-binary for PostgreSQL support, and alembic for migrations, which can be installed with the following command:

```
pip install sqlalchemy psycopg2-binary alembic
```

After installing the packages, you can configure a SQLAlchemy database URL, defining how FastAPI will connect to the database. It defines information such as database type, username, password, host, and database name. Here is how it would look for PostgreSQL:

```
from sqlalchemy import create_engine

DATABASE_URL = "postgresql://user:password@localhost/db_name"
engine = create_engine(DATABASE_URL)
```

In this code snippet, **`create_engine`** is the mechanism to establish the `engine` or the central part of SQLalchemy's database interactions. There is a pool of connection management that allows for various simultaneous requests by the application without having to open and then close database connections over and over again. This kind of connection pooling is most prized in high-traffic applications of FastAPI since one would optimize resource use through the reuse of existing connections and minimize latency. The engine bridges between FastAPI and the database, enabling the ORM or raw SQL queries to connect with the database smoothly. With that in place, you can now define your models, create tables, and begin querying the database.

Defining Models and Performing CRUD Operations

Here, we are defining a simple SQLAlchemy model to represent a `User` table in a relational database using FastAPI and SQLAlchemy's ORM.

Step-by-Step Explanation

1. **Define a Base Class:**

```
from sqlalchemy.ext.declarative import declarative_base
```

`declarative_base()` creates a base class from which all ORM models will inherit. This **`Base`** class provides the foundation for defining the tables and columns that represent our database's structure.

2. **Defining the User Model:**

```
class User(Base):
    __tablename__ = 'users'
    id = Column(Integer, primary_key=True, index=True)
    name = Column(String, index=True)
```

Here, we define a class **`User`**, which inherits from **`Base`**. This class represents a table in the database, with its name specified by **`__tablename__`**. In this case, the table will be named **`'users'`**.

- **Primary Key (`id` column):**

```
id = Column(Integer, primary_key=True, index=True)
```

The **id** column is defined as an integer and acts as the primary key for the users' table. The primary key uniquely identifies each record, and the **`index=True`** parameter allows for quicker lookups by indexing this column in the database.

- **Name (`name` column):**

```
name = Column(String, index=True)
```

The **name** column is a **String** type, intended to store the user's name. Like **id**, the **index=True** option here will create an index for the column in the database, making name-based searches more efficient.

Full Code

```
from sqlalchemy import Column, Integer, String
from sqlalchemy.ext.declarative import declarative_base

# Create the base class for model definitions
Base = declarative_base()

# Define the User model as a representation of the 'users' table
class User(Base):
    __tablename__ = 'users'
    id = Column(Integer, primary_key=True, index=True)  # Primary
key with index for faster lookup
    name = Column(String, index=True)  # Name column, indexed for
efficient searching
```

With the **User** model defined, SQLAlchemy now knows how to create the **users** table in the database, including an indexed primary key (id) and an indexed **name** column. This structure provides an efficient way to store and query user data in a FastAPI application. To complete the setup, you will typically configure a session with SQLAlchemy to manage database transactions, allowing you to perform CRUD operations on this table.

You can use SQLAlchemy sessions to handle database transactions in an efficient manner so that you may implement the core CRUD operations within your FastAPI application. Let's go through how each of these works:

- **Create:** To add a new record in the database, you first define a new instance of the model, for example, a User, and fill all its fields with the respective data. You then attach this instance to the session, and commit the transaction to commit the changes into the database.

  ```
  new_user = User(name="Alice")
  session.add(new_user)
  session.commit()
  ```

  Here, a new User with the name **"Alice"** is added to the database. **session.add()** queues the new user to be saved, and **session.commit()** applies the change.

- **Read:** Reading data allows you to fetch records from the database, either by querying all records in a table or filtering to retrieve specific ones.

  ```
  user = session.query(User).filter_by(name="Alice").first()
  ```

In this example, **session.query(User).filter_by(name="Alice").first()** searches for a user with the name **"Alice"** and returns the first match. You can use different filters to search by **id, name**, or other attributes.

- **Update:** Updating data requires fetching an existing record, modifying its fields, and committing the transaction.

```
user = session.query(User).filter_by(name="Alice").first()
user.name = "Alice Updated"
session.commit()
```

Here, we find the user named **"Alice"** and update their name to **"Alice Updated"**. **session.commit()** saves the change in the database.

- **Delete:** To delete a record, find the target record and remove it from the session, then commit the transaction to apply the change.

```
user = session.query(User).filter_by(name="Alice Updated").first()
session.delete(user)
session.commit()
```

This code snippet locates the user named **"Alice Updated"** and removes them from the database. **session.delete(user)** prepares the deletion and **session.commit()** finalizes it.

All these CRUD operations leverage the SQLAlchemy session for working with transactions. Sessions handle data consistency through the process of batching together a few operations and then rolling them back in case something goes wrong. So, the sessions are perfect for creating reliable database management within a FastAPI application.

Managing Database Sessions and Connections

This is basic for any application that needs to interact with a database and ensures that every operation is isolated and consistent. This session handling by SQLAlchemy with FastAPI provides a clean and effective way of keeping a connection to the database, making CRUD operations reliable and scalable.

Creating a Session with SQLAlchemy

To create a session, you will first use SQLAlchemy's `sessionmaker` function, which allows you to configure the session and bind it to the database engine. The **engine** here is what was initially defined when setting up the database URL with **create_engine**. Here is an example:

```
from sqlalchemy.orm import sessionmaker
SessionLocal = sessionmaker(bind=engine)
```

The **sessionmaker** function acts as a factory for producing new **Session** objects, which are tied to the database engine you configured. Defining **SessionLocal** in this way ensures that each time you call it, a new **`Session`** instance is created and bound to the **`engine`**. Using separate session instances is important in applications such as FastAPI, where requests are handled concurrently, and each request might need to perform independent transactions.

Using the Session in Your Application

To perform any database operation, you start by creating a session instance from `SessionLocal`. Here is how it looks:

```
db = SessionLocal()
```

This new **`db`** instance mirrors a connection to the database, which you can use while performing CRUD operations, or in querying tables, in order to make changes. Each session instance tracks all transactions that are pending as well as committed in the database. Having sessions in isolation ensures that when making changes within a session, they are not visible to any other sessions without their own being committed, thus meaning there is no data inconsistency.

Closing the Session: Preventing Connection Leaks

It is essential to close the session once you have finished your operations. If a session remains open, it keeps a connection to the database active, which can lead to connection leaks and exhaust the database's connection pool. SQLAlchemy does not automatically close sessions, so it is crucial to do this explicitly to ensure that resources are freed up.

```
db.close()
```

In FastAPI, you can automate session management by defining dependencies that create and close the session for each request. Here is an example of using FastAPI's dependency injection to create a session that automatically closes after use:

```
from fastapi import Depends

def get_db():
    db = SessionLocal()
    try:
        yield db
    finally:
        db.close()
```

The **`get_db`** function acts as a dependency, creating a new session and yielding it. When the request is completed, the **`finally`** block ensures that **`db.close()`** is called, releasing the connection. This setup allows you to pass `db` as a parameter to your endpoint functions with `Depends`:

```
@app.get("/users/{user_id}")
def read_user(user_id: int, db: Session = Depends(get_db)):
    return db.query(User).filter(User.id == user_id).first()
```

Using this pattern, FastAPI ensures that each request gets a fresh session, which is automatically closed afterwards. This approach avoids connection leaks, and makes your application more efficient and resilient.

It can help maintain database consistency by not leaking connections between the uses of SQLAlchemy with FastAPI. Sessions may be handled in isolation thanks to the `sessionmaker` of this software. It helps in the isolation of sessions using a given engine. However, there is an availability to create a bound session on this engine. So, one may need to manage them to perform isolated sessions, based on a particular request. Actually, for session management of this particular software, an automatically created connection and a subsequently closed one per request through its FastAPI dependency system help preserve application performance by saving used resources. This approach allows concurrent requests to be handled properly, an important requirement of a production-ready API.

Working with SQLite, PostgreSQL, and MySQL

SQLite is a small, file-based database suitable for development or testing, as it is easy and requires little setup. Because SQLite does not require running a separate server process and stores all data in one file, it is highly convenient for local development purposes, unlike larger database systems such as PostgreSQL or MySQL. The start using SQLite in your FastAPI project, give a file path in the database URL, usually ending in `.db`, and SQLAlchemy will take care of everything else. This way, you can play with models, CRUD operations and migrations, without complex configurations or managing a database server.

The use of SQLite with SQLAlchemy and FastAPI is not very complicated: to connect, and define an engine using `sqlite:///your_database.db`. SQLite is a good choice for rapid prototyping because it supports SQL syntax compatible with larger database systems, and it is easy to transition into PostgreSQL or MySQL for production. Remember that SQLite is highly convenient for development and prototyping, but it does not offer concurrency and scalability to handle production traffic. Now that your application is ready to be deployed, you will want to move the models and configurations over to something like PostgreSQL or MySQL; this way, your FastAPI application will remain healthy and scale nicely.

Setting Up SQLite for Development

SQLite is considered to be a lightweight and extremely simple in-process file-based database system. In general, it is applied for development and testing environments. SQLite does not require a separate server because all its data is stored within a single file on the disk. This makes the setup quick and hassle-free. It is ideal for local development, small applications, or environments where a full-scale database server is not required. SQLite is self-contained, so the developer will not have to bother himself with complex database configurations that might distract him from writing application logic.

To attach FastAPI to SQLite, you only need to set the database URL using a simple file path. Here is an example in your FastAPI application:

```
DATABASE_URL = "sqlite:///./test.db"
```

Here, **`sqlite:///./test.db`** is used to let SQLAlchemy know that it is to be used with SQLite and the **`test.db`** file needs to be created in the present working directory (**`./`**). The URL format provides SQLAlchemy with all it needs to create a connection. FastAPI will then take care of all CRUD operations on SQLite as if it were any other SQL database. It is quite advantageous for the rapid prototype of an API, testing, and executing automated tests without the need for the installation of servers. On the other hand, while SQLite is a piece of cake to work with, it is not really appropriate for a production environment with hundreds or thousands of people trying to hit a page at one time. You usually should be swapping into more robust, scalable databases such as PostgreSQL or MySQL for your production setup.

Connecting to PostgreSQL and MySQL in FastAPI

FastAPI supports connecting robust, server-based relational databases such as PostgreSQL and MySQL without any hassle. This makes them ideal for use in production environments because they scale and perform well. The applications can handle big datasets, high user traffic, and complex queries far better than file-based databases such as SQLite. To do this in FastAPI, one needs to install the drivers and configure the database URLs for each system.

- **PostgreSQL Connection:**

  PostgreSQL is a powerful, open-source relational database known for its advanced features and strong support for complex queries and data integrity. To connect FastAPI to a PostgreSQL database, you will need the **`psycopg2`** driver, which serves as the interface between Python and PostgreSQL. Install the driver using the following command:

  ```
  pip install psycopg2-binary
  ```

  Once installed, configure your database connection URL in FastAPI with the following format:

  ```
  DATABASE_URL = "postgresql://user:password@localhost/mydb"
  ```

  Replace **`user,`** **`password,`** **`localhost`**, and **`mydb`** with your PostgreSQL credentials, host, and database name. This URL structure allows SQLAlchemy to communicate with your PostgreSQL server, and perform database operations through FastAPI. PostgreSQL's compatibility with SQLAlchemy makes it a popular choice for FastAPI applications needing reliable data storage, transactions, and indexing capabilities for large datasets.

- **MySQL Connection:**

  MySQL is another widely used relational database, known for its high performance, ease of use, and strong community support. To connect FastAPI to MySQL, install the **`mysql-connector-python`** driver, which provides a secure and efficient connection between Python and MySQL. Install it with:

  ```
  pip install mysql-connector-python
  ```

  Then, configure the connection URL like so:

  ```
  DATABASE_URL = "mysql://user:password@localhost/mydb"
  ```

  Replace **`user, password, localhost`**, and **`mydb`** with the relevant credentials for your MySQL setup. SQLAlchemy's support for MySQL, combined with FastAPI's async capabilities, allows your application to handle a high volume of concurrent queries and users. This makes MySQL a good fit for applications that require quick read-write operations and scalability.

Once you have the connection URL and drivers installed, you can create the **`engine`** and set up a session factory with SQLAlchemy to manage interactions with either PostgreSQL or MySQL, just as you would with any database in FastAPI. This configuration allows FastAPI to support advanced database management, making it ideal for production-ready applications that demand performance, security, and reliability.

Handling Migrations with Alembic

Alembic is a strong tool that can track any changes made to your database schema over time, such that the database structure evolves as models of your application do. As a migration tool, Alembic integrates nicely with SQLAlchemy, so that you are able to modify your database schema, which might involve adding, modifying, or deleting tables or columns without having to update the database manually. Instead, Alembic will automatically generate migration files for you based on the last known state of your SQLAlchemy models, so code and database schema stay up to date while making changes easier to deploy across different environments.

To set up Alembic in a FastAPI project, start by initializing Alembic with the following command:

```
alembic init alembic
```

This command creates an `alembic` directory in your project, containing configuration files and scripts that Alembic will use to manage migrations. The main configuration file, **alembic.ini**, includes settings such as the database connection URL. Update this file with your **DATABASE_URL**, enabling Alembic to connect to your database.

When you are ready to create a migration, use:

```
alembic revision --autogenerate -m "Initial migration"
```

The **--autogenerate** flag instructs Alembic to scan your SQLAlchemy models and detect any differences between the models and the current database schema. Alembic then generates a migration file with SQL commands to update the database. The **-m** flag allows you to add a description (for example, **"Initial migration"**), which helps track migration history.

To apply the migration and update the database schema, use:

```
alembic upgrade head
```

This command applies the latest migration file, bringing the database in line with your models. Running migrations through Alembic ensures your database schema remains consistent across development, testing, and production environments. As you continue to add or modify models, you can use **alembic revision** and **alembic upgrade** to generate and apply new migrations, simplifying database maintenance and reducing errors due to schema mismatches.

Performing CRUD Operations on these Databases

These can be explained as adding, reading, updating, and deleting records from the database. The combination of FastAPI and SQLAlchemy has simplified executing all these operations, as the focus is on database systems that will host the code - SQLite in a local environment, PostgreSQL for a production setup, and MySQL for another; however, the code is basically the same, which actually makes the whole process very much simpler.

1. **Create:** To add a new record to the database, create an instance of the model class and add it to the session. For instance, in a FastAPI app, you could create a new user like this:

   ```
   new_user = User(name="Alice")
   db.add(new_user)
   db.commit()
   db.refresh(new_user)
   ```

   The **commit()** function saves the changes to the database, and **refresh()** updates the local instance with data from the database, such as the generated ID.

2. **Read:** Reading data involves querying the database to fetch records. Using SQLAlchemy's query interface, you can filter, sort, and retrieve data easily. For example:

   ```
   users = db.query(User).filter(User.name == "Alice").all()
   ```

   Here, **.all()** retrieves all matching results, while **.first()** could be used to fetch only the first record. This pattern allows for flexible querying regardless of the underlying database.

3. **Update:** Updating records involves modifying fields in an existing record and committing the session. SQLAlchemy tracks changes to objects, so modifying fields is simple:

   ```
   user = db.query(User).filter(User.name == "Alice").first()
   user.name = "Alicia"
   db.commit()
   ```

   SQLAlchemy will detect that **user.name** has changed and automatically generate the necessary SQL to update the record.

4. **Delete:** To delete records, query for the object, pass it to the session's **delete()** method, and commit. For example:

   ```
   user = db.query(User).filter(User.name == "Alicia").first()
   db.delete(user)
   db.commit()
   ```

   This ensures that the specified record is removed from the database, and SQLAlchemy handles all related SQL commands.

All of these CRUD operations become identical regardless of whether you are using SQLite, PostgreSQL, or MySQL due to FastAPI's abstraction for databases using SQLAlchemy. It really makes it invaluable during the development phase because you can start with a lightweight, local SQLite setup and easily migrate to a production-grade database such as PostgreSQL or MySQL once you are scaling. The database support and asynchronous nature of FastAPI also help your applications handle data-intensive workflows in an efficient and performance-oriented manner.

Using Tortoise ORM with FastAPI

Tortoise ORM is a lightweight and popular Python library designed for asynchronous applications. This helps to provide an easy way of interacting with databases using the **async/await** syntax. It is highly applicable for FastAPI applications because FastAPI features asynchronous capabilities, which can efficiently handle high-throughput applications. Tortoise ORM seems very intuitive concerning constructing models for the database, handling database connections, and helping CRUD operations not block the main event loop. It supports various databases, among which are PostgreSQL,

MySQL, and SQLite. When you need to switch over to a different database, it is very easy. Plus, the library is inspired by Django ORM as well, so if someone is familiar with Django, they could feel really comfortable working here.

To install Tortoise ORM in the FastAPI project, you start with modeling that maps directly to table definitions in the database. Each model class is inherited from `Model`, and fields are defined as attributes using Tortoise's **`fields`** module. Because Tortoise ORM is asynchronous, the database operations of creating, reading, updating, and deleting records are done through asynchronous methods. For example, querying the database requires using **`await`** to allow the server to handle other requests while waiting for the database response. It supports relationships between models, so related tables can be included for complex schemas, which will be a great feature to have for large applications. With all these features, Tortoise ORM is, therefore, a highly efficient and scalable data management tool in an asynchronous FastAPI environment, making development easier at the same time as maintaining performance.

Introduction to Tortoise ORM and Async Support

As such, Tortoise ORM is also an asynchronous ORM for Python and goes well with FastAPI's non-blocking nature. Primarily built with the intention of making databases easily accessible in high-speed applications, Tortoise essentially rules out the use of synchronous approaches toward database operations - something that is rather commonly associated with traditional approaches that may decelerate the whole async framework, should they come into play when used on top of FastAPI. Every one of the CRUD operations comes as asynchronous out-of-the-box support by way of Tortoise ORM that makes it possible for applications to have multiple DB requests carried out concurrently, and hence becomes even more efficient and improves throughput over time.

The greatest advantage of Tortoise ORM is that it is really easy to use. Being lightweight and focused on the design, it has a strong emphasis on async functionality and avoids some of the complexity found in more feature-heavy ORMs such as SQLAlchemy. Models in Tortoise are defined straightforwardly by listing fields and relationships. Developers can easily define the database schema quickly. It also supports the management of relationships, migrations, and efficient querying while maintaining an async workflow, which makes it an excellent choice for applications that require simple yet performant database integration with FastAPI.

Defining Models Using Tortoise ORM

Defining models in Tortoise ORM is pretty straightforward because it will help developers have a direct mapping of classes in Python to database tables. This makes the model definition somewhat similar to the ones in other Object-Relational Mapping (ORM) frameworks, thus allowing developers already familiar with the concept of ORM to quickly adapt to this application. Each model class, in this case, inherits from the `Model` base class supplied by Tortoise, hence providing the class with access to several ORM functionalities.

The following is an example where we have a model called **`User`** representing the user in the database. We use **id** as an **`IntField`** that we have declared to be a primary key for the table. That means each user is represented by a unique integer identifier, so it must make a distinction between records. The **name** field will be a **`CharField`**, which has a maximum of 50 characters. This sets an explicit limit on the `name` column, so the database does not accept an overly long string that can cause inefficiency or errors.

Tortoise ORM supports field types such as integers, strings, and booleans, as well as foreign keys and relationships. For example, to establish a relation with another model, you may use **`fields.ForeignKeyField`** to bind a `User` model with a **`Post`** model, for example. Furthermore, these field definitions also enable Tortoise ORM to do simple validation and data integrity checks. In any case, once the model classes are designed, Tortoise can, without much help, emit the SQL queries needed for the creation of respective database tables. This helps ensure that there are simple tools available for developers seeking to simplify setting up database interactions while making sure these follow the best schema design. In general, the declarative syntax definition of Tortoise ORM leaves little challenge in managing data interaction issues with asynchronous apps, for example, created using the FastAPI system.

Example:

```
from tortoise.models import Model
from tortoise import fields

class User(Model):
    id = fields.IntField(pk=True)
    name = fields.CharField(max_length=50)
```

This code snippet defines a `User` model using Tortoise ORM, which represents a database table for storing user information. The model inherits from **`Model`**, the base class provided by Tortoise, enabling it to utilize ORM functionalities. The `id` field is defined as an **`IntField`** and is marked as the primary key **(`pk=True`)**, ensuring that each user has a unique integer identifier. The **name** field is defined as a **`CharField`** with a maximum length of 50 characters, which imposes a constraint on the length of the user's name stored in the database. Together, these definitions establish the structure for the **`User`** table in the database, facilitating CRUD operations through Tortoise ORM.

Handling Database Operations Asynchronously

Tortoise ORM is designed to take full advantage of Python's asynchronous capabilities, allowing developers to perform database operations without blocking the event loop. This is particularly beneficial in applications that need to handle multiple requests simultaneously, such as web applications built with FastAPI. By leveraging async/await syntax, Tortoise ORM enables efficient handling of I/O-bound tasks, such as database queries, which can significantly improve overall application performance, especially under heavy loads.

In the provided example, the function **`get_user`** is defined as an asynchronous function that retrieves a user from the database based on their unique identifier (**`user_id`**). The use of the **`await`** keyword before the **`User.get(id=user_id)`** call indicates that the function will pause execution until the database query is completed, allowing other tasks to run concurrently during this wait time. This non-blocking behavior is crucial for maintaining responsiveness in applications where multiple users might be making requests at the same time.

When the database operation completes, the function resumes and returns the retrieved `user` object. If the user with the specified **`user_id`** exists in the database, this object contains all the information defined in the `User` model, making it easy to work with the retrieved data in a Pythonic way. If the user does not exist, the `get` method would raise a **`DoesNotExist`** exception, which can be handled appropriately to provide meaningful feedback to the application's users. Overall, the ability to handle database operations asynchronously with Tortoise ORM not only enhances performance but also contributes to a smoother user experience in FastAPI applications.

```
async def get_user(user_id: int):
    user = await User.get(id=user_id)
    return user
```

Practical Examples of Using Tortoise ORM

So, the Tortoise ORM has superiority in situations where there is high concurrency, as well as efficient operation within databases. Asynchronous functionality enables it to be the perfect application for applications processing and interacting with real-time data, so that developers can construct responsive and scalable systems.

- **Real-time dashboards:** In real-time dashboard applications, the expectation for such applications is that information should be current and not laggy or delayed. Tortoise ORM's asynchronous queries will let the application pull data from the database seamlessly. So, it ensures the real-time update of the metric, performance indicator, or analytics that the user expects. For instance, a live stock price financial dashboard can utilize Tortoise ORM to fetch the updated data in the background as the users work through the interface.

This way, the application processes several requests for data simultaneously and will therefore not delay the main event loop while it ensures that timely information is provided to the user.

- **Chat applications:** The scaling of user traffic requires chat applications to quickly and efficiently retrieve and store messages. The functionality of real-time updates in messages, indicators of presence, and management of a chat history can easily be added by developers who apply Tortoise ORM. So, for example, in the case of a sending message, it is also stored in the database but asynchronously, while an update of the chat interface could be made for all interested users at the same moment. This parallel processing of incoming and outgoing messages ensures that users get instant feedback about what they do, maintaining a fluid and interactive chatting experience.
- **IoT data processing:** IoT will produce huge amounts of data that will be generated from numerous devices; real-time processing is quite critical for a lot of applications. So, it is quite feasible for tortoise ORM to support throughputs in terms of data requests and hence serve the requirements of IoT-based applications, wherein data is being transmitted from different devices continuously. This is achieved by a smart home application gathering sensor readings from different devices, such as temperature, humidity, or motion sensors. Such data is then stored asynchronously in the database, which is managed by an ORM such as Tortoise so that the flow of incoming data streams can provide instant insight into any user's home environment–for example, alerts for unexplained activity or changes in temperature.

In a nutshell, Tortoise ORM is great for applications that are going to be highly concurrent and data-intensive. The ORM can be used for robust systems that can be deployed in real-time data, not only in financial dashboards or chat applications but even in IoT data processing. Such things bring about better experiences from the user's point of view, lower latency, and overall better performance for the application.

Real-World Scenarios and Solutions

The following section explores practical use cases that demonstrate how to apply FastAPI concepts in real projects. Each question highlights a common challenge and provides a step-by-step solution.

Question 1: Setting Up SQLite with SQLAlchemy in FastAPI

Goal: Create a simple FastAPI application integrated with SQLite using SQLAlchemy and set up a `User` table with basic CRUD capabilities.

Step 1: Set Up the FastAPI Project

1. **Install FastAPI and SQLAlchemy:**

   ```
   pip install fastapi sqlalchemy sqlite
   ```

2. **Create a basic project structure:**

   ```
   myproject/
   ├── main.py
   ├── database.py
   └── models.py
   ```

Step 2: Configure the Database (database.py)

```
from sqlalchemy import create_engine
from sqlalchemy.ext.declarative import declarative_base
from sqlalchemy.orm import sessionmaker

# SQLite Database URL
DATABASE_URL = "sqlite:///./test.db"

# Create the SQLAlchemy engine
engine = create_engine(DATABASE_URL, connect_args
={"check_same_thread": False})

# Configure the SessionLocal class
SessionLocal = sessionmaker(autocommit=False, autoflush=False,
bind=engine)

# Base class for models
Base = declarative_base()
```

Step 3: Define the User Model (models.py)

```
from sqlalchemy import Column, Integer, String
from .database import Base

class User(Base):
    __tablename__ = "users"

    id = Column(Integer, primary_key=True, index=True)
    name = Column(String, index=True)
    email = Column(String, unique=True, index=True)
```

Step 4: Create the Database Table

```
from .database import engine
from .models import Base

# This will create the table based on models defined
Base.metadata.create_all(bind=engine)
```

Step 5: Implement CRUD Operations (main.py)

1. **Initialize FastAPI:**

```
from fastapi import FastAPI, Depends
from sqlalchemy.orm import Session
from .database import SessionLocal, engine
from .models import User
from .database import Base

app = FastAPI()

# Dependency to retrieve the database session
def get_db():
    db = SessionLocal()
    try:
        yield db
    finally:
        db.close()
```

2. **Create a User:**

```
@app.post("/users/")
async def create_user(name: str, email: str, db: Session
= Depends(get_db)):
    user = User(name=name, email=email)
    db.add(user)
    db.commit()
    db.refresh(user)
    return user
```

3. **Retrieve All Users:**

```
@app.get("/users/")
async def get_users(db: Session = Depends(get_db)):
    return db.query(User).all()
```

This setup creates an SQLite database with a simple `User` model and CRUD endpoints.

Question 2: Integrating Tortoise ORM with FastAPI

Goal: Set up a **`Product`** model using Tortoise ORM with FastAPI and fetch all product entries asynchronously.

Step 1: Install Dependencies

```
pip install fastapi tortoise-orm
```

Step 2: Set Up Tortoise Configuration (main.py)

Define Tortoise Configuration:

```
from fastapi import FastAPI
from tortoise.contrib.fastapi import register_tortoise
from tortoise import fields, models

app = FastAPI()

class Product(models.Model):
    id = fields.IntField(pk=True)
    name = fields.CharField(max_length=255)
    description = fields.TextField()
    price = fields.FloatField()

# Register Tortoise with FastAPI
register_tortoise(
    app,
    db_url="sqlite://./test.db",
    modules={"models": ["main"]},
    generate_schemas=True,
    add_exception_handlers=True,
)
```

Step 3: Create API Endpoints for Products

Fetch All Products:

```
@app.get("/products/")
async def get_products():
    products = await Product.all()
    return products
```

This example shows how to use Tortoise ORM for asynchronous queries within FastAPI.

Question 3: Configuring PostgreSQL with SQLAlchemy

Goal: Set up FastAPI to use PostgreSQL with SQLAlchemy and perform basic CRUD operations.

Step 1: Install PostgreSQL and psycopg2-binary

```
pip install fastapi sqlalchemy psycopg2-binary
```

Step 2: Configure PostgreSQL Connection (database.py)

1. **Set up the database URL:**

```
DATABASE_URL = "postgresql://username:password@localhost/
mydatabase"
```

2. **Update SQLAlchemy engine:**

```
from sqlalchemy import create_engine
from sqlalchemy.ext.declarative import declarative_base
from sqlalchemy.orm import sessionmaker

engine = create_engine(DATABASE_URL)
SessionLocal = sessionmaker(autocommit=False, autoflush=False,
bind=engine)
Base = declarative_base()
```

Step 3: Define the Model and Create Tables

1. **Define a `Post` Model:**

```
from sqlalchemy import Column, Integer, String
from .database import Base
class Post(Base):
    __tablename__ = "posts"

    id = Column(Integer, primary_key=True, index=True)
    title = Column(String, index=True)
    content = Column(String)
```

2. **Create the Table:**

```
from .database import engine
from .models import Base

Base.metadata.create_all(bind=engine)
```

Step 4: Implement CRUD Endpoints (main.py)

1. **Initialize FastAPI:**

```
from fastapi import FastAPI, Depends
from sqlalchemy.orm import Session
from .database import SessionLocal, engine
from .models import Post

app = FastAPI()

def get_db():
    db = SessionLocal()
    try:
```

```
        yield db
    finally:
        db.close()
```

2. **Add CRUD Endpoints:**

   a. **Create a Post:**

```
@app.post("/posts/")
async def create_post(title: str, content: str, db: Session
= Depends(get_db)):
    post = Post(title=title, content=content)
    db.add(post)
    db.commit()
    db.refresh(post)
    return post
```

   b. **Get All Posts:**

```
@app.get("/posts/")
async def get_posts(db: Session = Depends(get_db)):
    return db.query(Post).all()
```

This example integrates PostgreSQL into a FastAPI project, demonstrating SQLAlchemy setup, model creation, and basic API functionality.

Question 4: Integrating a File Upload Feature with PostgreSQL in FastAPI

Goal: Implement a file upload feature in FastAPI that stores file metadata in a PostgreSQL database while saving the actual files to the local filesystem.

Step 1: Set Up the FastAPI Project and PostgreSQL Connection

1. **Install Required Packages:**

```
pip install fastapi sqlalchemy psycopg2-binary python-multipart
```

2. **Configure PostgreSQL Database (database.py):**

```
from sqlalchemy import create_engine
from sqlalchemy.ext.declarative import declarative_base
from sqlalchemy.orm import sessionmaker

DATABASE_URL = "postgresql://username:password@localhost/filedb"
engine = create_engine(DATABASE_URL)
SessionLocal = sessionmaker(autocommit=False, autoflush=False,
bind=engine)
Base = declarative_base()
```

Step 2: Define a Model for File Metadata (models.py)

```
from sqlalchemy import Column, Integer, String
from .database import Base

class FileMetadata(Base):
    __tablename__ = "file_metadata"
    id = Column(Integer, primary_key=True, index=True)
    filename = Column(String, index=True)
    file_path = Column(String, unique=True)
```

Step 3: Initialize the Database Tables

```
from .database import engine
from .models import Base

Base.metadata.create_all(bind=engine)
```

Step 4: Create File Upload API (main.py)

Set Up File Upload Endpoint:

```
from fastapi import FastAPI, File, UploadFile, Depends
from sqlalchemy.orm import Session
from .database import SessionLocal
from .models import FileMetadata

app = FastAPI()

def get_db():
    db = SessionLocal()
    try:
        yield db
    finally:
        db.close()

@app.post("/upload/")
async def upload_file(file: UploadFile = File(...), db: Session
= Depends(get_db)):
    file_location = f"files/{file.filename}"
    with open(file_location, "wb") as buffer:
        buffer.write(await file.read())

    # Save metadata to database
    file_metadata = FileMetadata(filename=file.filename,
file_path=file_location)
    db.add(file_metadata)
    db.commit()
    db.refresh(file_metadata)
```

```
        return {"info": "File uploaded", "filename": file_metadata.
    filename}
```

Step 5: Retrieve Uploaded Files

Fetch File Metadata:

```
@app.get("/files/")
async def get_files(db: Session = Depends(get_db)):
    return db.query(FileMetadata).all()
```

This solution enables file upload with metadata stored in PostgreSQL and files saved locally.

Conclusion

Connect the databases, and now you have equipped developers with something they actually need in order to properly manage information in a strong, highly scalable manner. SQLAlchemy also includes an extremely powerful ORM that makes smooth interactions possible with a relational database such as SQLite, PostgreSQL, and MySQL, or even simple SQL for more complex queries. Tortoise ORM then does the trick as the asynchronous approach to match with the non-blocking architecture of FastAPI. This chapter was designed to focus on the proper management of sessions, migrations via Alembic, and proper CRUD operations on any type of database system. So, understanding these integrations enables developers to have control over large-scale applications through efficient data organization while also having a future-proof design in place for the scaling up and growth of a project. Each method, whether it is SQLAlchemy or Tortoise, is ready to keep code clean and allow for performance optimization and best practices for the proper management of databases.

The chapter that follows is *Testing and Debugging*, which elaborates on essential processes towards stable and reliable FastAPI applications. Although connecting databases serves as a basis for data-related functionality, testing is pivotal in the identification of bugs, validation of functionalities, and prevention of unexpected failures in production environments. The next chapter will guide you through the process of how to create unit and integration tests using well-known testing tools such as Pytest, besides strategies for debugging in case of problems. From authenticating flows to database queries or middleware behavior, this framework will give you peace of mind with every deployment. Testing principles will ensure that the development process of the API and its usability by users go smoothly, with higher user satisfaction due to reliable, bug-free APIs.

Multiple Choice Questions

1. **Which ORM library is known for supporting both SQL and ORM interactions in FastAPI?**
   a. Tortoise ORM
   b. SQLAlchemy
   c. Django ORM
   d. Peewee
2. **What does ORM stand for?**
   a. Object Resource Mode
   b. Object Relational Mapping
   c. Organizational Relational Model
   d. Open Resource Management
3. **Which database is ideal for lightweight, file-based storage during development?**
   a. PostgreSQL
   b. MySQL
   c. SQLite
   d. MongoDB
4. **What is the purpose of Alembic in SQLAlchemy?**
   a. Data migration
   b. API routing
   c. Query optimization
   d. Session management
5. **Which keyword helps create asynchronous database queries in Tortoise ORM?**
   a. async
   b. defer

c. await

d. schedule

6. **What does CRUD stand for?**

a. Create, Retrieve, Update, Delete

b. Create, Read, Update, Drop

c. Cache, Remove, Update, Download

d. Create, Read, Use, Delete

7. **Which command initializes a new SQLAlchemy model?**

a. `model.init`

b. `Base.metadata.create_all`

c. `orm.setup()`

d. `database.connect()`

8. **What is the role of session management in SQLAlchemy?**

a. Managing API requests

b. Creating database tables

c. Handling database transactions

d. Encrypting data

9. **Which database management system is best suited for large-scale enterprise applications?**

a. SQLite

b. MySQL

c. PostgreSQL

d. Redis

10. **How do you define a foreign key in SQLAlchemy models?**

a. `Column(Integer)`

b. `Column(ForeignKey)`

c. `ForeignKey(Integer)`

d. `Field(Relation)`

11. **Which command installs Tortoise ORM via pip?**
    a. `pip install tortoise`
    b. `pip install tortoise-orm`
    c. `pip install tortoise_sql`
    d. `pip setup orm`
12. **What kind of architecture does Tortoise ORM follow?**
    a. Synchronous
    b. Asynchronous
    c. Event-driven
    d. Modular
13. **Which of the following is a relational database?**
    a. MongoDB
    b. SQLite
    c. Redis
    d. DynamoDB
14. **What method in Tortoise ORM saves a new entry to the database?**
    a. `.insert()`
    b. `.commit()`
    c. `.save()`
    d. `.write()`
15. **Why is using an ORM advantageous in FastAPI projects?**
    a. It simplifies API routes.
    b. It allows direct interaction with cloud storage.
    c. It abstracts database queries into Python objects.
    d. It improves web server performance.

Answers

Question	Answer
1	b
2	b
3	c
4	a
5	c
6	a
7	b
8	c
9	c
10	b
11	b
12	b
13	b
14	c
15	c

CHAPTER 10
Testing and Debugging

Introduction

In this chapter, we will dive into the core practices of testing and debugging–practices that are crucial when building robust FastAPI applications. This is to ensure that your application is both functional and reliable in the long run. Testing provides a structured way to validate the behavior of your code against expected outcomes, allowing you to catch errors early in the development lifecycle. Debugging, on the other hand, focuses on diagnosing and resolving issues that arise during development or after deployment. Together, these practices form the backbone of any well-engineered software project, helping developers maintain high standards of code quality while minimizing downtime and unexpected failures.

Testing is critical for verifying that individual components of your FastAPI application, as well as their interactions, work as intended. In this chapter, you will be introduced to testing methodologies such as unit testing, which takes one piece of functionality in isolation and tests it. Integration testing, on the other hand, checks for many components working together nicely. We use a widely used testing framework, **`pytest`**, to demonstrate how to write clean, efficient, and scalable test cases. Developers can enjoy the confidence to make changes in their application since the robust testing strategy adopted would enable catching any regressions or errors very early during the process.

Debugging complements testing to spot issues that testing would otherwise miss, especially those related to real-world use cases, deployment environments, or unforeseen user behavior. This chapter will discuss debugging tools and practices that are used with FastAPI applications, such as interactive debuggers like pdb, IDE-based debugging features, and best practices related to logging. Proper debugging not only accelerates resolution times but also helps to understand the root causes of problems, allowing developers to avoid similar mishaps in the future. We also discuss strategies for debugging asynchronous code, as commonly found in FastAPI applications, which involves using specific tools and techniques for tracing the execution flow.

Mastering the concepts of testing and debugging can lead to the construction of applications that handle both expected and unexpected cases graciously. This chapter really hammers in the adoption of a TDD mentality, and strongly advocates test coverage for maximum reliability. It also gives practical tips on setting up reproducible debugging environments and eventually helps in identifying the root causes of issues efficiently. Equipped with these skills, you can ensure that your FastAPI application is not only functional but resilient, scalable, maintainable, and ready to support user and business needs.

Structure

In this chapter, we will cover the following topics:

- **Writing Unit Tests with pytest**
    - Introduction to pytest: Setting Up and Configuring **`pytest`** for FastAPI Applications
    - Writing Basic Unit Tests to Cover Individual Functions and Methods
    - Mocking Dependencies to Isolate and Test Specific Application Components
    - Utilizing pytest's Fixtures to Streamline Test Preparation and Teardown
    - Best Practices for Writing Maintainable Unit Tests
- **Integration Testing**
    - Understanding Integration Tests and Their Importance in FastAPI
    - Setting up Integration Tests to Validate API Routes and Endpoints
    - Testing Against Database Interactions and Ensuring API Compatibility
    - Managing Authentication and Authorization in Integration Tests
    - Using FastAPI's Built-In **`TestClient`** to Simulate Requests and Responses
- **Debugging Techniques and Tools**
    - Setting up Debugging Configurations in IDEs (VSCode, PyCharm)
    - Using `pdb` and Other Python Debugging Tools
    - Techniques for Isolating and Diagnosing Runtime Errors
    - Using FastAPI's Error Handling Features and Logging for Troubleshooting
    - Best Practices for Debugging

Writing Unit Tests with pytest

Unit testing is the practice of proving the smallest pieces of your FastAPI application's correctness–each function or endpoint behaves exactly as expected in isolation. The popular testing framework for Python, pytest, makes it quite intuitive and powerful to write and manage these tests. With easy syntax, an extensive ecosystem of plugins, and great support for fixtures, it is easy to test even very complex FastAPI applications.

Introduction to pytest: Setting Up and Configuring `pytest` for FastAPI Applications

The widely used Python testing framework, Pytest, is known for its power, flexibility, and ease of use. Its clean and intuitive syntax lets developers write concise and readable test cases, thus making the testing process both more efficient and enjoyable. Unlike many testing frameworks, pytest minimizes boilerplate code while still offering advanced features, such as fixtures, parameterized tests, and built-in assertions. These characteristics make `pytest` an excellent tool for modern software development, including testing FastAPI applications, involving asynchronous operations, and dynamic behaviors.

The rich plugin ecosystem of **`pytest`** stands out. This ecosystem is what makes the framework even more powerful to suit a wide variety of projects: for example, asyncio test cases with **`pytest-asyncio`** are essential when working with an async-based architecture. Similarly, plugins such as **`pytest-cov`** enable comprehensive code coverage analysis so that developers can be sure that every part of their application has been tested sufficiently. It is also very flexible in regards to including additional plugins, making pytest a versatile tool to be tailored to the specific needs of your project, regardless of its complexity.

Setting up pytest for a FastAPI project is easy and usually starts with pip installing the framework via **`pip install pytest`**. It can be structured further by having your test suite in the form of test files, prefixed with **`test_`**, along with test functions prefixed with **`test_`**. For FastAPI, you can use its built-in TestClient to simulate HTTP requests and responses so you can easily test API endpoints. Furthermore, it can be configured to work with plugins such as **`pytest-asyncio`** so that asynchronous endpoints are tested in a seamless manner; fixtures also allow setting up reusable resources such as test databases or mock dependencies for tests.

`pytest` integrated into the development workflow can make your test suite reliable and scalable. Powerful features of **`pytest`** simplify writing and executing tests and promote best practices such as modular and reusable code; whether you are building small APIs or large applications, **`pytest`** gives you the tools you need to keep it of high quality and catch bugs as early in the cycle as possible. This further leads to more robust applications and a smoother development process.

Steps to configure:

Configuring pytest for a FastAPI project involves a few simple but crucial steps to setting up an organized, efficient testing environment. Proper configuration ensures smooth execution of your test suite and enhances test reusability and maintainability as your project grows. Here are the detailed steps:

1. **Install pytest**

   Begin by installing `pytest` in your development environment. This can be done using the command:

   ```
   pip install pytest
   ```

   A Pytest installation is easy, and the framework is thus available to write and run tests. It is also good practice to include **`pytest`** in your project **`requirements.txt`** or **`pyproject.toml`** to ensure consistency across environments. For projects that support asynchronous testing, which is very common with FastAPI applications, you can install the **`pytest_asyncio`** plugin:

   ```
   pip install pytest-asyncio
   ```

2. **Create a Dedicated `tests/` Directory**

   Organizing your test files is important for keeping it clear and scalable. The first thing to do is to create a directory called **`tests/`** in the root of your project. At this point, create one or more test files named with the convention **`test_`**, for example, **`test_routes.py`** or **`test_models.py`**. This naming scheme is important because pytest detects and runs test files and functions that follow this naming scheme. An orderly **`tests/`** directory allows your test suite to stay organized even as your application grows.

3. **Set Up a `conftest.py` File**

   In **`tests/`** create a file **`conftest.py`**. This is a special pytest configuration file to define reusable fixtures and other configurations for your test suite. Fixtures are a powerful pytest feature that allows you to create reusable setups for your tests. These are, for example, initializing test databases, mock clients, or even overriding dependencies. Here is how you might define a fixture to create a **`TestClient`** for your FastAPI app:

   ```
   import pytest
   from fastapi.testclient import TestClient
   from myapp.main import app  # Replace with your app module

   @pytest.fixture
   def client():
       return TestClient(app)
   ```

   With this setup, you can use the **`client`** fixture in your tests, eliminating the need to initialize the **`TestClient`** repeatedly.

4. **Execute Tests Using the `pytest` Command**

   Once your test files and configurations are ready, you can run all tests by simply executing the `pytest` command in your terminal:

   ```
   Pytest
   ```

   Pytest will automatically discover and execute all test cases in the **`tests/`** directory. The output provides a summary of test results, including any failures, making it easy to identify issues. You can also use additional options, such as `-v` for verbose output or **`--maxfail=3`** to stop after three failed tests.

By following these steps, you can create a well-configured testing environment that is easy to maintain and scale. The combination of organized test files, reusable fixtures, and pytest's powerful execution capabilities ensures a smooth and efficient testing process for your FastAPI application.

Writing Basic Unit Tests to Cover Individual Functions and Methods

Unit testing is the basis upon which a robust testing strategy is built. Testing, here, targets the smallest components in your application–individual functions, classes, or methods–are tested in isolation. In other words, each component of your code should behave in exactly the manner specified, with no influence from other parts of the application. Unit tests for a FastAPI project are primarily useful to validate utility functions, business logic, or any helper method that operates in isolation from the API layer.

For effective unit tests, the function or method under test should always be separated from its dependencies, such that the test results reflect correctness in the code itself and not external factors. Utility functions or business logic may be isolated from the test along with API routes, databases, and other components. Structuring your test files to mirror your application's modules also makes it easier to maintain and locate tests as the project evolves. For example, if you have an application module called **`utils.py`**, you could then have a matching test file under **`tests/`** such as **`test_utils.py`**.

```
# myapp/utils.py
def add(a, b):
    return a + b
# tests/test_utils.py
from myapp.utils import add
def test_add():
    assert add(2, 3) == 5  # Positive case
    assert add(-1, 1) == 0  # Edge case with negative numbers
    assert add(0, 0) == 0  # Edge case with zeros
```

In this example:

- The **add** function is simple and self-contained, making it ideal for unit testing.
- The test file mirrors the application module structure, keeping the test suite organized.
- Multiple assertions are used to test the function under different scenarios, ensuring comprehensive coverage.

For more complex functions, you can follow a similar strategy. If the function interacts with external dependencies, consider using **mocking** to simulate those dependencies and isolate the function's behavior. For example, if a function interacts with an external API, you can use pytest-mock or unittest.mock to simulate API responses.

By focusing on small, isolated components, unit testing helps catch bugs early in the development cycle. It also ensures that changes to one part of your application will not inadvertently break other parts. This makes unit testing a critical step in building reliable and maintainable FastAPI applications.

Mocking Dependencies to Isolate and Test Specific Application Components

In FastAPI, isolating tests against external services means that the tests should not depend on anything except the functionality being tested. FastAPI allows one to make dependencies easily overridable using the **Depends** mechanism, thus making it possible to replace actual dependencies with mock objects/functions when testing. For example, if your endpoint relies upon a database query or an external API call, you could override these dependencies using mock implementations that would return known responses. This would ensure that tests are always independent of external systems and, therefore, more robust and faster to run. Using FastAPI's dependency injection system in this effective way allows for strong, maintainable test suites around your application.

Example:

```
from fastapi import FastAPI, Depends

app = FastAPI()

def get_db():
    return {"key": "value"}  # Example dependency

@app.get("/items/")
def read_items(db=Depends(get_db)):
    return db
```

```
def test_read_items():
    def mock_get_db():
        return {"mock_key": "mock_value"}

    app.dependency_overrides[get_db] = mock_get_db

    with TestClient(app) as client:
        response = client.get("/items/")
        assert response.json() == {"mock_key": "mock_value"}
```

Utilizing pytest's Fixtures to Streamline Test Preparation and Teardown

Fixtures in pytest are a powerful feature that simplifies test setup and teardown by creating reusable resources that can be shared across multiple tests. You make your code consistent regarding the test environment and avoid duplication of code. For instance, in a FastAPI application, you might use fixtures to initialize a **`TestClient`** for simulating API requests or to prepare mock data when testing interactions with a database. Fixtures are declared using **`@pytest.fixture`**, and can have setup logic run prior to the test execution, and can have optional teardown code executed after test completion. They can also be parameterized so that a variety of inputs or scenarios can be checked with little effort. Use your fixtures efficiently, and you will have smoothed out your test process, cleaner code, and ensured that your tests are reliable and scalable with the growth of your application.

Example:

```
import pytest
from fastapi.testclient import TestClient
from app.main import app

@pytest.fixture
def client():
    return TestClient(app)

def test_example(client):
    response = client.get("/")
    assert response.status_code == 200
```

Best Practices for Writing Maintainable Unit Tests

Writing maintainable unit tests is critical to ensure the long-term reliability and scalability of your FastAPI application. Not only does best practice make your tests more readable and easier to debug but also effective when changes happen in your codebase. Here are some key guidelines:

- **Write concise, single-purpose tests:**

  Each test should be aimed at proving a particular behavior or functionality of the unit under test. This way, if it fails, the problems are easily pointed out, and its purpose is clear. Avoid combining unrelated behaviors in a single test through multiple assertions, as it seems to obscure what is failing in the code.

- **Use descriptive test names:**

  The test names should depict what is being tested; for example, instead of writing a test named **`test_user`**, it may be descriptive to name it as **`test_create_user_with_valid_data`**. This makes it easier for other developers–and also your future self–to see at one glance what this test is for.

- **Mock dependencies when interacting with external services:**

  When your application talks to external systems, for example, to the database, API, or message queue, the correct approach for unit testing is to mock the dependencies. In other words, it is a process of isolating the code being under test from external systems, because external systems may introduce variability or latency in your application. Use libraries such as **`pytest-mock`** or **`unittest.mock`** when simulating API responses or database queries.

- **Ensure tests are idempotent:**

  Tests should be deterministic; that is, they should always produce the same results, no matter how often they are run. Generally, mutable states, random data, and even things such as system time and network conditions cannot be assumed to be consistent. For example, if a test creates a database entry, it should clean up after itself to ensure a consistent state for subsequent test runs.

- **Regularly run the test suite to catch regressions early:**

  Frequent execution of the test suite is the only way through which problems are caught early in the development process. Integrate your tests into the CI/CD pipeline to ensure they will run automatically whenever some changes are made to the codebase. This helps identify problems right away, making debugging much easier and preventing problems from escalating in production.

Integration Testing

Integration testing focuses on validating how different components of an application work together, ensuring that the combined system behaves as expected. Unlike unit tests, which test individual functions or modules in isolation, integration tests examine the interactions between modules, such as API endpoints communicating with databases or external services. These tests are crucial for identifying issues that may arise due to mismatches or dependencies between components.

Understanding Integration Tests and Their Importance in FastAPI

Usually, during integration testing of a FastAPI application, the entire API endpoints are tested by sending them against the underlying business logic, database, and other dependencies to ensure they interact appropriately. Usually, tools such as **`TestClient`** simulate HTTP requests to the application and check responses. Besides that, mocking or using the test database helps to create isolation from production environments to allow you to test interactions without actually affecting real data. Integration testing focuses on the validation of workflows and ensuring the smooth functioning of system interconnections.

Integration tests within your development workflow can catch errors that will not surface during unit tests, ensuring that your FastAPI application works correctly in real scenarios.

Setting Up Integration Tests to Validate API Routes and Endpoints

Integration testing is a critical step that ensures, by far, that your FastAPI application's API routes and endpoints function properly with the underlying business logic, databases, and external dependencies. Proper environment creation for integration tests simulates the real world while keeping it isolated from production. Thus, here is an in-depth guide to the correct setup of integration tests.

1. **Create a Separate Database for Testing**

   Another method to ensure your tests do not interfere with the production data is to have a separate database for testing. An in-memory database provided by SQLite, for instance, is an excellent testing choice because it is lightweight, fast, and resets with every test run. You can configure your FastAPI application to point to this test database during the testing phase by overriding the database URL in your settings. For instance, replace the production database URL with `sqlite:///:memory:` when running tests.

2. **Use `pytest` Fixtures for Setup and Teardown**

   Pytest fixtures provide a structured way to handle setup and teardown tasks, ensuring a clean slate for each test. Create a fixture to initialize the database, set up tables, and populate them with test data. For example:

```
import pytest
from sqlalchemy import create_engine
from sqlalchemy.orm import sessionmaker
from myapp.database import Base, get_db

@pytest.fixture
def test_db():
    engine = create_engine("sqlite:///:memory:")
    Base.metadata.create_all(bind=engine)
    SessionLocal = sessionmaker(autocommit=False, autoflush=False,
bind=engine)
    yield SessionLocal
    Base.metadata.drop_all(bind=engine)
```

This fixture ensures that a fresh in-memory database is available for each test run and that resources are cleaned up afterward. You can use the **test_db** fixture to override the default database dependency in your FastAPI application during tests.

3. **Configure FastAPI to Use Mock or Test Dependencies**

   FastAPI's dependency injection system makes it easy to replace real dependencies with mock or test versions during integration tests. For example, you can override the default database session with the test database session using the **dependency_overrides** attribute of the FastAPI app:

```
from fastapi.testclient import TestClient
from myapp.main import app
from myapp.database import get_db

@pytest.fixture
def client(test_db):
    app.dependency_overrides[get_db] = lambda: test_db()
    yield TestClient(app)
```

   This setup allows your API routes to interact with the test database instead of the production database when you are testing. In a similar way, you can mock out external services such as APIs or message queues by overriding their respective dependencies.

With integration tests set up along with their own database, pytest fixtures, and mock dependencies, you essentially create an environment that closely resembles production but is isolated and safe for testing. This approach ensures validation of your API routes and endpoints on all sides so that integration issues can be caught early, and you can deliver a more robust FastAPI application.

Example of creating a testing database:

```
from sqlalchemy import create_engine
from sqlalchemy.orm import sessionmaker
from app.database import Base

SQLALCHEMY_DATABASE_URL = "sqlite:///./test.db"
engine = create_engine(SQLALCHEMY_DATABASE_URL)
TestingSessionLocal = sessionmaker(autocommit=False,
autoflush=False, bind=engine)

def setup_test_db():
    Base.metadata.create_all(bind=engine)
    return TestingSessionLocal()

def teardown_test_db():
    Base.metadata.drop_all(bind=engine)
```

Testing Against Database Interactions and Ensuring API Compatibility

Indeed, API endpoint integration testing is a guarantee that the routes of your FastAPI application behave as expected and interface with differing aspects, such as, but not limited to, the database, external APIs, and the business logic behind which you are creating the API. The key focus is mostly on behavior, so that where interaction occurs, whether it is getting routes, query parameters, request bodies, or the response, it behaves as it should under real-world scenarios.

- **Testing Routes**: We should validate routes that are reachable and return the correct HTTP statuses. For example, we could check if a **`GET`** request to **`/items`** successfully retrieves a list of items or if a **`POST`** request to **`/items`** correctly adds a new item. We can use FastAPI's `TestClient` to simulate these requests and verify that the appropriate endpoints are hit. This goes with guaranteeing the proper setup of your route definitions and HTTP methods.
- **Validating Query Parameters:** You will notice that most API endpoints depend on query parameters to filter, sort, or paginate data. Integration tests should therefore check that these parameters are correctly processed. For example, if your endpoint does support pagination, you could verify whether returning page number 2 with the parameter **`?page=2`** returns the expected subset of results. In case an endpoint accepts filters, like **`?category=books`**, you can test if the answer holds the specified filter.
- **Testing Request Bodies:** In the case of endpoints that accept request bodies, such as `POST` or PUT routes, validation is essential because such routes would

then forward input data in the right way. Testing the scenarios of valid and invalid inputs, as well as edge cases, should be included to ensure the endpoint works appropriately with input data. For example, you can test whether the API returns **422 Unprocessable Entity** when required fields are missing or invalid data types are passed. This ensures your Pydantic models and validation logic are strong.

- **Verifying Responses:** Finally, and most importantly, the endpoint responses must be checked. Validating the HTTP status codes, response structure, and data content will do this. For example, if your **`GET /items`** endpoint is expected to return a list of items, the test should verify that the response contains an array, matches the expected schema, and includes the correct data. Tests should also ensure that for invalid or unexpected requests, error responses such as **404 Not Found** or **500 Internal Server Error** are returned.

Example of testing a GET endpoint:

```
from fastapi.testclient import TestClient
from app.main import app

client = TestClient(app)

def test_read_items():
    response = client.get("/items/")
    assert response.status_code == 200
    assert response.json() == {"items": []}
```

Example of testing a POST endpoint:

```
def test_create_item():
    response = client.post("/items/", json={"name": "Test Item"})
    assert response.status_code == 201
    assert response.json() == {"name": "Test Item", "id": 1}
```

This way, all these aspects of API endpoints will be well-tested to ensure that your application functions as expected under any conditions, from common ones to extreme edge cases. Such tests are crucial for catching issues that arise from interference between components, ensuring that your FastAPI application is reliable and user-friendly.

Conclusion of API Compatibility

If integration tests are being performed with database interactions, then you should use a temporary or isolated database so that the production data is not affected. FastAPI supports dependency overriding, which means you can inject a test database or mock service into your application while you are performing tests. For example, you can use a different SQLite in-memory database for the tests themselves, so each starts fresh and no data is persisted to the end of one test for use or interference in another. Such an arrangement isolates all database interactions and checks how well the application handles database queries, transactions, and models without changing real-world data.

Other than checking on how the API interacts with a database, compatibility with the underlying database schema and business logic should be ensured. Creating, updating, and deleting records through API endpoints were some of the test scenarios for this purpose, verifying that the correct data was stored in the test database. You should also test edge cases, such as how your application will handle missing or invalid database records, and how it ensures returning proper error messages. Only by validating the database operations and by validating API responses together can you be sure that your application works as expected in a real-world environment where the API and database components interact seamlessly.

Example:

```
from sqlalchemy import create_engine
from sqlalchemy.orm import sessionmaker
from app.database import Base, get_db
from app.main import app

SQLALCHEMY_DATABASE_URL = "sqlite:///./test.db"
engine = create_engine(SQLALCHEMY_DATABASE_URL)
TestingSessionLocal = sessionmaker(autocommit=False, autoflush=-
False, bind=engine)

Base.metadata.create_all(bind=engine)

def override_get_db():
    db = TestingSessionLocal()
    try:
        yield db
    finally:
        db.close()

app.dependency_overrides[get_db] = override_get_db
```

This example demonstrates setting up a SQLite test database and overriding the default database dependency.

Managing Authentication and Authorization in Integration Tests

Testing authentication and authorization functions on endpoints ensures that all integration tests guarantee that security mechanisms are working as expected. In

FastAPI, you will mostly generate test tokens or mock credentials to demonstrate a user authenticated under various conditions. For instance, you can use a test user and generate a JWT token or any other authentication token that your application uses. Once a token is generated, you can add it to the request headers for protected endpoints to verify that access control has been implemented correctly. Testing with both valid and invalid authentication cases, such as an expired token or unauthorized access attempts, will ensure that your application secures endpoints appropriately and returns relevant HTTP status codes, such as **401 Unauthorized** or **403 Forbidden**. This process will help verify that your authentication and authorization systems are robust, meaning that only authorized users can access restricted resources.

Example:

```
from fastapi.testclient import TestClient
from app.auth import create_access_token

client = TestClient(app)

def test_protected_route():
    token = create_access_token({"sub": "testuser"})
    headers = {"Authorization": f"Bearer {token}"}
    response = client.get("/protected-route", headers=headers)
    assert response.status_code == 200
```

Using FastAPI's Built-In `TestClient` to Simulate Requests and Responses

FastAPI's inbuilt **`TestClient`** allows for testing through simulated requests and responses in integration tests, so you can test how your API endpoints are working without even having to start up a live server. The TestClient acts like real HTTP requests, such as **`GET`**, **`POST`**, **`PUT`**, and **`DELETE`**, and gives back the response for validation purposes. This makes it perfect for testing interactions with your FastAPI application's routes, whereby endpoints return the expected status code, headers, and response body. For integration tests dealing with external services such as payment gateways or third-party APIs, the **`TestClient`** is used in conjunction with mocking tools to mimic the behavior of these external interactions: Now you will be able to validate how your API behaves if these external services return different responses (for example, success, failure, or timeouts) without really hitting the live services. These tests guarantee your application's resilience in different scenarios, as tests are fast and highly isolated.

Example:

- **Mocking external APIs** using the **responses** library:

```
import responses

@responses.activate
def test_external_api():
    responses.add(responses.GET, "https://api.example.com/data",
json={"key": "value"}, status=200)
    response = client.get("/external-data/")
    assert response.status_code == 200
    assert response.json() == {"key": "value"}
```

Debugging Techniques and Tools

Debugging is an important step in the development process; it enables developers to track issues in the codebase and promptly resolve them. In FastAPI, there are several methods for debugging and ways to make your application easier to debug. You can set up debugging configurations in your IDE, such as Visual Studio Code, which enables you to set breakpoints, inspect variables, and step through your code. This proves to be especially useful for tracing complex logic and understanding the flow of data, and diagnosing issues in real time during development. By configuring a debugger of your IDE, you can pause execution at specific points, examine the current state of the application, and test potential fixes interactively.

Integrating **pdb**, or Python Debugger, directly into your code, or employing tools such as `fastapi-debugtoolbar` can help track issues within production-like environments while analyzing the requests and responses within the FastAPI app itself.

Setting Up Debugging Configurations in IDEs

Establishing debugging configurations in an Integrated Development Environment, or IDE, is an important step in efficient problem-solving for developers. It allows them to track down issues in the application easily by configuring their IDE to handle breakpoints, step through code, and inspect variables. Most of the modern IDEs, such as Visual Studio Code, are known to provide intuitive interfaces to configure and run debuggers directly from within an editor. This configuration allows you to stop your code wherever it might be and analyze the state of the application, thus gaining deeper insights into the execution flow and the root causes of errors.

Debugging with VSCode

VSCode supports the debugging of Python applications very solidly through its built-in debugger and Python and Pylance extensions. To debug a FastAPI project, one needs to configure the `launch.json` file in VSCode. This specifies how the application is to be run and how the debugger should attach to it. You can specify the entry point of your application and usually the main FastAPI instance, and set breakpoints to point out difficult issues. It is even allowed to configure remote debugging to run FastAPI inside containers or remote environments to step through the code, see what is in the request and response objects, and know the value of variables easily to pinpoint and resolve issues. In VSCode, the friendly user interface makes debugging a powerful tool to increase development efficiency and code quality.

To set up debugging:

1. Open the project in VSCode.
2. Navigate to the "Run and Debug" sidebar and create a new launch configuration.
3. Use the following sample configuration for FastAPI:

```
{
    "version": "0.2.0",
    "configurations": [
        {
            "name": "Python: FastAPI",
            "type": "python",
            "request": "launch",
            "program": "main.py",
            "args": ["run", "--reload"],
            "console": "integratedTerminal"
        }
    ]
}
```

4. Place breakpoints in your code and start the debugger.

Debugging with PyCharm

Out of all the popular IDEs for Python development, PyCharm has built-in debugging tools that are specifically optimized for Python applications, including FastAPI projects. The debugging interface in PyCharm is very intuitive, allowing you to set breakpoints, step through your code, and inspect variables and stack traces with ease. With PyCharm, you can begin a debugging session by simply running your FastAPI app in debug mode, and where the IDE automatically pauses execution at your set breakpoints.

The PyCharm debugger allows you to view and modify the state of variables, track the flow of execution, and evaluate expressions in real-time, giving you lots of depth on what is happening in your application. PyCharm also supports remote debugging. So if you are running your FastAPI application within a Docker container or on a remote server, you can connect to the process and debug it as if it were running locally.

With inline variable values, multi-threaded debugging, and flawless integration with FastAPI's async features, PyCharm offers a robust and friendly debugging experience to help developers identify and fix issues efficiently.

1. Open the FastAPI project in PyCharm.
2. Configure the project interpreter with the required environment.
3. Create a new Run/Debug configuration:
   - Select "**Python**" as the configuration type.
   - Set the script path to the FastAPI entry point (for example, **`main.py`**).
   - Add any necessary arguments for running the server (for example, **`uvicorn main:app --reload`**).
4. Start the debugger and step through the code using breakpoints.

Using pdb and Other Python Debugging Tools

The built-in Python debugger is **`pdb`**, a lightweight but powerful tool for runtime diagnosis. It works right from your terminal or command-line interface, which makes it highly accessible and versatile for debugging your Python applications, including projects that contain FastAPI. `pdb` allows you to stop code execution at any arbitrary points, inspect what your variables are, or step line by line in your application to see how data is flowing, and where the bugs are being introduced. The granular control over code execution really pays off when debugging complex logic or identifying subtle bugs.

A breakpoint can be inserted into your code with the **`breakpoint()`** function newly available in Python 3.7, or you can explicitly invoke **`import pdb; pdb.set_trace()`**. At this point, when a breakpoint is reached, the program goes into pdb interactive mode. Here you can enter commands such as **`n`** (next) to go to the next line, **`c`** (continue) to continue execution, and **`p <variable>`** to print the value of some specific variable. You may also examine the call stack using the **`where`** command, or jump to a given line of code using **`jump <line_number>`**.

For deeper debugging, there are **`ipdb`**, an enhanced version of **`pdb`** with IPython support, or `pudb`, another text-based visual debugger that includes syntax highlighting, navigation, and more user-friendly interfaces. You can also use the `debugpy` library, which integrates into modern IDEs such as VSCode or PyCharm, so you might combine `pdb`'s functionality with the convenience of an interactive GUI debugger.

Debuggers by `pdb` and related tools allow developers to pull and fix issues within their FastAPI applications based on minimal external dependency, which could otherwise be time-consuming with the help of these tools. The debugger tools are also well-suited for environments where IDE support is limited, such as a remote server or in a containerized deployment.

Example usage:

1. Insert a `pdb` breakpoint in your code:
   ```
   import pdb; pdb.set_trace()
   ```
2. Run the application, and execution will pause at the breakpoint.
3. Use commands such as **`n`** (next), **`c`** (continue), or **`p variable_name`** (print variable) to navigate and inspect.

Other tools:

- **`ipdb`**: An enhanced version of `pdb` with more interactive features.
- **Visual Debugging Tools**: Libraries such as `debugpy` integrate with IDEs for graphical debugging interfaces.

Techniques for Isolating and Diagnosing Runtime Errors

- **Reproduce the Error**: Always attempt to replicate the issue under controlled conditions to narrow down its cause.
- **Divide and Conquer**: Isolate smaller components of the application and test them independently.
- **Logging**: Use Python's `logging` module to add meaningful logs at critical points. **For example:**
  ```
  import logging
  logging.basicConfig(level=logging.DEBUG)
  logging.debug("Debug information")
  ```
- **Tracebacks**: Examine error tracebacks carefully to identify the root cause and pinpoint the line of code causing the issue.
- **Dependency Analysis**: Verify the compatibility of installed dependencies and ensure that the environment matches the application's requirements.

Using FastAPI's Error Handling Features and Logging

FastAPI provides built-in features for handling and logging errors effectively:

- **Custom Exception Handlers**: Define custom handlers for specific exceptions to provide user-friendly error messages:

```
from fastapi import FastAPI, HTTPException
app = FastAPI()

@app.exception_handler(HTTPException)
async def custom_http_exception_handler(request, exc):
    return JSONResponse(
        status_code=exc.status_code,
        content={"message": "Custom error: " + exc.detail},
    )
```

- **Middleware for Logging**: Use middleware to capture and log requests and responses for better debugging insights:

```
from starlette.middleware.base import BaseHTTPMiddleware
class LoggingMiddleware(BaseHTTPMiddleware):
    async def dispatch(self, request, call_next):
        response = await call_next(request)
        print(f"Request: {request.url}")
        print(f"Response: {response.status_code}")
        return response
app.add_middleware(LoggingMiddleware)
```

- **`uvicorn` Logs**: Leverage uvicorn's logging configuration to capture application-level details: Run with:

```
uvicorn main:app --reload --log-level debug
```

Best Practices for Debugging

- **Always test in an isolated environment to prevent unwanted side effects:** Running tests in a controlled environment ensures that your debugging process cannot interfere with your production system or other services. Something like Docker or a virtual environment lets you reproduce the runtime conditions under which your application runs precisely.
- **Use meaningful log messages to describe application state:** Effective logging is crucial for understanding what went wrong. Use structured logging formats (for example, JSON) where possible to make logs easier to parse and analyze
- **Leverage tools like `pytest`'s built-in debugging options for unit and integration tests**: Pytest provides debugging tools such as **`--pdb`** or **`--trace`**, helping identify issues during the test run. For example, if you run `pytest --pdb`, you will be dropped into an interactive session on every failed test so that you can inspect variables and execution state.

- **Regularly update and review dependencies to mitigate compatibility issues:** Older versions of libraries can also bring in bugs or vulnerabilities. Use tools such as **`pip-tools`** or `poetry` to manage dependency systematically. Regularly check for updates and review changelogs to ensure that upgrading a library is not going to break your application.

Would you like a conclusion and quiz for this chapter, or shall we proceed to the next one?

Conclusion

Testing and debugging are critical parts of software development, ensuring that your FastAPI applications are reliable and easy to maintain. Through this chapter, you have learned how to write solid unit tests using **`pytest`**, leverage integration tests to test entire workflows, and use `pdb` and IDE configurations in debugging for pinpointing and resolving issues. By using the best practices, you can ensure that your FastAPI application is stable and scalable, with each module performing as expected and possible errors resolved efficiently.

The next chapter, *Deployment and Scalability*, focuses on operationalizing your FastAPI application, from hosting strategies and configuration of the environments in which to deploy to handling scalability through load balancing and monitoring. Whether you are shipping out to cloud-based providers such as AWS or containerized, Dockerized, and Kubernetes-based environments, this chapter provides you with the roadmap for ensuring your application will be ready for production and scale well without pre-optimization by performance.

Multiple Choice Questions

1. **Which IDE allows seamless integration for debugging FastAPI applications?**
    a. Notepad++
    b. Eclipse
    c. VSCode
    d. Sublime Text
2. **What is the purpose of the `pdb` module in Python?**
    a. To create unit tests
    b. To debug Python programs
    c. To format code
    d. To write SQL queries

3. **Which Python debugging tool offers enhanced interactivity compared to `pdb`?**
    a. pytest
    b. ipdb
    c. uvicorn
    d. MyPy
4. **What does the `logging` module help achieve in debugging?**
    a. Generate SQL queries
    b. Inspect runtime errors
    c. Add runtime information to logs
    d. Create unit tests
5. **Which configuration file is used in VSCode for FastAPI debugging?**
    a. **`launch.json`**
    b. **`settings.json`**
    c. **`debug.config`**
    d. **`tasks.json`**
6. **What command starts `uvicorn` with debug-level logs?**
    a. **`uvicorn main:app --log-level info`**
    b. **`uvicorn main:app --log-level debug`**
    c. **`uvicorn main:app --debug`**
    d. **`uvicorn main:app -trace`**
7. **Which tool simulates requests and responses for integration testing in FastAPI?**
    a. TestClient
    b. pytest
    c. `uvicorn`
    d. Tortoise ORM

8. **What is the primary function of middleware in FastAPI debugging?**
    a. Handle database queries
    b. Log requests and responses
    c. Generate fixtures
    d. Process JSON responses
9. **What command is used to step through code using pdb?**
    a. `run`
    b. `trace`
    c. `n`
    d. `step`
10. **Which FastAPI feature allows custom error handling?**
    a. Middleware
    b. Exception Handlers
    c. Dependency Injection
    d. HTTP Router

Answers

Question	Answer
1	c
2	b
3	b
4	c
5	a
6	b
7	a
8	b
9	c
10	b

CHAPTER 11
Deployment and Scalability

Introduction

Effective deployment and scaling of applications is a foundation of delivering reliable, high-performing software solutions that do indeed meet user expectations. This chapter discusses the underlying strategies and tools necessary to push your FastAPI application from being in development to being actually ready for production. This points to structured deployment processes with goals toward zero downtime, better security, and higher maintainability. By mastering these principles, developers can ensure their applications remain reliable under diverse operating conditions and ready to adapt to evolving requirements.

A key focus of this chapter is containerization, a modern approach to packaging applications and their dependencies into portable units. Through tools such as Docker, you will learn how to create lightweight, consistent environments that simplify deployment across different systems. Containerization ensures that your FastAPI application runs smoothly, irrespective of the underlying infrastructure, thus reducing compatibility issues and increasing development and testing efficiency. It also forms the basis of scalable and manageable deployment pipelines that are crucial for modern software ecosystems.

The chapter extends its scope to orchestration, a critical component for managing complex, distributed systems at scale. Leveraging Kubernetes, you will explore how to automate the deployment, scaling, and management of containerized applications. Kubernetes empowers developers to handle high availability, load balancing, and resource allocation with precision, ensuring your FastAPI application can meet growing traffic demands effortlessly. By integrating these tools, the chapter demonstrates how to build a resilient architecture capable of adapting to dynamic workloads.

Finally, it addresses scalability: it explains what you can do in terms of both horizontal and vertical scaling for your FastAPI application. The chapter addresses real practices of performance optimization: load balancing, database scaling, caching, and other techniques by which you will be able to cope with increased traffic without reliability or performance losses. These principles, regardless of the size of your application or system, will equip you to deliver smooth user experiences in any scenario.

Structure

In this chapter, we will cover the following topics:

- **Deploying FastAPI Applications**
  - Preparing Your FastAPI Project for Deployment
  - Configuring Environments (development, staging, production)
  - Deployment Strategies (manual, automated, CI/CD pipelines)
  - Hosting Options: AWS, Azure, GCP, and Heroku
  - Configuring HTTPS and Domain Management
- **Using Docker and Kubernetes**
  - Introduction to Containerization with Docker
  - Writing and Optimizing Dockerfiles for FastAPI
  - Orchestrating Deployments Using Kubernetes
  - Managing Scalability and High Availability with Kubernetes
  - Practical Example of Deploying FastAPI with Docker and Kubernetes
- **Scaling Applications with FastAPI**
  - Load Balancing Strategies for FastAPI
  - Horizontal and Vertical Scaling Approaches
  - Monitoring Performance and Managing Resources
  - Integrating Caching Solutions to Optimize Response Times

Deploying FastAPI Applications

FastAPI should be deployed in a properly configured environment to ensure robustness and security. For hosting, you can choose a cloud provider such as AWS, Google Cloud, or Azure, or use containerization with Docker. The deployment environment must support web servers capable of handling asynchronous requests, such as Uvicorn or Gunicorn. Additionally, setting up HTTPS for secure communication, configuring domain names, and enabling logging and monitoring tools are essential steps. Together, these measures ensure that the application is secure, accessible, and capable of delivering optimal performance and reliability in a production environment.

Preparing Your FastAPI Project for Deployment

Deploying a FastAPI application begins with preparing the project to meet the requirements of a production environment. A well-structured project, which organizes folder structure for clarity, scalability, and maintainability as the application grows, is easier to manage and debug, making the deployment pipeline smoother. Also, it locks library dependencies in a **`requirements.txt`** file so that there is identical usage of versions in all deployment stages, from development up to production, so that applications behave the same across all the different environments, and so that compatibility issues are minimized.

Another important deployment management step deals with the handling of configurations over different environments: development, staging, and production. **`.env`** files or **`python-decouple`** are secure means of storing and retrieving such sensitive data, including API keys, database credentials, and environment-specific settings. Configuration detail separation from the codebase further increases security but makes switching between environments a straightforward process. For instance, developers can mimic production settings without taking risks with sensitive data in the staging environment to test thoroughly before they go live.

One other set of tools required during deployment are version control systems. An example is Git. In it, version control has proven invaluable to the process: with this functionality, every single modification of the code is recorded. In this way, a group can develop while effectively being able to move forward from previous versions, should problems occur in the new ones. This streamlined code management establishes a foundation for implementing the deployment pipelines that can automatically prompt the builds and deployments with limited human intervention, ensuring an always-up-to-date application able to meet user demands.

Configuring Environments

Setting up environments is an important step in deploying a FastAPI application. It ensures the application runs optimally through all the stages of development and production. Environments include development, staging, and production, defined by their respective configurations, which meet particular needs. For example, the development environment usually has debugging enabled, uses localhost servers, and gives detailed error messages to help developers during the coding phase. This configuration enables fast prototyping and debugging without worrying about exposing sensitive information or optimizing for large-scale use.

1. **Development**

   This environment of development allows the building and early testing of the application. It is a productivity-friendly and flexible environment, suitable for quick changes and iterative testing. It should also feature debugging so that the application can display detailed error messages and stack traces when issues occur. For instance, a FastAPI application in development might use the built-in **`uvicorn`** server to run locally on http://127.0.0.1:8000, with features such as **`reload=True`** to automatically restart the server upon code changes. Dummy databases or SQLite files may also be used instead of production-grade databases to simplify setup and avoid accidental data corruption. These environment variables in development are stored within `a.env` file. So, for example, details such as **`DEBUG=True`, `DATABASE_URL=sqlite:///development.db`**, or **`API_KEY=dev-key`** are stored and used.

2. **Staging**

   The staging environment is a pre-production space where developers can test the application under conditions closely mimicking production. It serves as a sandbox for quality assurance, performance testing, and integration verification. In this environment, debugging is disabled, and real-world data or realistic test datasets are often used to simulate user interactions. For instance, a FastAPI application can connect to a database, hosted on cloud services specifically for staging, **`DATABASE_URL=postgresql://staging-user@staging-db.server.com/staging`**. Usually, in staging, there is the creation of continuous integration and deployment pipelines, or CI/CD pipelines, where they automatically deploy the most updated changes from a staging branch version. Testing third-party integrations, such as payment gateways or APIs, focuses on ensuring that all these parts work together smoothly. By fairly closely mimicking production, staging minimizes the risk of important unexpected issues after deployment.

3. **Production**

   The production environment is where the application is deployed for end-users and needs to be optimized for security, reliability, and scalability. Debugging is disabled in order not to expose sensitive information, and the application runs on hardened, monitored servers. For example, a FastAPI application could be served using Gunicorn or Uvicorn workers behind a reverse proxy such as Nginx, with HTTPS enabled for secure communication. Environment variables in production may consist of DEBUG=False, **`DATABASE_URL=postgresql://prod-user@prod-db.server.com/production`**, and **`API_KEY=secure-prod-key`**, where all sensitive details are separated and stored. High availability techniques such as load balancing and horizontal scaling may be utilized to take care of traffic spikes using Kubernetes. Monitoring and logging tools such as Prometheus and Grafana might be included in the stack for better performance insights and the easy identification and resolution of issues. These measures collectively ensure that the application provides a seamless experience for users, even under heavy demand.

Deployment Strategies

Deploying applications is a choice of strategy to ensure smooth and reliable delivery of updates into production environments. The strategies of deployment can be broadly categorized into manual and automated deployments, each suited to different project sizes and requirements. Manual deployment is simple and direct, but it often involves repetitive steps for every update, which is better suited for small projects with infrequent changes. Whereas the deployment is automated, CI/CD pipelines will be used so as to streamline and scale up the process. Automated deployment is therefore more suited for larger, dynamic projects.

- **Manual Deployment**: This is often used for small-scale applications or in the early stages of development when the deployment process is straightforward. The manual deployment process usually involves uploading code to the server, restarting services, and updating configuration files manually. For example, in a FastAPI project, a developer might use SSH to log into a remote server, pull the latest code from a Git repository, run `pip install -r requirements.txt` to install dependencies, and restart the Uvicorn server. This approach may be simple and provide full control over each step, but it is also very time-consuming and error-prone for larger projects. The latter also lacks consistency because, more than anything, the process relies on the developer's attention to detail, which can often lead to discrepancies over time during deployment.
- **Automated Deployment**: Automation, which eliminates repetitive tasks and hence avoids human errors, boosts speed, and reliability in deployments; tools such as GitHub Actions, Jenkins, or GitLab CI/CD are used in creating such pipelines. For example, an AWS-hosted FastAPI application might use GitHub Actions to automate the following process: pushing changes to the main branch will trigger a pipeline that builds a Docker image, pushes it to a container registry, and then deploys it to an AWS Elastic Beanstalk environment. Automated deployment means every change is tested and verified before hitting production, significantly reducing bugs and downtime. This also features rollback mechanisms, which means it can easily revert to a stable version if problems occur and is ideal for projects with frequent updates or large user bases.

Choosing the Right Strategy

The choice between manual and automated deployment depends on the scale and complexity of the project. For smaller projects with minimal updates, manual deployment can be sufficient if the deployment process is documented and followed rigorously. However, as the project grows and deployment frequency increases, transitioning to automated pipelines becomes essential for maintaining consistency and efficiency. It is possible to use a hybrid approach; start with manual deployment, and then gradually introduce automation tools with the progression of the project.

This flexibility will ensure that the deployment strategy matches the project's needs and resources, paving the way for scalability and efficiency in the future.

Hosting Options

Selecting a hosting solution is the key to launching FastAPI applications because this decision impacts their performance, scalability, and cost efficiency. Based on the scale, requirements, and resources, developers can use any number of hosting options. From using cloud provider flexibility, the PaaS simplicity, to on-premise servers' control, everything is at their fingertips. Each approach comes with its unique benefits and considerations, which allows the developer to tailor the hosting environment to their specific needs.

- **Cloud Providers**: The use of cloud platforms such as AWS, Microsoft Azure, and Google Cloud Platform (GCP) gives robust and scalable hosting options for FastAPI applications. It supports deploying applications in virtual machines, containerized environments, or serverless architectures, depending on the size and complexity of the project. For instance, the deployment of a FastAPI application on AWS might include Elastic Beanstalk for managed services or Elastic Kubernetes Service (EKS) for container orchestration. This may include simplified deployment through automation of scaling and resource management using GCP's App Engine or Azure App Services. These platforms also give some advanced features such as distributed databases, monitoring tools, and global CDNs that ensure applications are performant and accessible to users globally. Cloud hosting offers scalability and flexibility but requires cost management to optimize resource usage.
- **Platform-as-a-Service (PaaS)**: Platform-as-a-Service solutions, such as Heroku, provide more simplified hosting for FastAPI, which is great for speedy, hassle-free deployment without the need for developers having to worry about the backend infrastructure. PaaS largely abstracts much of underlying infrastructure management, so developers can now focus on their application's code. For example, when deploying a FastAPI-based application on Heroku, it is simply a push to a Git repository, following which Heroku takes control over the build, deployments, and scaling. With the add-ons of PostgreSQL databases, logging, and monitoring integrated into the PaaS, it is suitable for small to medium-sized projects or prototypes. However, it comes with a price tag as the PaaS solutions might be more expensive than the other hosting options for bigger projects or applications with high traffic.
- **On-Premise Servers**: On-premise hosting is a traditional approach where organizations manage their own infrastructure to host FastAPI applications. This option gives maximum control over the server environment, which can include custom configurations, strict security measures, and compliance with specific regulatory requirements. For instance, an organization may deploy

a FastAPI application on an internal server running Linux, using Nginx as a reverse proxy and a self-hosted PostgreSQL database. Businesses that involve confidential data, such as finance and healthcare, prefer on-premise hosting as data residency is critical for such types. However, it would incur a great amount of maintenance for the hardware as well as for the networks. It is not appropriate when the project size or even the size of a development team is small, with an inadequate budget.

Choosing the Right Option

It really depends on the size of the application, expected traffic, and organizational needs in choosing between cloud, PaaS, and on-premise hosting. Cloud providers are best for scalable, global applications; PaaS platforms are excellent for rapid deployment and ease of use; and on-premise servers are ideal for organizations requiring full control and compliance. The developers can pick a hosting option that would balance performance, scalability, and cost-effectiveness through careful evaluation of the requirements of the project.

Configuring HTTPS and Domain Management

The security and reliability of a FastAPI application are important; hence, when it is to be deployed for production use. HTTPS configuration and domain names management are a part of the steps toward these two goals. HTTPS encrypts the communication between clients and servers, thus securing from interception the sensitive information regarding user credentials, API keys, and other data between the transmission of such pieces of information. Domain management also assists in mapping a friendly domain name to your application's IP address so that it is easily accessible and builds trust with users.

Configuring HTTPS using SSL/TLS Certificates

Configuring HTTPS needs an SSL/TLS certificate that authenticates the server's identity and creates a secure connection with the client. Free and widely trusted services such as Let's Encrypt provide SSL/TLS certificates that can be integrated into your application with minimal effort. For example, if you are using Nginx as a reverse proxy for your application, you might use the Certbot tool to automatically get and set up a Let's Encrypt certificate. You might execute commands such as **`sudo certbot -nginx`** to create and insert the certificate into your Nginx configuration. HTTPS not only protects user data but also improves search engine rankings and builds user confidence, as browsers display a padlock icon for secure websites.

Domain Management and DNS Configuration

Mapping a domain name to your API's IP address is a crucial step in making your application accessible through a human-readable URL. This process involves configuring DNS (Domain Name System) records for your domain. For instance, an `A` record points your domain, for example, **`api.example.com`** to the IP address of your server. A `CNAME` record, on the other hand, can point your subdomains to another domain or service. Most domain registrars have friendly interfaces to configure DNS settings, allowing you to set additional information such as TTL (time-to-live) values for cache. Proper management of the domain ensures seamless access to your application and simplifies the user experience.

Using Reverse Proxies for Traffic Routing

Nginx or Traefik is the tools that are used in HTTPS configuration and domain management. These tools act as reverse proxies, which handle incoming traffic, route requests to the appropriate application server, and terminate SSL/TLS connections. For example, Nginx allows you to have multiple server blocks for managing multiple domain names, and you can enable HTTPS by pointing it to the SSL certificate and key files in the Nginx configuration file. In addition, Traefik features dynamic routing, allowing Traefik to automatically request SSL/TLS certificates through Let's Encrypt. More importantly, both of these tools support load balancing, caching, and logging, which make your FastAPI application more robust and responsive.

All the same, long-term security means renewing SSL/TLS certificates before they expire. Let's Encrypt, in this regard, makes renewal pretty easy through automated renewal scripts. Finally, with HSTS (HTTP Strict Transport Security), your browsers are strictly connected to your application through HTTPS. All these are practices that make sure that your application is secure, scalable, and easily accessed by users if the proper DNS configuration and reverse proxy setup are followed.

Using Docker and Kubernetes

In all fairness, Docker and Kubernetes transformed how applications are deployed as well as managed by introducing these notions: containerization and orchestration. Docker simplifies application and dependency packaging into an image that is portable while guaranteeing consistent behavior. It is, for instance, possible to containerize a FastAPI application and its runtime environment in **`Dockerfile`** and then build its container image. This image can then be shared across teams or deployed directly to servers, eliminating the "it works on my machine" problem. Kubernetes complements Docker by managing these containers at scale, automating tasks such as deployment, scaling, and recovery. Together, these tools provide a robust foundation for modern application deployment.

Introduction to Containerization with Docker

Containers allow applications to run from secluded environments, encapsulating any code, libraries, or runtime needed for execution within the container. Docker further aids developers in creating these easy containerizations. A simple fast-

API **Dockerfile** may look as simple as using a Python-based image, installing dependencies for each version of the application from within **requirements.txt**, and exporting the application on a local port. The Docker engine builds the container image from this file. This application can then run locally or be deployed onto a cloud platform. Compose makes multi-container application management easier than with Docker: manage FastAPI and PostgreSQL using one YAML file. This keeps it portable and consistent, helping the development workflow all the way to deployment.

Writing and Optimizing Dockerfiles for FastAPI

A Dockerfile is an essential component when deploying a FastAPI application using Docker. It defines a series of instructions to build a Docker image that encapsulates the application and its dependencies. The following is an example of a basic Dockerfile tailored for a FastAPI project:

```
# Use the official Python image
FROM python:3.10-slim

# Set the working directory inside the container
WORKDIR /app

# Copy the requirements file and install dependencies
COPY requirements.txt .
RUN pip install --no-cache-dir -r requirements.txt

# Copy the application code to the container
COPY . .

# Expose port 8000, the default port for FastAPI
EXPOSE 8000

# Command to start the FastAPI application
CMD ["uvicorn", "main:app", "--host", "0.0.0.0", "--port", "8000"]
```

This example ensures that the Docker container is lightweight and efficient. It uses a slim Python image, installs only the necessary dependencies from **requirements.txt**, and sets up the FastAPI application to run with Uvicorn as the ASGI server.

Optimizations for Production

To make the Docker image more suitable for production environments, several optimizations can be applied:

- **Use Smaller Base Images**

  Switching to smaller base images, such as **python:3.10-alpine**, significantly reduces the size of the Docker image. Alpine-based images are minimal and include only the essential components. For example:

```
FROM python:3.10-alpine
```

However, be aware that Alpine images might require additional effort to ensure compatibility with some Python packages, as they use **`musl`** instead of **`glibc`**.

- **Multi-Stage Builds**

  Multi-stage builds allow you to separate the build environment from the runtime environment, resulting in a cleaner and smaller production image. This approach is especially useful for applications with build-time dependencies (for example, compilers). Here is an example:

```
# Stage 1: Build dependencies
FROM python:3.10-slim as builder
WORKDIR /app
COPY requirements.txt .
RUN pip install --no-cache-dir --prefix=/install -r requirements.
txt

# Stage 2: Runtime
FROM python:3.10-alpine
WORKDIR /app
COPY --from=builder /install /usr/local
COPY . .
EXPOSE 8000
CMD ["uvicorn", "main:app", "--host", "0.0.0.0", "--port", "8000"]
```

  This strategy ensures that only the essential dependencies are included in the final image, resulting in a leaner and more secure image.

- **Cache Optimization**

  By structuring the Dockerfile to take advantage of Docker's layer caching, you can speed up builds. Place instructions that change frequently (such as copying application code) towards the end of the Dockerfile. For example, installing dependencies after copying only **`requirements.txt`** ensures that this step is cached until **`requirements.txt`** changes:

```
COPY requirements.txt .
RUN pip install --no-cache-dir -r requirements.txt
COPY . .
```

- **Secure Image Configuration**

  - Use non-root users to reduce potential security risks:

```
RUN adduser -D appuser
USER appuser
```

- Limit file permissions in the container to prevent unauthorized access.

By applying these optimizations, you can create a Docker image that is not only efficient but also secure and production-ready. This ensures smoother deployments and better performance in a production environment.

Orchestrating Deployments with Kubernetes

Kubernetes provides open-source container orchestration software meant to automate and enhance the deployment, scaling, and management of containers in large clusters to suit large distributed systems. However, due to the need to abstract the containers over all the clusters as shown, it allows developers to focus purely on the application while in their production environment, delivering scalability as well as robustness in the system. It is Docker integrative, hence people would easily pick it up. Kubernetes simplifies resource management, enables zero-downtime deployments, and provides mechanisms for scaling applications dynamically based on demand.

Key Kubernetes Concepts

- **Pods:** A Pod is the smallest deployable unit in Kubernetes, and it can be a wrapper of one or more tightly coupled containers. In most cases, only one container is running within a Pod, such as the FastAPI container, though more than one container could be used to support other tasks, such as logging or monitoring. Pods share networking and storage resources for efficient communication between containers. For instance, a Pod running a FastAPI container can also include a sidecar container meant for metrics collection.
- **Services:** Kubernetes Services offer stable network endpoints for Pods, which can live and die. With services, the front-end application gets decoupled from its underlying Pods, giving the application consistent communication as a result of changes within its Pods' lifecycle. For example, it can route traffic between components within the cluster. Then there is the `LoadBalancer` service, which exposes the application outward towards external users. So, during deploying an application such as FastAPI, use Service for exposing the API endpoint such that users or another service can access it smoothly.
- **Deployments:** Deployments describe the desired state of an application and govern the rollout process to achieve that state. They are responsible for managing tasks such as scaling the number of Pods, updating the images of containers, and recovering from failures. A Deployment ensures that the given number of replicas (Pods) are running at any given time and distribute traffic uniformly while ensuring high availability. For example, a FastAPI Deployment can specify three replicas so that the application remains accessible even if one of the Pods fails.

Deployment YAML Example

Below is an example of a Deployment configuration for a FastAPI application, illustrating how to define and manage the application in a Kubernetes cluster:

```
apiVersion: apps/v1
kind: Deployment
metadata:
  name: fastapi-deployment
spec:
  replicas: 3  # Number of Pods to run
  selector:
    matchLabels:
      app: fastapi  # Label selector to identify the Pods
  template:
    metadata:
      labels:
        app: fastapi  # Labels assigned to the Pods
    spec:
      containers:
      - name: fastapi-container  # Name of the container
        image: your-docker-image  # Replace with your Docker image
        ports:
        - containerPort: 8000  # Exposed container port
```

Explanation of the YAML File:

- **`apiVersion: apps/v1`**: Specifies the API version for the Deployment resource.
- **`kind: Deployment`**: Indicates that the resource is a Deployment.
- **`metadata`**: Contains metadata about the Deployment, such as its name (`fastapi-deployment`).
- **`replicas`**: Defines the number of Pods to run concurrently. In this case, three replicas ensure high availability.
- **`selector`**: Matches the Deployment with Pods that have the label **`app: fastapi`**.
- **`template`**: Specifies the configuration for the Pods managed by this Deployment. It includes labels (**`app: fastapi`**) and the container configuration.
- **`containers`**: Lists the containers to run in the Pod. The `image` field specifies the Docker image for the FastAPI application, and `ports` defines the container's exposed port (8000).

Benefits of Using Kubernetes for FastAPI Applications

- **Automated Scaling**: Kubernetes can automatically scale Pods up or down based on resource usage or traffic demands using Horizontal Pod Autoscalers.

- **Rolling Updates and Rollbacks**: Deployments support seamless updates to application containers, minimizing downtime. If an update fails, Kubernetes can roll back to the previous state.
- **Load Balancing**: Services distribute incoming traffic across Pods, ensuring efficient utilization and reliability.
- **Resilience**: Kubernetes monitors Pods and restarts them if they fail, maintaining application availability.
- **Infrastructure Abstraction**: Kubernetes abstracts the underlying infrastructure, allowing applications to run consistently on any cloud provider or on-premises cluster.

By combining these features with the flexibility of FastAPI, Kubernetes provides an ideal solution for deploying and managing high-performing, scalable applications in production environments.

Managing Scalability and High Availability with Kubernetes

Kubernetes is designed to handle the challenges of scaling applications and ensuring their high availability, making it a critical tool for modern deployment strategies. By automating the management of containerized applications, Kubernetes provides dynamic scaling and robust failover mechanisms that help maintain optimal performance even during traffic spikes or unexpected failures. These features ensure that your FastAPI application remains responsive and available to users, regardless of workload fluctuations.

Horizontal Scaling for Dynamic Workloads

Horizontal Pod Autoscaling (HPA) in Kubernetes allows the platform to automatically adjust the number of Pods in response to workload changes. This scaling is based on metrics such as CPU utilization, memory usage, or custom metrics defined by the application. For example, if your FastAPI application experiences a sudden surge in API requests, Kubernetes can increase the number of Pods to distribute the load effectively. Conversely, during periods of low activity, it scales down Pods to optimize resource usage and reduce costs.

To implement HPA, you can define a configuration like this:

```
apiVersion: autoscaling/v2
kind: HorizontalPodAutoscaler
metadata:
  name: fastapi-hpa
spec:
```

```
scaleTargetRef:
  apiVersion: apps/v1
  kind: Deployment
  name: fastapi-deployment
minReplicas: 2
maxReplicas: 10
metrics:
- type: Resource
  resource:
    name: cpu
    target:
      type: Utilization
      averageUtilization: 50
```

In this example, the HPA scales the number of replicas for the **`fastapi-deployment`** between 2 and 10, aiming to maintain CPU utilization around 50%. This ensures the application can dynamically adapt to changing demands without manual intervention.

Load Balancers for High Availability

To maintain high availability, Kubernetes employs load balancers to distribute incoming traffic evenly across all active Pods. This approach prevents any single Pod from being overwhelmed with requests, enhancing both performance and reliability. Kubernetes Services, such as **`LoadBalancer`** or **`NodePort`**, act as the entry point for incoming traffic and route requests to the appropriate Pods.

For example, defining a LoadBalancer Service for a FastAPI application might look like this:

```
apiVersion: v1
kind: Service
metadata:
  name: fastapi-service
spec:
  type: LoadBalancer
  selector:
    app: fastapi
  ports:
  - protocol: TCP
    port: 80
    targetPort: 8000
```

In this configuration:

- The Service listens on port 80 for incoming traffic and forwards it to port 8000 in the Pods.
- The **`LoadBalancer`** type automatically provides a cloud-based load balancer, making the application accessible over the internet.

This setup ensures consistent performance and availability, even when individual Pods are restarted or replaced.

Failover and Self-Healing Mechanisms

Kubernetes includes built-in mechanisms to handle failures, ensuring that applications remain operational with minimal downtime. If a Pod becomes unhealthy or crashes, Kubernetes automatically replaces it with a new one to maintain the desired number of replicas specified in the Deployment. Liveness and readiness probes can be defined to monitor the health of each Pod, ensuring that only healthy Pods receive traffic.

For example, adding health probes to a FastAPI Deployment might look like this:

```
livenessProbe:
  httpGet:
    path: /health
    port: 8000
  initialDelaySeconds: 5
  periodSeconds: 10
readinessProbe:
  httpGet:
    path: /ready
    port: 8000
  initialDelaySeconds: 5
  periodSeconds: 10
```

- **Liveness Probe**: Ensures the container is still running. If the probe fails, Kubernetes restarts the container.
- **Readiness Probe**: Determines if the container is ready to serve traffic. Pods failing this probe are removed from the Service endpoints temporarily.

Benefits of Scalability and High Availability with Kubernetes

By utilizing Kubernetes scaling and load-balancing functionalities, FastAPI applications manage varied levels of traffic in the most efficient manner while also wasting fewer resources. Automation helps avoid the requirement of human intervention during peak usage and therefore ensures smooth usage without being interrupted. High availability by ensuring load balancing along with failover mechanisms ensures minimal service interruptions for users, even in the case of failures such as Pod and nodes. These features of Kubernetes are a must-have when a scalable and resilient FastAPI deployment has to be operated on a production level.

Practical Example: Deploying FastAPI with Docker and Kubernetes

Firstly, the process of deploying an application with FastAPI will include creating a Docker image, making it available to a container registry, and then using Kubernetes to handle and manage its deployment. It results in ensuring the application is properly containerized, version-controlled, and easily scalable. Here is the detailed outline of each step involved in this process.

1. **Build the Docker Image**

   The first step is to containerize the FastAPI application by creating a Docker image. A Dockerfile, which contains the instructions for building the image, must already be prepared. For example, the Dockerfile might look like this:

```
# Use the official Python image
FROM python:3.10-slim

# Set working directory
WORKDIR /app

# Copy requirements file and install dependencies
COPY requirements.txt .
RUN pip install --no-cache-dir -r requirements.txt

# Copy the application code
COPY . .

# Expose port 8000 for FastAPI
EXPOSE 8000

# Command to run the FastAPI application
CMD ["uvicorn", "main:app", "--host", "0.0.0.0", "--port", "8000"]
```

   Once the Dockerfile is ready, build the image using the `docker build` command:

```
docker build -t fastapi-app .
```

- **`-t fastapi-app`**: Tags the image with the name **`fastapi-app`** for easy reference.
- **`.`**: Refers to the current directory, which contains the Dockerfile and application code.

   This step creates a Docker image locally, encapsulating the application and its dependencies.

2. **Push the Image to a Container Registry**

   After building the image, push it to a container registry such as Docker Hub, AWS Elastic Container Registry (ECR), or Google Container Registry (GCR). This ensures that Kubernetes clusters can access the image.

   First, tag the image with a specific repository name and version:

   ```
   docker tag fastapi-app your-dockerhub-user/fastapi-app:latest
   ```

   Here, your-dockerhub-user is your Docker Hub username, and the latest is the version tag. Next, push the image to the registry:

   ```
   docker push your-dockerhub-user/fastapi-app:latest
   ```

- Authentication: Ensure you are logged in to the registry using **`docker login`**.
- Registry Visibility: Depending on your requirements, the image can be made public or private.

   After pushing, the image is accessible globally for deployment.

3. **Apply Kubernetes Configuration**

   Create a Kubernetes configuration file (**`deployment.yaml`**) to define how the application should be deployed. Below is an example configuration for a FastAPI application:

```
apiVersion: apps/v1
kind: Deployment
metadata:
  name: fastapi-deployment
spec:
  replicas: 3
  selector:
    matchLabels:
      app: fastapi
  template:
    metadata:
      labels:
        app: fastapi
    spec:
      containers:
      - name: fastapi-container
        image: your-dockerhub-user/fastapi-app:latest
        ports:
        - containerPort: 8000
---
apiVersion: v1
kind: Service
metadata:
```

```
  name: fastapi-service
spec:
  type: LoadBalancer
  selector:
    app: fastapi
  ports:
  - protocol: TCP
    port: 80
    targetPort: 8000
```

- **Deployment Section:**
  - **`replicas: 3`** ensures high availability with three instances of the application running concurrently.
  - **`image: your-dockerhub-user/fastapi-app:latest`** specifies the container image to deploy.
- **Service Section:**
  - **`type: LoadBalancer`** exposes the application to the internet.
  - **`port: 80` and `targetPort: 8000`** forward traffic from port 80 (external) to port 8000 (internal application).

Apply the configuration using **`kubectl`**:

```
kubectl apply -f deployment.yaml
```

This command creates the necessary Pods, Deployments, and Services as defined in the YAML file.

4. **Verify the Deployment**

After applying the configuration, verify that the Pods are running and the application is accessible:

- **Check Pod Status:**

```
kubectl get pods
```

- **Check Service Details:**

```
kubectl get services
```

The output will include an external IP address for the **`LoadBalancer`** Service. Access the FastAPI application in a browser or via **`curl`** using the external IP address.

This workflow demonstrates a practical approach to deploying FastAPI applications using Docker and Kubernetes. By containerizing the application and leveraging Kubernetes' scalability and orchestration features, you can deploy robust and production-ready applications that handle varying traffic demands efficiently.

Scaling Applications with FastAPI

Scaling applications is critical to handling varied loads and performance with increasing traffic. FastAPI, known for performance efficiency, has available options for scaling applications horizontally and vertically. Through these, you can ensure your FastAPI application remains a safe bet both in the present and the future.

Load Balancing Strategies for FastAPI

Load balancing is a crucial strategy to distribute incoming requests across multiple servers or application instances. This distribution helps prevent any single server from becoming a bottleneck, thereby improving the overall performance and reliability of the application.

- **Reverse Proxy**: Tools such as **nginx** or **Traefik** act as reverse proxies, managing and distributing requests across backend FastAPI application instances. These proxies ensure that each request is sent to the least busy server, maintaining optimal load across all instances.
- **Cloud Load Balancers**: Services such as **AWS Elastic Load Balancing**, **GCP Load Balancer**, and **Azure Load Balancer** automatically handle traffic distribution. These cloud-managed solutions provide scalability without the need for manual intervention, balancing incoming requests across a cluster of instances with minimal latency and high availability.

Combining reverse proxies with cloud load balancing not only distributes traffic but also enhances fault tolerance, making the application more resilient to failures. This ensures a seamless experience for users even during spikes in traffic.

Horizontal and Vertical Scaling Approaches

Horizontal Scaling involves adding more application instances to handle increasing numbers of concurrent requests. This approach is ideal for web applications such as FastAPI because it can scale dynamically in response to demand.

- **Horizontal Scaling**: By adding more instances, you distribute the load, which helps manage peak traffic periods more effectively. For example, if your FastAPI application experiences a surge in requests, you can simply launch additional instances to handle the load. This method is particularly beneficial for microservices architecture, where each service can be independently scaled and managed.
- **Vertical Scaling**: **Vertical Scaling**, on the other hand, refers to upgrading the resources of a single server, such as adding more CPU or memory. While simpler to implement, vertical scaling has its limitations due to physical

constraints, such as the maximum capacity of the hardware. This method is often used for workloads that do not require multiple instances but benefit from increased resources. For instance, a heavily used FastAPI application with high computational needs might opt for a more powerful server.

Monitoring Performance and Managing Resources

Using tools such as Prometheus and Grafana, you can monitor metrics such as response times, request rates, and CPU usage. Proper monitoring helps identify bottlenecks and optimize resource allocation. Kubernetes also offers resource quotas and limits for managing application performance efficiently.

Efficiently managing resources and monitoring application performance are critical to the success of a scaled FastAPI deployment.

- **Monitoring**: Tools such as **Prometheus** and **Grafana** are commonly used for tracking performance metrics such as response times, request rates, CPU usage, and memory consumption. These tools allow administrators to set up alerts and visualize data to quickly identify bottlenecks and optimize resource allocation. For instance, if an increase in CPU usage correlates with response time degradation, this data can trigger an automatic scaling action to add more instances.
- **Kubernetes Resource Quotas and Limits**: Kubernetes offers mechanisms such as resource quotas and limits to manage and control the consumption of resources by applications. These settings help prevent overuse of CPU and memory, ensuring that the application does not exhaust available resources and impact performance. By applying these controls, administrators can ensure stable operation even as the number of application instances increases.

Integrating Caching Solutions

Caching reduces the load on APIs by storing frequent responses temporarily. FastAPI can integrate with caching tools such as Redis or Memcached to improve response times for repetitive queries. For example, caching database query results can significantly enhance performance.

Caching is another effective strategy for scaling FastAPI applications, particularly to handle repetitive queries efficiently.

- **Caching**: FastAPI can integrate with caching solutions such as **Redis** or **Memcached** to store frequently accessed data in memory. Caching can significantly reduce the load on APIs by storing the results of expensive database queries or API calls, thus improving response times. For example, a database query that takes 200ms can be cached, and subsequent requests for the same data are served almost instantaneously. This not only enhances performance but also reduces latency and load on the database, making the application more responsive during high-demand periods.

Combining load balancing, efficient resource management, and caching optimizations ensures that FastAPI applications are not only scalable but also capable of maintaining high performance and reliability under varied and growing workloads. This comprehensive approach to deployment and scaling is crucial for the sustained success of modern web applications.

Conclusion

The chapter on **Deployment and Scalability** looked into critical concepts to make sure FastAPI applications are ready for production and able to cope with user demands effectively. Starting with detailed strategies for deploying FastAPI applications, the chapter emphasized the use of reliable platforms and environments, both traditional hosting and modern containerized solutions. It included Docker for containerization, allowing for consistency and portability of applications, and Kubernetes for orchestration, which is critical in managing large-scale systems and maintaining uptime during high-demand scenarios. It also discussed practical approaches to scaling, including both vertical and horizontal scaling techniques that could handle traffic surges. Tools such as load balancers, monitoring systems such as Prometheus and Grafana, and caching mechanisms such as Redis were emphasized in the optimization of application performance and resource distribution. Finally, it insisted that security should be paramount at the time of deployment and scaling. Its APIs must remain robust and vulnerability-proof.

We continue to the next chapter, **Managing Application Configuration**, which is one of the most under-appreciated aspects of application development but an essential one. This chapter discusses best practices of organizing and managing application settings to maintain consistency and secure configurations across environments. Starting with handling environment variables, leveraging configuration files, and up until integrating secure secret management solutions, the following chapters provide guidance on maintaining scalability and flexibility in your FastAPI application while reducing risks and minimizing errors. Read on to take a deep dive into configuration management for your application.

Multiple Choice Questions

1. **What is the primary advantage of using Docker for deploying FastAPI applications?**
   a. Faster application runtime
   b. Consistent and portable application environment
   c. Increased memory usage
   d. Simplified debugging
2. **Which tool is commonly used for container orchestration in production?**
   a. Apache
   b. Kubernetes
   c. PostgreSQL
   d. Redis
3. **What is the function of a load balancer in a FastAPI deployment?**
   a. Managing API keys
   b. Distributing traffic among multiple application instances
   c. Monitoring application logs
   d. Managing database migrations
4. **What command is used to build a Docker image for a FastAPI application?**
   a. `docker start`
   b. `docker-compose`
   c. `docker build`
   d. `docker image create`
5. **Which of the following is an example of horizontal scaling?**
   a. Increasing CPU cores on a single server
   b. Adding more instances of the application to a load balancer
   c. Using a higher-performance SSD
   d. Upgrading the application code

6. **What file format is typically used for defining Kubernetes configurations?**
   a. JSON
   b. YAML
   c. XML
   d. INI
7. **Which tool is often used to monitor application metrics in a containerized environment?**
   a. Redis
   b. Prometheus
   c. PostgreSQL
   d. Celery
8. **What is the role of a reverse proxy in FastAPI deployment?**
   a. Manage API routing and caching
   b. Handle database migrations
   c. Generate API documentation
   d. Secure the application's source code
9. **Which Kubernetes object is used to expose FastAPI services to external users?**
   a. Pod
   b. Service
   c. Deployment
   d. Ingress
10. **What is the primary use of Redis in scaling FastAPI applications?**
    a. Authentication
    b. Caching responses to reduce database queries
    c. Monitoring logs
    d. Running migrations

Answers

Question	Answer
1	b
2	b
3	b
4	c
5	b
6	b
7	b
8	a
9	d
10	b

CHAPTER 12
Managing Application Configuration

Introduction

FastAPI deployments will make seamless transitions between the environments, such as development, testing, and production, easier. FastAPI has tools and design patterns to maintain configuration settings from the application logic, and hence supports flexibility, scalability, and maintainability. This chapter deals with the need for environment variables, handling of sensitive data through file-based configuration, and the utilization of libraries such as Pydantic Settings and dynaconf, which are mighty for structured and dynamic configuration management.

Environment variables are vital for storing sensitive information such as API keys, database credentials, and secret tokens outside of the application code. Beyond that, file-based configurations, such as `.env` files or YAML/JSON files, provide an added layer of organization, as it is easier to maintain environment-specific settings. Libraries such as **`python-dotenv`** allow developers to load and manage these configurations effectively during local development. Moreover, Pydantic Settings enhances this process further by combining type validation with environment-aware settings in order to provide robust and error-free configurations.

Security is the primary concern, especially when in production environments, where mishandling sensitive data may expose vulnerabilities. This chapter, therefore, emphasizes best practices such as avoiding hardcoding credentials and limiting access to configuration files. Advanced tools such as dynaconf also support hierarchical and dynamic configuration management that helps to manage complex deployment scenarios.

By the end of this chapter, you will understand how to design adaptable and secure configurations for FastAPI applications. With these skills, you will be able to maintain clear code, protect sensitive information, and ensure that behavior is reliable across diverse deployment environments.

Structure

In this chapter, we will cover the following topics:

- **Using Environment Variables for Configuration**
  - Introduction to Environment Variables and Their Significance
  - Methods to Access Environment Variables in FastAPI
  - Examples for Setting and Retrieving Configurations from Environment Variables
- **Managing Configuration for Different Environments**
  - Why Separate Configurations for Different Environments Are Crucial
  - Strategies to Switch Configurations Dynamically
  - Examples of Environment-Based Configurations
- **Config File Formats**
  - Overview of Popular Configuration File Formats (YAML, JSON, .env)
  - Pros and Cons of Each Format
  - Example Structures for FastAPI Applications
- **Securely Handling Sensitive Data**
  - Techniques for Managing Sensitive Information (for example, API keys, passwords)
  - Leveraging Secret Managers or Encrypted Storage Solutions
  - Best Practices to Prevent Leaks of Sensitive Data
- **Configuration Management Tools and Libraries**
  - Introduction to Pydantic Settings and Dynaconf
  - Step-by-Step Guides to Implementing These Tools in FastAPI Projects
  - Comparing Features and Scenarios for Choosing the Right Tool

Using Environment Variables for Configuration

Environment variables are a secure and flexible way to manage configuration settings in FastAPI applications. They allow sensitive information such as API keys, database credentials, and secret tokens to be stored outside the source code, reducing the risk of exposure. Tools such as **`python-dotenv`** can be used to load these variables from `.env` files during development, while production environments can directly access system-level variables. For example, **`os.getenv()`** can retrieve environment-specific values, enabling dynamic behavior such as switching between development and production configurations. This approach ensures portability and enhances security across different environments.

Introduction to Environment Variables and Their Significance

Environment variables are key-value pairs defined outside of the application code that help configure the app's behavior without altering the codebase. They ensure portability, enabling the same application to run in different environments (for example, local, testing, production) with specific settings such as database URLs or API keys. Using environment variables reduces the risk of exposing sensitive data, which might otherwise be hardcoded into the application. FastAPI offers high support in working with environment variables to make configuration easier.

Methods to Access Environment Variables in FastAPI

FastAPI leverages Python's built-in **os** module to interact with environment variables. These variables can be accessed using **os.getenv()** or **os.environ**. Below is an example of how to use environment variables in FastAPI:

```
import os
from fastapi import FastAPI

app = FastAPI()

DATABASE_URL = os.getenv("DATABASE_URL", "sqlite:///default.db")
# Default value as a fallback

@app.get("/")
def read_root():
    return {"Database URL": DATABASE_URL}
```

In this example, **DATABASE_URL** is fetched from the environment. If it is not set, the application falls back to a default value.

Examples for Setting and Retrieving Configurations

Configuration settings help manage environment-specific variables such as database connections, API keys, and logging levels. You can set and retrieve configurations using environment variables, configuration files, or built-in frameworks such as Pydantic in FastAPI.

- **Setting Environment Variables**
  - **In Linux/Mac:**
    ```
    export DATABASE_URL="postgresql://user:password@
    localhost:5432/mydb"
    ```
  - **In Windows (Command Prompt):**
    ```
    set DATABASE_URL=postgresql://user:password@localhost:5432/
    mydb
    ```
- **Using `.env` Files**

  A **`.env`** file stores environment variables locally. Use libraries such as **`python-dotenv`** to load these variables into the application:

  ```
  from dotenv import load_dotenv
  import os

  load_dotenv()  # Load variables from a .env file
  SECRET_KEY = os.getenv("SECRET_KEY")
  ```

  Example `.env` file:

  ```
  DATABASE_URL=postgresql://user:password@localhost:5432/mydb
  SECRET_KEY=mysecretkey
  ```

  By using environment variables effectively, developers can create scalable, secure, and environment-agnostic applications.

Managing Configuration for Different Environments

The separation of configurations for different environments is very important for the smooth operation of applications across the development, testing, and production stages. Each environment has a different purpose and different requirements, such as debugging in development and high security and performance in production. Separate configurations prevent accidental exposure of sensitive data such as API keys or database credentials, which is critical for safeguarding your application. By segregating settings, you also minimize the risks of deploying development-specific settings to production, thereby giving you stability and reliability.

Importance of Separate Configurations for Different Environments

FastAPI applications usually run in multiple environments, for example, development, testing, and production. Each environment has different configuration needs; for example, a development setup might use SQLite, which is lightweight, while production may require high-performance PostgreSQL. Separate configurations ensure flexibility, avoid hardcoded environment-specific settings, and prevent sensitive production data from being exposed accidentally during development or testing.

Strategies for Managing Configurations

Effectively managing configurations involves adopting strategies that promote security, scalability, and maintainability across different environments. A common approach is to use environment variables to store sensitive or environment-specific settings, such as database URLs and API keys. These variables can be accessed using libraries such as **os** in Python or tools such as dotenv for loading them from **.env** files. Another strategy involves leveraging configuration management libraries, such as Pydantic or Dynaconf, to centralize and validate settings, ensuring consistency and reducing errors. These strategies enable seamless transitions between environments while maintaining secure and efficient operations.

- **Using Environment-Specific Files**

  Define separate **.env** files or configuration files for each environment:

  - **.env.dev**: Contains configurations for the development environment.
  - **.env.test**: Includes settings for testing.
  - **.env.prod**: Stores production-specific variables.

  Load the appropriate file based on the environment:

  ```
  from dotenv import load_dotenv
  import os

  environment = os.getenv("ENV", "dev")  # Defaults to "dev"
  load_dotenv(f".env.{environment}")  # Load specific environment
  variables
  DATABASE_URL = os.getenv("DATABASE_URL")
  ```

- **Environment Variables for Environment Selection**

  Use a single environment variable (for example, **ENV**) to determine the active environment. This approach simplifies deployment pipelines by ensuring configurations align with the environment automatically.

- **Configuration Using Python Classes**

  Python's `pydantic` library provides an elegant way to manage configurations through strongly typed classes:

```
from pydantic import BaseSettings

class Config(BaseSettings):
    database_url: str
    debug_mode: bool = False

    class Config:
        env_file = ".env"

settings = Config()
print(settings.database_url)
```

Examples of Environment-Based Configurations

Here is how to differentiate configurations for development, testing, and production:

- **Development**: Enable verbose logging, debug mode, and a lightweight database.
- **Testing**: Use isolated database instances and mock external services.
- **Production**: Optimize performance, restrict debug output, and integrate production-grade services (for example, caching).

Best Practices for Configuration Management Across Environments

- **Segregate Configurations**: Always use separate files for sensitive environments such as production.
- **Secure Configuration Files**: Restrict access to production configuration files to minimize security risks.
- **Version Control**: Avoid committing sensitive configuration files to repositories; use templates instead (for example, **`.env.example`**).
- **Automate Configurations**: Automate the selection of environment configurations during deployment to prevent human errors.

This modular approach ensures that your FastAPI application remains scalable, secure, and adaptable to varied environments.

Config File Formats (YAML, JSON, .env)

Configuration files, essentially, are the bases for managing application settings, offering a single-point interface for handling environment-specific variables. YAML, JSON, and .env files are a popular format, each with its strengths. YAML files are great at being read, as they can represent complex hierarchies that make them ideal for large-scale configurations. JSON files are also widely supported and easy to parse. They provide a structured format that can easily integrate with APIs and libraries .env files are lightweight and straightforward, and are primarily used for storing key-value pairs such as API keys and environment-specific secrets.

Overview of Popular Configuration File Formats

FastAPI supports several configuration file formats, each suited to different needs. The most commonly used formats are **YAML**, **JSON**, and **.env**. Each offers unique features and levels of simplicity, making them versatile tools for managing application configurations effectively.

- **YAML (Yet Another Markup Language)**: Ideal for complex, nested configurations, YAML is favored for its readability and integration with tools such as Kubernetes.
- **JSON (JavaScript Object Notation)**: Lightweight and API-friendly, JSON works well for projects with frequent communication between frontend and backend systems.
- **.env Files**: Simple and concise, `.env` files store environment variables, often used for managing sensitive or environment-specific configurations.

Pros and Cons of Each Format

Here is the tabular view of Pros and Cons

Format	Pros	Cons
YAML	Human-readable, supports nesting	Requires additional parsing library
JSON	Simple, widely supported, native to Python	Difficult for deeply nested configs
.env	Easy setup, minimalistic	Limited structure, only key-value pairs

Table 12.1: *Pros and cons of each format*

Example Structures for FastAPI Applications

Here is the syntactic example:

- **YAML Example:**

```
app:
  name: FastAPIApp
  version: 1.0
database:
  host: localhost
  port: 5432
```

- **JSON Example:**

```
{
  "app": {
    "name": "FastAPIApp",
    "version": "1.0"
  },
  "database": {
    "host": "localhost",
    "port": 5432
  }
}
```

- **.env Example:**

```
APP_NAME=FastAPIApp
APP_VERSION=1.0
DB_HOST=localhost
DB_PORT=5432
```

These file formats enable clear, scalable, and secure application configuration management, catering to varied development and deployment needs.

Securely Handling Sensitive Data

Securing sensitive data is very critical as the applications are protected from vulnerability and unauthorized access. Any sensitive information, such as database credentials, API keys, or encryption secrets, should never be hardcoded into the source code. Instead, they are stored in environment variables or the secret management tools provided by cloud platforms such as AWS Secrets Manager, Azure Key Vault, or Google Secret Manager. The least privilege principle dictates that only those services or individuals that require access to these secrets should be granted such access. Additionally, encryption of data both at rest and in transit will ensure further security and industry compliance.

Techniques for Managing Sensitive Information

Handling sensitive information such as API keys, database credentials, and passwords is critical in any FastAPI application to ensure data privacy and security. Here are some effective techniques:

- **Environment Variables**: Store sensitive data in environment variables using `.env` files and libraries such as **`python-dotenv`**. This ensures secrets are kept out of the source code.
- **Configuration Files**: Encrypt sensitive data in configuration files and restrict access to these files by setting proper file permissions.
- **Secret Management Services**: Use tools such as AWS Secrets Manager, Azure Key Vault, or HashiCorp Vault to store and retrieve sensitive data securely. These services provide encryption, access controls, and rotation features.

Example using `python-dotenv`:

```
from dotenv import load_dotenv
import os

load_dotenv()  # Load environment variables from .env file
DATABASE_URL = os.getenv("DATABASE_URL")
```

Leveraging Secret Managers or Encrypted Storage Solutions

Secret management tools allow for centralized, secure handling of sensitive data:

- **AWS Secrets Manager**: Automatically rotates secrets and provides secure access through APIs.
- **HashiCorp Vault**: A robust open-source tool for storing and accessing secrets, with encryption, audit logs, and access control policies.
- **Kubernetes Secrets**: For containerized environments, Kubernetes allows storing secrets in **`ConfigMaps`** or as encrypted data, accessible only by the pods requiring them.

Example: Storing a secret in HashiCorp Vault:

1. **Store a secret:**

   ```
   vault kv put secret/api-key value=my-secret-key
   ```

2. **Access the secret in Python:**

```
import hvac
client = hvac.Client(url="http://127.0.0.1:8200")
client.token = "your-vault-token"
secret = client.secrets.kv.v2.read_secret_version(path="api-key")
print(secret["data"]["data"]["value"])
```

Best Practices to Prevent Leaks of Sensitive Data

Protecting sensitive data is crucial to maintaining security and privacy in applications. Best practices include storing secrets in environment variables, using encrypted vaults, restricting access with proper permissions, and avoiding hardcoding credentials in source code.

- **Avoid Hardcoding Secrets**: Never embed sensitive data directly in source code or version control systems such as Git.
- **Access Control**: Ensure only authorized personnel and services can access sensitive data.
- **Encryption**: Always encrypt sensitive data both in transit (for example, TLS/SSL) and at rest (for example, AES).
- **Regular Rotation**: Rotate API keys, passwords, and certificates periodically to limit exposure in case of leaks.
- **Audit and Monitoring**: Track access to sensitive data and implement monitoring tools to detect anomalies.
- **Secrets in Containers**: Use `docker secrets` or Kubernetes secrets to handle sensitive data in containerized applications.

By implementing these techniques and best practices, FastAPI developers can effectively safeguard sensitive information, ensuring compliance with security standards and protecting application data from breaches.

Configuration Management Tools and Libraries

Robust tools for configuration management should give flexibility, scalability, and security. Among the popularly used libraries to simplify managing configurations in FastAPI are Pydantic Settings and Dynaconf. In the case of Pydantic Settings, it actually uses Pydantic models. The developers can now define and validate configuration data using Python classes, maintaining consistency and type safety. On the other hand,

Dynaconf provides a very flexible mechanism for loading configuration values from a variety of sources: environment variables, files (YAML, JSON, TOML), and even remote services such as Vault or S3. These tools provide central management of application configurations and ensure that configurations can be easily adjusted across different environments.

Introduction to Pydantic Settings and Dynaconf

Effective configuration management is vital for FastAPI applications to handle diverse environments and maintain scalability. Two widely used tools for managing configurations in Python-based projects are **Pydantic Settings** and **Dynaconf**. Both libraries simplify handling configurations and enable secure, modular setups for development, testing, and production environments.

- **Pydantic Settings**: Part of the Pydantic library, it enables defining configurations as structured models. It provides type validation, environment variable support, and seamless integration with FastAPI.
- **Dynaconf**: A versatile library for managing settings dynamically. It supports multiple configuration sources (for example, environment variables, .env files, YAML, JSON) and offers layered configurations for various environments.

Step-by-Step Guide to Implementing Pydantic Settings

A step-by-step guide to implementing Pydantic Settings involves defining a Pydantic model to structure and validate the configuration data, followed by loading environment variables or configuration files. By using Pydantic's **`BaseSettings`**, you can automatically load and validate settings while ensuring type safety and consistency across different environments.

1. **Install Pydantic:**

   ```
   pip install pydantic
   ```

2. **Define a Configuration Class:**

   Use the **`BaseSettings`** class from Pydantic to define your settings.

   ```
   from pydantic import BaseSettings

   class Settings(BaseSettings):
       database_url: str
       api_key: str
   ```

```
    class Config:
        env_file = ".env"
```

3. **Load Settings in FastAPI:**

   Instantiate the `Settings` class and use it across your app.

   ```
   from fastapi import FastAPI
   app = FastAPI()
   settings = Settings()

   @app.get("/")
   def read_config():
       return {"database_url": settings.database_url}
   ```

4. **Environment File Example:**

   ```
   DATABASE_URL=postgresql://user:password@localhost/dbname
   API_KEY=12345
   ```

Step-by-Step Guide to Implementing Dynaconf

A step-by-step guide to implementing Dynaconf involves installing the library, creating a configuration file (for example, `settings.toml`), and defining settings in a centralized manner. Dynaconf allows you to load configurations from multiple sources, including environment variables, and supports multi-environment setups to manage development, staging, and production configurations seamlessly.

1. **Install Dynaconf:**

   ```
   pip install dynaconf
   ```

2. **Initialize Configuration:**

   Create a `settings.py` file and configure Dynaconf.

   ```
   from dynaconf import Dynaconf
   settings = Dynaconf(
       settings_files=["settings.yaml", ".secrets.yaml"]
   )
   ```

3. **Use Configuration in FastAPI:**

   Access settings directly in your application.

   ```
   @app.get("/")
   def read_dynaconf():
       return {"db_url": settings.database_url}
   ```

4. **Example `settings.yaml`:**

```
default:
  database_url: "sqlite:///default.db"
development:
  database_url: "sqlite:///dev.db"
```

5. **Environment-Specific Configurations:**

   Run the application with different environments:

   `export ENV_FOR_DYNACONF=development`

Comparing Features and Scenarios for Choosing the Right Tool

Here is the comparison between these two scenarios:

Feature	Pydantic Settings	Dynaconf
Validation	Strong type validation	Flexible, less strict
Ease of Use	Simple, direct	Rich, more customizable
Environment Support	Built-in	Advanced layered support
Configuration Sources	.env only	.env, YAML, JSON, etc.
Best For	Lightweight apps	Complex multi-env setups

Table 12.2: *Comparing Features and Scenarios for Choosing the Right Tool*

Choosing the Right Tool

- Use **Pydantic Settings** for smaller projects requiring strict validation and minimal configurations.
- Opt for **Dynaconf** for larger applications with multi-environment needs and diverse configuration sources.

Both tools enhance configuration management in FastAPI applications, enabling secure, scalable, and maintainable setups tailored to diverse requirements.

Conclusion

Managing application configuration is a cornerstone of developing robust, scalable, and secure FastAPI applications. This chapter explored essential strategies for handling configurations effectively, catering to different environments such as development, testing, and production. By leveraging environment variables, developers can decouple sensitive settings such as API keys and database credentials from the source code, reducing the risk of accidental leaks. The comparison of popular configuration file formats, including .env, YAML, and JSON, highlighted their strengths and use cases, providing practical guidance for choosing the right format for a project. The chapter also emphasized securely handling sensitive data, discussing methods such as secret managers, encrypted storage solutions, and adherence to best practices. Tools such as Pydantic Settings and Dynaconf were introduced to streamline configuration management, with detailed, step-by-step implementations to showcase their functionality in FastAPI. These tools not only simplify managing configurations but also enable dynamic adjustments for environment-specific settings, enhancing flexibility and maintainability. By the end of the chapter, readers should feel equipped to implement comprehensive configuration strategies that enhance the scalability and security of their applications, laying a strong foundation for handling real-world challenges.

With a solid understanding of managing application configurations, the next chapter shifts focus to ***Building Practical Projects.*** This chapter will bring all the foundational concepts covered so far into actionable scenarios by guiding readers through the development of real-world FastAPI applications. Readers will learn to integrate features such as authentication, database management, and file handling into cohesive, functional projects. Whether it is creating a task manager or a blog platform, the chapter will provide step-by-step tutorials, emphasizing modularity and scalability. This hands-on approach will solidify the theoretical knowledge and empower readers to build their own solutions tailored to specific requirements.

CHAPTER 13
Building Practical Projects

Introduction

Mastery of FastAPI is achieved through the creation of hands-on projects that integrate all the concepts learned during the book. This chapter closes the gap between practice and theory by walking you through three practical projects intended to solidify FastAPI's fundamental features, ranging from routing, dependency injection, and database integration. The Simple To-Do API is the first project, which prioritizes simple CRUD operations, request validation, and data storage, and it is a great starting point for beginners. The second, a more sophisticated E-commerce API, adds model relationships, user authentication, cart management, and order processing–providing a deeper exploration of intermediate-level FastAPI features.

The third project, a Social Media API, models key functionality of Twitter or Instagram-style platforms. It features user authentication, posting creation, handling of interactions, and database performance optimization for scalability. As a whole, these projects double as exercises and reusable templates for actual APIs. By progressing from simple to complex implementations, you will build a strong foundation in API development, covering everything from CRUD to secure, scalable architecture. Let us now explore the structure of this chapter and how each project is laid out.

Structure

In this chapter, we will cover the following topics:

- **Example Project 1: Simple To-Do API**
  - Setting Up the Project Environment and Structure
  - CRUD Operations for Managing Tasks
  - Request Validation Using Pydantic Models
  - Data Persistence Using an SQLite Database

- **Example Project 2: E-commerce API**
  - Setting Up the Project with User Authentication
  - Designing Models for Products, Categories, and Orders
  - Implementing Cart and Checkout Functionality
  - Managing User Authentication with JWT
- **Example Project 3: Social Media API**
  - Setting Up the Social Media Project
  - Creating User Registration and Authentication Systems
  - Implementing Post Creation, Deletion, and Interaction Features (likes/ comments)
  - Database Optimization for Handling Large Volumes of Data
  - Structuring APIs for Scalability and Modularity

Example Project 1: Simple To-Do API

To start creating the Simple To-Do API, it is crucial to have a clean and well-structured project environment. This involves creating a virtual environment, installing FastAPI and other dependencies, and having a logical folder structure for routes, models, and configuration. Having this setup in place ensures that the project is scalable and maintainable as it evolves.

Setting Up the Project Environment and Structure

Begin by creating a new FastAPI project. Install the required dependencies using `pip`:

```
pip install fastapi uvicorn pydantic sqlalchemy
```

Next, organize the project directory. A suggested structure:

```
to_do_api/
│
├── main.py  # Entry point
├── models.py  # Database models
├── schemas.py  # Pydantic models for validation
├── database.py  # Database connection setup
├── crud.py  # CRUD operation logic
└── requirements.txt  # Dependencies
```

CRUD Operations for Managing Tasks

Define basic CRUD endpoints in **main.py**:

- **Create a Task**: Add a task to the database.
- **Read Tasks**: Retrieve all tasks or a specific task.
- **Update a Task**: Modify task attributes.
- **Delete a Task**: Remove a task by its ID.

Example:

```
from fastapi import FastAPI
from schemas import TaskCreate
from crud import create_task

app = FastAPI()

@app.post("/tasks/")
def add_task(task: TaskCreate):
    return create_task(task)
```

Request Validation Using Pydantic Models

In **schemas.py**, define the Pydantic models for tasks:

```
from pydantic import BaseModel

class TaskBase(BaseModel):
    title: str
    description: str

class TaskCreate(TaskBase):
    pass

class Task(TaskBase):
    id: int

    class Config:
        orm_mode = True
```

This ensures data integrity for incoming and outgoing requests.

Data Persistence Using an SQLite Database

Set up the database connection in **database.py** and create a Task model in **models.py** using SQLAlchemy:

```
from sqlalchemy import Column, Integer, String
from database import Base

class Task(Base):
    __tablename__ = "tasks"
    id = Column(Integer, primary_key=True, index=True)
    title = Column(String, index=True)
    description = Column(String)
```

Run migrations to create the database schema.

Optional Features:

- **Task Prioritization**: Add a priority field to tasks.
- **Completion Status**: Include a **`completed`** Boolean flag.

Example Use Case:

1. User submits a POST request to **`/tasks/`** to create a task.
2. Task details are validated using Pydantic models and stored in the database.
3. User retrieves tasks via a GET request, optionally filtered by priority or status.

Example Project 2: E-Commerce API

The E-Commerce API project introduces a more complex application structure involving users, products, carts, and orders. Before implementing the features, it is important to prepare the environment by installing necessary libraries, setting up the database, and configuring authentication. A well-organized project setup will streamline development and allow easy expansion as more features are added.

Setting up the E-Commerce API Project

Begin by setting up a FastAPI environment for the e-commerce API. Install the necessary dependencies:

```
pip install fastapi uvicorn sqlalchemy pydantic
```

Organize the project directory structure for better scalability:

```
ecommerce_api/
│
├── main.py          # Entry point for the API
├── models.py        # Database models
├── schemas.py       # Pydantic schemas
├── database.py      # Database setup
├── crud.py          # Business logic for CRUD operations
└── requirements.txt # Project dependencies
```

Database Models for Products and Orders

In **models.py**, define database models using SQLAlchemy for **Product** and **Order** tables:

```
from sqlalchemy import Column, Integer, String, Float
from database import Base

class Product(Base):
    __tablename__ = "products"
    id = Column(Integer, primary_key=True, index=True)
    name = Column(String, index=True)
    description = Column(String)
    price = Column(Float)
    stock = Column(Integer)

class Order(Base):
    __tablename__ = "orders"
    id = Column(Integer, primary_key=True, index=True)
    product_id = Column(Integer)
    quantity = Column(Integer)
    total_price = Column(Float)
```

CRUD Endpoints for Products

Add endpoints in **main.py** for managing products:

- **Create Product**: Add a new product to the inventory.
- **Read Products**: Retrieve the list of products or a specific product by ID.
- **Update Product**: Modify product details, such as price or stock.
- **Delete Product**: Remove a product by ID.

Example for adding a product:

```
from fastapi import FastAPI
from schemas import ProductCreate
from crud import create_product

app = FastAPI()

@app.post("/products/")
def add_product(product: ProductCreate):
    return create_product(product)
```

Order Management

Define endpoints for managing orders:

- **Place an Order**: Validate the product's availability, calculate the total price, and reduce stock.
- **Retrieve Orders**: Fetch all orders or specific orders by ID.
- **Cancel an Order**: Restore stock if an order is canceled.

Example of an order schema in **schemas.py**:

```
from pydantic import BaseModel

class OrderCreate(BaseModel):
    product_id: int
    quantity: int

class Order(BaseModel):
    id: int
    product_id: int
    quantity: int
    total_price: float

    class Config:
        orm_mode = True
```

Validation and Error Handling

Use Pydantic models to validate incoming requests, such as checking for stock availability before placing an order. Return appropriate error messages for invalid inputs.

Optional Features:

- Add user authentication for order management.
- Include product categories for better organization.
- Implement pagination for large product lists.

Example Project 3: Social Media API

The Social Media API project aims to replicate core features of modern social platforms, such as user interactions, posts, and comments. Setting up this project involves configuring the database for relational data, installing dependencies, and preparing modules for authentication and content handling. A solid initial setup is crucial to ensure the system remains scalable and responsive under heavy user activity.

Setting Up the Social Media API

The Social Media API project focuses on core functionalities such as user management, posts, comments, and likes. Start by setting up the environment:

Install necessary libraries:

```
pip install fastapi uvicorn sqlalchemy pydantic
```

Organize the project structure:

```
social_media_api/
│
├── main.py            # Application entry point
├── models.py          # Database models for users, posts, and comments
├── schemas.py         # Pydantic schemas for request and response models
├── database.py        # Database connection and initialization
├── crud.py            # CRUD logic for database operations
└── requirements.txt   # Dependencies
```

Database Models for Users and Posts

In **models.py**, define tables for **User**, **Post**, and **Comment** using SQLAlchemy:

```
from sqlalchemy import Column, Integer, String, Text, ForeignKey
from database import Base
from sqlalchemy.orm import relationship

class User(Base):
    __tablename__ = "users"
    id = Column(Integer, primary_key=True, index=True)
    username = Column(String, unique=True, index=True)
    email = Column(String, unique=True, index=True)
    hashed_password = Column(String)

    posts = relationship("Post", back_populates="owner")

class Post(Base):
    __tablename__ = "posts"
    id = Column(Integer, primary_key=True, index=True)
    title = Column(String)
    content = Column(Text)
    owner_id = Column(Integer, ForeignKey("users.id"))

    owner = relationship("User", back_populates="posts")
```

```
    comments = relationship("Comment", back_populates="post")

class Comment(Base):
    __tablename__ = "comments"
    id = Column(Integer, primary_key=True, index=True)
    content = Column(Text)
    post_id = Column(Integer, ForeignKey("posts.id"))

    post = relationship("Post", back_populates="comments")
```

User Authentication

Set up user registration and authentication using FastAPI's **`OAuth2PasswordBearer`** and `JWT` tokens. Include endpoints for:

- **Register User**: Accept a username, email, and password. Hash the password before storing it.
- **Login User**: Verify credentials and return a JWT token.

Example for user registration:

```
from fastapi import FastAPI, HTTPException
from schemas import UserCreate
from crud import create_user

app = FastAPI()

@app.post("/register/")
def register_user(user: UserCreate):
    try:
        return create_user(user)
    except Exception as e:
        raise HTTPException(status_code=400, detail=str(e))
```

Post and Comment Management

Define endpoints to create, retrieve, update, and delete posts and comments:

- **Create Post**: Accept a title and content and associate it with the authenticated user.
- **List Posts**: Retrieve all posts with optional filters (for example, by user).
- **Add Comment**: Allow users to comment on posts.
- **List Comments**: Fetch all comments for a specific post.

Example endpoint for adding a post:

```
from fastapi import Depends, HTTPException
from schemas import PostCreate
from crud import create_post
from dependencies import get_current_user

@app.post("/posts/")
def add_post(post: PostCreate, user: User = Depends(get_current_
user)):
    return create_post(post, user.id)
```

Like and Follow Functionality

Extend the API to include social interactions:

- **Like Post**: Toggle a like for a post by a user.
- **Follow User**: Allow users to follow/unfollow each other.
- **List Followers/Following**: Retrieve a user's follower/following list.

Security and Data Validation

Use Pydantic schemas for request validation and ensure security best practices:

- Hash and securely store passwords.
- Validate all inputs (for example, for special characters or SQL injection).
- Secure sensitive endpoints using JWT tokens.

Testing and Deployment

Test the Social Media API with pytest for unit and integration tests. Deploy the application on a cloud platform (for example, AWS or Heroku) with Docker for containerization.

Code

The complete code for this section will be available on our GitHub page: https://github.com/OrangeAVA/Building-High-Performance-Web-APIs-with-FAST-API

Code for Simple To-Do API

Directory Structure

```
simple_todo_api/
├── main.py            # Application entry point
├── models.py          # SQLAlchemy models
├── schemas.py         # Pydantic schemas
├── crud.py            # CRUD operations
├── database.py        # Database configuration
├── dependencies.py    # Dependencies for authentication
├── tests/             # Unit and integration tests
│   ├── test_todo.py
└── requirements.txt  # Dependencies
```

Dependencies (`requirements.txt`)

```
fastapi==0.95.1
uvicorn==0.23.0
sqlalchemy==2.0.10
pydantic==1.10.7
asyncpg==0.30.0
```

Install using

```
pip install -r requirements.txt
```

Database Configuration (`database.py`)

```
from sqlalchemy import create_engine
from sqlalchemy.ext.asyncio import create_async_engine,
AsyncSession
from sqlalchemy.orm import sessionmaker, declarative_base
from sqlalchemy.future import select

DATABASE_URL = "postgresql+asyncpg://user:password@localhost/
todo_db"  # Use asyncpg for PostgreSQL

# Create the async engine
engine = create_async_engine(DATABASE_URL, echo=True)

# SessionLocal for async database session
AsyncSessionLocal = sessionmaker(
    engine, class_=AsyncSession, expire_on_commit=False, future=True
)

Base = declarative_base()

# Dependency to get async DB session
```

```
async def get_db():
    async with AsyncSessionLocal() as session:
        yield session
```

Models (`models.py`)

```
from sqlalchemy import Column, Integer, String, Boolean
from database import Base

class ToDoItem(Base):
    __tablename__ = "todo_items"

    id = Column(Integer, primary_key=True, index=True)
    title = Column(String, index=True)
    description = Column(String, nullable=True)
    completed = Column(Boolean, default=False)
```

Schemas (`schemas.py`)

```
from pydantic import BaseModel
class ToDoBase(BaseModel):
    title: str
    description: str | None = None

class ToDoCreate(ToDoBase):
    pass

class ToDoUpdate(BaseModel):
    title: str | None = None
    description: str | None = None
    completed: bool | None = None

class ToDoResponse(ToDoBase):
    id: int
    completed: bool

    class Config:
        orm_mode = True
```

CRUD Operations (`crud.py`)

```
from sqlalchemy.ext.asyncio import AsyncSession
from sqlalchemy.future import select
from models import ToDoItem
from schemas import ToDoCreate, ToDoUpdate
from fastapi import HTTPException

async def create_todo_item(db: AsyncSession, todo: ToDoCreate):
    db_item = ToDoItem(**todo.dict())
```

```
    db.add(db_item)
    await db.commit()
    await db.refresh(db_item)
    return db_item

async def get_todo_items(db: AsyncSession):
    result = await db.execute(select(ToDoItem))
    return result.scalars().all()

async def get_todo_item_by_id(db: AsyncSession, item_id: int):
    result = await db.execute(select(ToDoItem).filter(ToDoItem.id
== item_id))
    return result.scalars().first()

async def update_todo_item(db: AsyncSession, item_id: int, todo_
update: ToDoUpdate):
    db_item = await get_todo_item_by_id(db, item_id)
    if not db_item:
        raise HTTPException(status_code=404, detail="Item not
found")
    for key, value in todo_update.dict(exclude_unset=True).
items():
        setattr(db_item, key, value)
    await db.commit()
    await db.refresh(db_item)
    return db_item

async def delete_todo_item(db: AsyncSession, item_id: int):
    db_item = await get_todo_item_by_id(db, item_id)
    if not db_item:
        raise HTTPException(status_code=404, detail="Item not
found")
    await db.delete(db_item)
    await db.commit()
    return db_item
```

Main Application (main.py)

```
from fastapi import FastAPI, Depends, HTTPException
from sqlalchemy.orm import Session
from database import Base, engine, get_db
from schemas import ToDoCreate, ToDoResponse, ToDoUpdate
from crud import create_todo_item, get_todo_items, update_todo_
item, delete_todo_item

Base.metadata.create_all(bind=engine)

app = FastAPI()
```

```
@app.post("/todos/", response_model=ToDoResponse)
async def add_todo(todo: ToDoCreate, db: Session = Depends
(get_db)):
    return await create_todo_item(db, todo)

@app.get("/todos/", response_model=list[ToDoResponse])
async def list_todos(db: Session = Depends(get_db)):
    return await get_todo_items(db)

@app.get("/todos/{item_id}/", response_model=ToDoResponse)
async def get_todo(item_id: int, db: Session = Depends(get_db)):
    item = await get_todo_item_by_id(db, item_id)
    if not item:
        raise HTTPException(status_code=404, detail="Item not
found")
    return item

@app.put("/todos/{item_id}/", response_model=ToDoResponse)
async def modify_todo(item_id: int, todo_update: ToDoUpdate, db:
Session = Depends(get_db)):
    return await update_todo_item(db, item_id, todo_update)

@app.delete("/todos/{item_id}/", response_model=ToDoResponse)
async def remove_todo(item_id: int, db: Session = Depends(get_
db)):
    return await delete_todo_item(db, item_id)
```

FastAPI Routes:

- **`POST /todos/`**: Create a new to-do item.
- **`GET /todos/`**: List all to-do items.
- **`GET /todos/{item_id}/`**: Get a specific to-do item.
- **`PUT /todos/{item_id}/`**: Update an existing to-do item.
- **`DELETE /todos/{item_id}/`**: Delete a to-do item.

Testing

Create unit tests to verify the API works as expected.

tests/test_todo.py

```
from fastapi.testclient import TestClient
from main import app

client = TestClient(app)
```

```
def test_create_todo():
    response = client.post("/todos/", json={"title": "Test Todo",
"description": "Test Description"})
    assert response.status_code == 200
    assert response.json()["title"] == "Test Todo"

def test_list_todos():
    response = client.get("/todos/")
    assert response.status_code == 200
    assert isinstance(response.json(), list)

def test_update_todo():
    # Assume the first item exists
    response = client.put("/todos/1/", json={"title": "Updated
Todo"})
    assert response.status_code == 200
    assert response.json()["title"] == "Updated Todo"

def test_delete_todo():
    response = client.delete("/todos/1/")
    assert response.status_code == 200
```

Run and Test

1. **Run the server:**

   ```
   uvicorn app.main:app --reload
   ```

2. **Open your browser and navigate to:**
   - API docs: **`http://127.0.0.1:8000/docs`**
   - Test endpoints interactively.

E-commerce API Code

Directory Structure:

```
ecommerce_api/
├── main.py            # Application entry point
├── models.py          # SQLAlchemy models
├── schemas.py         # Pydantic schemas
├── crud.py            # CRUD operations
├── database.py        # Database configuration
├── dependencies.py    # Dependencies for authentication
├── tests/             # Unit and integration tests
│   ├── test_products.py
│   ├── test_orders.py
└── requirements.txt   # Dependencies
```

Dependencies (`requirements.txt`)

```
fastapi==0.95.1
uvicorn==0.23.0
sqlalchemy==2.0.10
pydantic==1.10.7
```

User Management

Define the User model, authentication routes, and token management.

```
from fastapi import FastAPI, Depends, HTTPException, status
from pydantic import BaseModel
from sqlalchemy import create_engine, Column, Integer, String,
Boolean
from sqlalchemy.ext.declarative import declarative_base
from sqlalchemy.orm import sessionmaker
from passlib.context import CryptContext
from jose import JWTError, jwt
from datetime import datetime, timedelta

# Basic setup
SECRET_KEY = "your_secret_key"
ALGORITHM = "HS256"
ACCESS_TOKEN_EXPIRE_MINUTES = 30

Base = declarative_base()
engine = create_engine("sqlite:///ecommerce.db")
SessionLocal = sessionmaker(bind=engine)

app = FastAPI()

# Models
class User(Base):
    __tablename__ = "users"
    id = Column(Integer, primary_key=True, index=True)
    username = Column(String, unique=True, index=True)
    email = Column(String, unique=True, index=True)
    hashed_password = Column(String)
    is_admin = Column(Boolean, default=False)
    is_active = Column(Boolean, default=True)

Base.metadata.create_all(bind=engine)

# Password hashing
pwd_context = CryptContext(schemes=["bcrypt"], deprecated="auto")

def verify_password(plain_password, hashed_password):
```

```
    return pwd_context.verify(plain_password, hashed_password)

def get_password_hash(password):
    return pwd_context.hash(password)

# Token generation
def create_access_token(data: dict, expires_delta: timedelta
= None):
    to_encode = data.copy()
    if expires_delta:
        expire = datetime.utcnow() + expires_delta
    else:
        expire = datetime.utcnow() + timedelta(minutes=15)
    to_encode.update({"exp": expire})
    return jwt.encode(to_encode, SECRET_KEY, algorithm=ALGORITHM)

# Schemas
class UserCreate(BaseModel):
    username: str
    email: str
    password: str

class Token(BaseModel):
    access_token: str
    token_type: str

@app.post("/signup")
def signup(user: UserCreate):
    hashed_password = pwd_context.hash(user.password)
    db_user = User(username=user.username, email=user.email,
hashed_password=hashed_password, is_admin=False)
    session.add(db_user)
    session.commit()
    return {"message": "User registered successfully"}

@app.post("/login")
def login(user: UserLogin):
    db_user = session.query(User).filter(User.email == user.
email).first()
    if not db_user or not pwd_context.verify(user.password, db_
user.hashed_password):
        raise HTTPException(status_code=401, detail="Invalid
credentials")
    access_token = create_access_token(data={"sub": db_user.user-
name, "is_admin": db_user.is_admin})
    return {"access_token": access_token}
```

Product Management

Define models, schemas, and routes to manage products.

```
class Product(Base):
    __tablename__ = "products"
    id = Column(Integer, primary_key=True, index=True)
    name = Column(String, index=True)
    description = Column(String)
    price = Column(Integer)
    stock = Column(Integer)

class ProductCreate(BaseModel):
    name: str
    description: str
    price: int
    stock: int

@app.get("/products")
def get_products(search: str = None, min_price: int = 0, max_
price: int = 100000):
    query = session.query(Product)
    if search:
        query = query.filter(Product.name.ilike(f"%{search}%"))
    if min_price or max_price:
        query = query.filter(Product.price.between(min_price,
max_price))
    return query.all()

@app.post("/products")
def add_product(product: ProductCreate, user: User = Depends
(get_current_user)):
    if not user.is_admin:
        raise HTTPException(status_code=403, detail="Permission
denied")
    db_product = Product(**product.dict())
    session.add(db_product)
    session.commit()
    return {"message": "Product added successfully"}
```

Cart Management

Add, update, and view items in the cart.

```
class Cart(Base):
    __tablename__ = "cart"
    id = Column(Integer, primary_key=True, index=True)
    user_id = Column(Integer)
    product_id = Column(Integer)
```

```
    quantity = Column(Integer)

@app.post("/cart")
def add_to_cart(cart_item: CartItemCreate, user: User = Depends
(get_current_user)):
    product = session.query(Product).filter(Product.id == cart_
item.product_id).first()
    if not product or product.stock < cart_item.quantity:
        raise HTTPException(status_code=400, detail="Insufficient
stock")
    existing_cart_item = session.query(Cart).filter(Cart.user_id
== user.id, Cart.product_id == cart_item.product_id).first()
    if existing_cart_item:
        existing_cart_item.quantity += cart_item.quantity
    else:
        db_cart_item = Cart(user_id=user.id, **cart_item.dict())
        session.add(db_cart_item)
    session.commit()
    return {"message": "Cart updated"}

@app.get("/cart/{user_id}")
def get_cart(user_id: int):
    session = SessionLocal()
    cart_items = session.query(Cart).filter(Cart.user_id == user_
id).all()
    session.close()
    return cart_items
```

Wishlist

Manage wishlist functionality.

```
class Wishlist(Base):
    __tablename__ = "wishlist"
    id = Column(Integer, primary_key=True, index=True)
    user_id = Column(Integer)
    product_id = Column(Integer)

@app.post("/wishlist")
def add_to_wishlist(product_id: int, user: User = Depends
(get_current_user)):
    db_wishlist = Wishlist(user_id=user.id, product_id=product_id)
    session.add(db_wishlist)
    session.commit()
    return {"message": "Added to wishlist"}

@app.get("/wishlist")
def get_wishlist(user: User = Depends(get_current_user)):
```

```
    wishlist_items = session.query(Wishlist).filter(Wishlist.user_
id == user.id).all()
    return wishlist_items
```

Order Processing and Payment Integration

Handle order placement and payment.

```
class Order(Base):
    __tablename__ = "orders"
    id = Column(Integer, primary_key=True, index=True)
    user_id = Column(Integer)
    product_id = Column(Integer)
    quantity = Column(Integer)
    total_price = Column(Integer)

@app.post("/orders")
def create_order(user: User = Depends(get_current_user)):
    cart_items = session.query(Cart).filter(Cart.user_id == user.
id).all()
    if not cart_items:
        raise HTTPException(status_code=400, detail="Cart is empty")
    for item in cart_items:
        product = session.query(Product).filter(Product.id == item.
product_id).first()
        if product.stock < item.quantity:
            raise HTTPException(status_code=400, detail=f"Insuffi-
cient stock for {product.name}")
        product.stock -= item.quantity
        db_order = Order(user_id=user.id, product_id=item.product
_id, quantity=item.quantity, total_price=product.price * item.
quantity)
        session.add(db_order)
        session.delete(item)
    session.commit()
    return {"message": "Order placed successfully"}
```

Advanced Features

- **Customer Reviews:** Allow users to leave reviews and ratings for products.

```
class Review(Base):
    __tablename__ = "reviews"
    id = Column(Integer, primary_key=True)
    user_id = Column(Integer)
    product_id = Column(Integer)
    rating = Column(Integer)
    review_text = Column(String)
```

```
@app.post("/reviews")
def add_review(review: ReviewCreate, user: User = Depends(get_
current_user)):
    db_review = Review(user_id=user.id, **review.dict())
    session.add(db_review)
    session.commit()
    return {"message": "Review added successfully"}
```

- **Promotions and Coupons:** Allow users to apply promo codes for discounts.

```
class Coupon(Base):
    __tablename__ = "coupons"
    id = Column(Integer, primary_key=True)
    code = Column(String, unique=True)
    discount_percentage = Column(Integer)
    is_active = Column(Boolean, default=True)

@app.post("/apply-coupon")
def apply_coupon(code: str, user: User = Depends(get_current_
user)):
    coupon = session.query(Coupon).filter(Coupon.code == code,
Coupon.is_active == True).first()
    if not coupon:
        raise HTTPException(status_code=400, detail="Invalid or
expired coupon")
    return {"message": f"Coupon applied. {coupon.discount_
percentage}% discount available"}
```

Social Media API Code

User Management

```
class User(Base):
    __tablename__ = "users"
    id = Column(Integer, primary_key=True, index=True)
    username = Column(String, unique=True, index=True)
    email = Column(String, unique=True, index=True)
    hashed_password = Column(String)

# Registration and login
@app.post("/signup")
def signup(user: UserCreate):
    hashed_password = pwd_context.hash(user.password)
    db_user = User(username=user.username, email=user.email,
hashed_password=hashed_password)
    session.add(db_user)
    session.commit()
    return {"message": "User registered successfully"}
```

```
@app.post("/login")
def login(user: UserLogin):
    db_user = session.query(User).filter(User.email == user.
email).first()
    if not db_user or not pwd_context.verify(user.password,
db_user.hashed_password):
        raise HTTPException(status_code=401, detail="Invalid
credentials")
    access_token = create_access_token(data={"sub": db_user.user-
name})
    return {"access_token": access_token}
```

User Posts

```
class Post(Base):
    __tablename__ = "posts"
    id = Column(Integer, primary_key=True)
    user_id = Column(Integer, ForeignKey("users.id"))
    content = Column(String)
    created_at = Column(DateTime, default=datetime.utcnow)

@app.post("/posts")
def create_post(post: PostCreate, user: User = Depends
(get_current_user)):
    db_post = Post(user_id=user.id, **post.dict())
    session.add(db_post)
    session.commit()
    return {"message": "Post created successfully"}

@app.get("/posts")
def get_user_posts(user: User = Depends(get_current_user)):
    posts = session.query(Post).filter(Post.user_id == user.id).
all()
    return posts
```

Likes and Comments

```
class Like(Base):
    __tablename__ = "likes"
    id = Column(Integer, primary_key=True)
    user_id = Column(Integer, ForeignKey("users.id"))
    post_id = Column(Integer, ForeignKey("posts.id"))

class Comment(Base):
    __tablename__ = "comments"
    id = Column(Integer, primary_key=True)
    user_id = Column(Integer, ForeignKey("users.id"))
```

```
    post_id = Column(Integer, ForeignKey("posts.id"))
    comment = Column(String)

@app.post("/like")
def like_post(post_id: int, user: User = Depends(get_current_
user)):
    db_like = Like(user_id=user.id, post_id=post_id)
    session.add(db_like)
    session.commit()
    return {"message": "Post liked"}

@app.post("/comment")
def comment_on_post(post_id: int, comment: str, user: User
 = Depends(get_current_user)):
    db_comment = Comment(user_id=user.id, post_id=post_id,
comment=comment)
    session.add(db_comment)
    session.commit()
    return {"message": "Comment added"}
```

Notifications

```
class Notification(Base):
    __tablename__ = "notifications"
    id = Column(Integer, primary_key=True)
    user_id = Column(Integer, ForeignKey("users.id"))
    message = Column(String)
    is_read = Column(Boolean, default=False)

@app.post("/notifications")
def create_notification(user: User, message: str):
    db_notification = Notification(user_id=user.id,
message=message)
    session.add(db_notification)
    session.commit()
    return {"message": "Notification sent"}

@app.get("/notifications")
def get_notifications(user: User = Depends(get_current_user)):
    notifications = session.query(Notification).filter(Notification.
user_id == user.id).all()
    return notifications
```

Friendships

```
class Friendship(Base):
    __tablename__ = "friendships"
    id = Column(Integer, primary_key=True)
    user1_id = Column(Integer, ForeignKey("users.id"))
```

```
    user2_id = Column(Integer, ForeignKey("users.id"))
    status = Column(String)  # 'pending', 'accepted', 'rejected'

@app.post("/friend-request")
def send_friend_request(friend_id: int, user: User = Depends(get_
current_user)):
    db_request = Friendship(user1_id=user.id, user2_id=friend_id,
status="pending")
    session.add(db_request)
    session.commit()
    return {"message": "Friend request sent"}

@app.post("/accept-friend-request")
def accept_friend_request(request_id: int, user: User = De-
pends(get_current_user)):
    db_request = session.query(Friendship).filter(Friendship.id ==
request_id).first()
    if not db_request:
        raise HTTPException(status_code=404, detail="Request not
found")
    db_request.status = "accepted"
    session.commit()
    return {"message": "Friend request accepted"}
```

Conclusion

This chapter provided an in-depth journey into creating real-world applications using FastAPI. Through the development of a To-Do API, an E-commerce API, and a Social Media API, we explored the nuances of building scalable, secure, and feature-rich systems. Each project showcased modern API best practices, including robust user authentication, efficient database interactions, and thoughtful error handling. These examples are designed to be comprehensive templates, equipping developers with the skills to craft production-ready applications, while also addressing edge cases and scalability challenges.

The next chapter, *Future of FastAPI*, delves into the evolving landscape of FastAPI and its role in modern web development. We will examine upcoming features, trends in asynchronous programming, and how FastAPI is adapting to emerging technologies such as serverless architectures and AI-driven APIs. This chapter will also highlight community contributions, industry adoption, and practical insights into preparing your FastAPI projects for the future. Stay tuned to explore how FastAPI continues to shape the API development ecosystem

CHAPTER 14
Future of FastAPI

Introduction

The last chapter deals with the dynamic evolution of FastAPI, including its roadmap and exciting features, considering the ever-changing landscape of web development, which is one of the most rapidly growing frameworks for building modern web applications. This chapter outlines upcoming features aimed at improving performance, developer experience, and compatibility with emerging technologies. Even enhanced dependency injection, advanced WebSocket support, and deeper integration with some of the popular tools are some of the preview features. With these developments, FastAPI has ensured that the framework is ahead of the next-generation applications and ready for use in the near future.

Going beyond the technological advancements, the chapter also sheds light on a very vibrant, supportive, and active ecosystem established by the community of FastAPI. The framework's growth is fueled by a collaborative environment where developers actively contribute, share knowledge, and create resources such as tutorials, plugins, and best practices. FastAPI's extensive documentation, community-driven projects, and forums provide invaluable support for both new and experienced developers. By embracing this ecosystem, developers can stay ahead of industry trends and continuously refine their skills. Finally, FastAPI is positioning itself not just as a tool, but rather as a cornerstone for scalable, high-performance web applications in this fast-evolving digital world.

Structure

In this chapter, we will cover the following topics:

- Upcoming Features and Roadmap
    - Key Enhancements Planned for FastAPI
    - The Vision for Asynchronous Programming Advancements
    - Integration with Emerging Trends Such As Serverless Architecture and AI/ML APIs

- Community and Resources for Ongoing Learning
  - Contributions by the FastAPI Community
  - Exploring Repositories, Blogs, and Video Tutorials
  - Leveraging Resources Such As FastAPI's Documentation and Forums

Upcoming Features and Roadmap

The roadmap of FastAPI has been directed to add more performance, scalability, and developer experience-related features. This means more support for robust WebSocket communication, better real-time data streams handling, and further improvements in dependency injection to make complex applications more manageable. Simultaneously, efforts are put into asynchronous operation streamlining and optimization of the startup time in large-scale deployment. All this is to build FastAPI's reputation as a high-performance framework that can deliver modern web development challenges.

Key Enhancements Planned for FastAPI

FastAPI has an ambitious roadmap designed to enhance its capabilities and maintain its status as a leading web framework.

- **Improved Dependency Injection:** FastAPI plans to refine its dependency injection system, making it even more flexible for complex use cases. This will simplify the creation of modular and reusable components across applications.
- **Performance Optimizations:** The development team is committed to ensuring that FastAPI remains one of the fastest frameworks. Upcoming updates will include further optimizations in request handling, response generation, and data validation.
- **Support for Emerging Standards:** FastAPI intends to incorporate cutting-edge protocols such as HTTP/3, which promises better performance and reliability for modern web applications. It also aims to extend support for WebSockets, enabling real-time communication in APIs.
- **Advanced Developer Tools:** Tools such as schema generators, enhanced code editors, and more intuitive error reporting will be prioritized. These improvements aim to make developers more productive and reduce the learning curve for new users.

The Vision for Asynchronous Programming Advancements

FastAPI has been a trailblazer in leveraging Python's asynchronous programming capabilities, and the future roadmap envisions even greater strides in this area.

- **Streamlined Async Features:** FastAPI aims to refine asynchronous support for complex use cases, such as streaming large datasets and handling long-running tasks efficiently. The framework will enhance middleware and background task processing to ensure non-blocking operations.
- **Async Database Integrations:** While FastAPI already supports async database interactions, future updates aim to provide seamless integration with modern, async-first ORMs and drivers, enabling high-performance CRUD operations without sacrificing readability.
- **Event-Driven APIs:** There are plans to support event-driven architecture out of the box, allowing APIs to be triggered by events such as Kafka streams, message queues, or custom signals. This aligns with the growing adoption of event-driven microservices.

Integration with Emerging Trends such as Serverless Architecture and AI/ML APIs

FastAPI's flexibility makes it an ideal candidate for serverless deployments. The roadmap includes better integrations with serverless platforms such as AWS Lambda and Google Cloud Functions. Additionally, FastAPI is actively aligning with the growing demand for AI/ML APIs. This includes streamlined support for integrating machine learning models and enabling efficient inference at scale.

- **Serverless-Ready Framework:** FastAPI is looking to strengthen its compatibility with serverless platforms such as AWS Lambda, Google Cloud Functions, and Azure Functions. The goal is to minimize cold start times and optimize resource utilization in serverless deployments.
- **AI and Machine Learning APIs:** As AI continues to shape the tech landscape, FastAPI is evolving to cater to the needs of ML engineers and data scientists. Upcoming updates may include built-in support for integrating with popular ML libraries, serving pre-trained models, and simplifying endpoint creation for real-time inference.
- **Focus on Scalability with Modern Architectures:** The framework aims to provide first-class support for microservices and distributed systems, making it easier to scale applications horizontally. Tools for monitoring, debugging, and managing distributed applications are also on the horizon.

Community and Resources for Ongoing Learning

The FastAPI community is a great facilitator of collaboration and knowledge sharing among developers. It provides a lot of resources, including detailed documentation, interactive tutorials, and an ever-growing library of third-party extensions. Developers can engage through forums, GitHub discussions, and social media platforms, gaining insights and exchanging best practices. The community also hosts webinars and coding sessions, ensuring developers of all levels can continue learning and stay updated with the latest advancements in FastAPI.

Contributions by the FastAPI Community

The FastAPI community plays a pivotal role in its development, contributing to its growth through open-source initiatives and educational content.

- **Open-Source Contributions:** Developers from around the world actively contribute to the framework by submitting pull requests, fixing bugs, and enhancing features. The community also develops third-party libraries, plugins, and integrations to extend FastAPI's functionality.
- **Workshops and Meetups:** Regular workshops and meetups are organized by the community to share knowledge and best practices. These events provide a platform for newcomers and seasoned developers alike to connect, collaborate, and learn.

Exploring Repositories, Blogs, and Video Tutorials

Exploring well-maintained repositories, technical blogs, and video tutorials helps in staying updated with the latest trends and best practices. These resources provide real-world examples, hands-on guidance, and expert insights to enhance learning and problem-solving skills.

Let us explore the repositories, blogs, and video tutorials in brief:

- **GitHub Repositories:** FastAPI's official GitHub repository is a treasure trove of code samples, feature implementations, and discussions. Many community-maintained repositories provide ready-to-use templates and tools for common use cases.
- **Educational Blogs:** Developers frequently share in-depth tutorials, problem-solving techniques, and architectural patterns on platforms such as Medium,

Dev.to, and individual blogs. These resources are valuable for tackling real-world challenges.

- **Video Tutorials and Courses:** YouTube channels and online learning platforms offer a wide range of content, from beginner-friendly introductions to advanced FastAPI techniques. These tutorials are particularly useful for visual learners.

Leveraging Resources such as FastAPI's Documentation and Forums

FastAPI's official documentation and community forums are valuable resources for learning and troubleshooting. The documentation provides in-depth guides and examples, while forums and discussion platforms help resolve issues through shared knowledge and expert advice.

- **Official Documentation:** The official FastAPI documentation remains the most comprehensive and reliable resource for understanding the framework's features and APIs. It is continuously updated to reflect the latest changes and best practices.
- **Community Forums and Q and A Platforms:** Platforms such as Stack Overflow, Reddit, and the FastAPI Discord channel serve as interactive hubs for troubleshooting, sharing knowledge, and staying updated on the framework's developments.

Conclusion

The "**Future of FastAPI**" chapter is forward-looking on how this amazing framework will grow and develop. Getting to know its future outlook and the new capabilities in asynchronous programming gives FastAPI its edge in rapidly evolving technology landscapes. With its perfectly fit integration with serverless architecture and AI/ML trends, the framework shows that it can adapt to modern use cases. Finally, community contributions and easily accessible resources bring to the limelight how FastAPI is helping developers innovate and continuously improve. This chapter tells a story of a promising and dynamic future for FastAPI.

The last chapter, *Appendices*, is a very practical companion to the book in the sense that it gathers together essential reference materials, including installation guides, a glossary of key terms, and additional resources for advanced learning. This chapter will reinforce all the concepts covered in the book and provide readers with a quick-access toolkit for implementing FastAPI in diverse projects. Whether you are a beginner or an advanced developer, the appendices will ensure that your journey with FastAPI remains smooth and resourceful.

CHAPTER 15
Appendices

Introduction

This chapter on appendices provides an all-inclusive, hands-on reference that gathers the fundamental concepts, tools, and resources covered in the book. It will act as a ready-reference guide for developers at all skill levels to refer to just-in-time summaries of critical topics, such as routing, dependency injection, data validation, and asynchronous programming. Whether one intends to refresh the best practices for deploying FastAPI applications or wants a quick refresh on how to integrate third-party tools, this section will ensure that you have all the important information at your fingertips.

Beyond the core concepts, the appendices include handy code snippets, troubleshooting tips, and links to additional resources such as official documentation, community forums, and popular libraries. These elements make it an indispensable tool for developers navigating real-world FastAPI projects. For beginners, it is a confidence-boosting resource to quickly resolve common challenges, while experienced developers can rely on it to streamline their workflows and dive deeper into advanced features.

Structure

In this chapter, we will cover the following topics:

- Additional Resources
- Further Reading
- FastAPI Cheat Sheet

Additional Resources

FastAPI is blessed with the highest quality resources a developer would wish to have in their improvement journey-from documentation to community-led content.

Starting from the basic resource to highly complex topics, there is just too much material at one's fingertips.

- **Documentation and Official Guides:** The official FastAPI documentation is at the heart of learning, which covers everything and more about this framework. Everything from routing to data validation through to dependency injection and asynchronous tasks is covered by the documentation. Real-world use cases and best practices further ensure that developers can bring their knowledge to life.
- **Community Forums and Discussions:** FastAPI's active community fosters collaboration and troubleshooting through platforms such as GitHub Discussions (https://github.com/fastapi/fastapi/discussions), where developers can share insights, report issues, and propose improvements. Additionally, platforms such as Stack Overflow and Reddit host vibrant discussions, offering quick solutions to technical challenges and a space for exchanging innovative ideas.
- **Educational Content:** An ever-growing selection of blogs, articles, and tutorials provides curated learning paths tailored to different skill levels. Trusted authors and educators offer insights into FastAPI best practices, while dedicated YouTube channels and online courses provide hands-on demonstrations and walkthroughs, making it easier to grasp complex concepts.
- **Other Framework Integrations:** Resources for integrating FastAPI with tools such as Celery for task queues, Redis for caching, and various database libraries are invaluable for developers who want to build more complex applications. Integrations such as these allow for handling advanced use cases such as GraphQL APIs or real-time communication through WebSockets, making FastAPI applicable and versatile in a wide range of situations.

Further Reading

This can significantly improve your level of expertise beyond the basic knowledge of FastAPI and create further opportunities in application development. The following resources add more depth to the explorations of higher-order topics, industry trends, and related technologies.

- **Books and Advanced Tutorials:** Curated books related to Python development, REST APIs, and async programming are listed below. Book titles that particularly discuss FastAPI and its entire ecosystem provide valuable discussions on making applications scalable and maintainable. More advanced tutorials enable developers to learn how to prepare their FastAPI applications for prime performance, such as optimizing queries, middleware implementation, and asynchronous workflow.

- **Industry Trends and Case Studies:** Good lessons have been learned as a result of Uber and Netflix's adoption of FastAPI. Case studies of how these companies use FastAPI in real-world scenarios reveal strategies for managing high-traffic applications, implementing scalable microservices, and ensuring overall system reliability. In reality, these case studies reveal the potential of the framework and inspire innovative solutions to ordinary challenges.
- **Related Technologies:** Complementary technologies such as Docker, Kubernetes, and CI/CD pipelines come into play during modern FastAPI development. All the resources mentioned above give great practical insights to containerize your applications, orchestrate deployments, and automate your build and release pipelines. Furthermore, advanced usage of libraries such as Pydantic to validate data structures and SQLAlchemy to manage databases enhances the understanding of how to best handle the complex requirements of an application.

FastAPI Cheat Sheet

This is the FastAPI cheat sheet, which can be treated as a one-page summary about the framework and all its major syntax, tools, and patterns - as a sort of quick guide for developers in most cases, helping to decide between defining routes, setting dependency injection, handling request validation, and many more. Commonly used decorators such as `@app.get` and `@app.post` are also included, along with tips on how to include middleware or handle exceptions with Pydantic models for request and response validation. As developers work in fast-paced environments, this resource eliminates the need to search through extensive documentation, thereby saving so much time and streamlining the development process.

In addition to core syntax, the cheat sheet contains examples of advanced features such as asynchronous route handling, custom dependencies, and OAuth2 authentication mechanisms. It also showcases best practices on structuring a FastAPI project, environment variables, and managing database connections through tools such as SQLAlchemy. By offering a snapshot of FastAPI's capabilities, the cheat sheet is particularly valuable for quick troubleshooting, onboarding new team members, or revisiting essential concepts during development. It ensures that developers can work efficiently without sacrificing the quality or security of their applications.

1. **Basic App Setup**

```
from fastapi import FastAPI
app = FastAPI()

@app.get("/")
async def read_root():
    return {"Hello": "World"}
```

2. **Request Models with Pydantic**

```
from pydantic import BaseModel

class Item(BaseModel):
    name: str
    price: float

@app.post("/items/")
async def create_item(item: Item):
    return item
```

3. **Dependency Injection**

```
from fastapi import Depends

async def common_dependency():
    return "dependency result"

@app.get("/")
async def read_item(dep_result: str = Depends(common_dependency)):
    return {"dep_result": dep_result}
```

4. **Database Connection**
   - Examples for SQLAlchemy and Tortoise ORM initialization and queries.
5. **Authentication Example**
   - JWT and OAuth2 basic token generation snippets.

This cheat sheet serves as a short and highly accessible reference for the core features of FastAPI. It provides instant guidance for efficient project development and gives developers immediate access to key tools and best practices, including defining routes, handling requests, integrating dependencies, and validating data. Tailored for both new and experienced developers, this guide simplifies the development workflow by presenting key concepts in an easy-to-digest format, ensuring developers can quickly implement or revisit important FastAPI functionalities without delving into extensive documentation.

Conclusion

The appendices chapter is a vital cornerstone for developers, offering a treasure trove of practical tools, curated resources, and actionable insights to deepen their understanding of FastAPI. As the final chapter of this book, it consolidates the knowledge gained throughout, acting as a quick-reference guide that developers can rely on as they build, optimize, and scale their applications. Whether this is a critique of critical concepts, advanced uses, or techniques for troubleshooting, this chapter was designed to fill the reader's need for greater confidence and lucidity in managing real-world applications.

The appendices, apart from just reinforcing the knowledge learned from the book, would serve as an invaluable resource to be continued through one's learning journey and in mastering it. Links to official documentation, community forums, and advanced tutorials give an incentive for further exploration and continuous learning. This chapter winds up the journey toward understanding FastAPI but also serves as a launching pad for the developer to innovate, solve complex problems, and get ahead in this ever-evolving world of modern web development.

Index

E

P

Q

R

S